# STUBBORN BUGGERS

# TIM BOWDEN

# STUBBORN BUGGERS

## Survivors of the infamous POW gaol that made Changi look like heaven

ALLEN&UNWIN
SYDNEY · MELBOURNE · AUCKLAND · LONDON

Allen & Unwin
83 Alexander Street
Crows Nest NSW 2065
Australia
Phone:   (61 2) 8425 0100
Email:    info@allenandunwin.com
Web:     www.allenandunwin.com

Cataloguing-in-Publication details are available from the
National Library of Australia
www.trove.nla.gov.au

ISBN 978 1 74331 442 5

Typeset in 12/17pt Minion by Midland Typesetters, Australia
Printed and bound in Australia by Griffin Press

10 9 8 7 6 5 4 3 2

MIX
Paper from
responsible sources
FSC® C009448

The paper in this book is FSC® certified.
FSC® promotes environmentally responsible,
socially beneficial and economically viable
management of the world's forests.

*For all the gutsy survivors of Outram Road Gaol but particularly the twelve men whose narratives have supported this book.*

*Ken Bird*
*Stan Davis*
*Penrod Dean*
*Frank Martin*
*John McGregor*
*Chris Neilson*
*Bert Rollason*
*James Taylor*
*Herb Trackson*
*Rod Wells*
*John Wyett*
*Bill Young*

# CONTENTS

# INTRODUCTION

I started writing this book nearly thirty years ago. It had its genesis in two major series of oral history programs that I made for ABC Radio over a period of four years in the early 1980s. The series were the sixteen-part *Prisoners of War: Australians Under Nippon* followed by a ten-part series, *Survival*. *Survival* profiled the remarkable experiences of eight ex-prisoners of war, including the accounts of Signaller Chris Neilson and Sister Vivian Bullwinkel, the sole survivor of a massacre of Australian nurses on Banka Island, Sumatra.

Neilson had been a prisoner in Singapore's Outram Road Gaol, a brutal nineteenth-century establishment where torture and punishment accompanied solitary confinement in tiny cells in the three-storey stone and concrete British gaol. Neilson's account of his experiences in and out of Outram Road was one of the most singular of the Australian former inmates I interviewed from that awful place. It symbolised for me the sheer grit, determination and mental toughness that enabled people to go on living, even when starved, beaten and facing a future seemingly with no hope except a slow death.

Formerly Pearl's Hill Prison, built in 1847, it was condemned and scheduled to be demolished in 1912 but the British did not get around to doing so. Always referred to by gaolers and its inmates as 'Outram Road Gaol', it was a military prison where the Japanese also sent their own soldiers and officers who had committed serious crimes. This was a place of punishment and death, where executions by beheading by samurai sword, hanging, or shooting took place continuously from 1942 to 1945. No one knows how many prisoners were executed, or simply died of malnutrition and untreated disease. The estimates are in the thousands, not hundreds. Chinese civilians accused of sabotage were routinely murdered and buried in unmarked mass graves.

In the mid 1980s, I had finished my ABC Radio documentaries on the experiences of Australian prisoners of war of the Japanese in camps that stretched from Timor to Manchuria, but the stories of the Outram Road men in Singapore stayed in my mind. Through the late 1980s and early 1990s, I sought out more survivors, and teased out their vivid memories, sometimes returning to interview them twice because I planned to write a book about their extraordinary survival against the odds.

This book tells the story of twelve Outram Road men. Eleven of them were soldiers, and one—the brave and courageous medical doctor, James Taylor—was a civilian. Two had died before I could record them. John McGregor had fortunately written a self-published book about what happened to him. His fellow escapee from Changi, Penrod Dean, planned to write his own book, and refused to talk to me until he had done so. I was unable to convince him to speak to me before he died, but was able to draw on his published memoir. The other nine spoke freely and evocatively about why they were sent to Outram Road Gaol, and what happened to them there.

It is a matter of personal regret that there were only two of my interviewees alive by the time I finished writing this book in 2013. But they all knew of my ambition to tell their stories. The memories of the twelve men provided me with extraordinary accounts of how they survived unimaginable hardships and lived to tell the tale. This book is based on their testimonies.

Following the fall of Singapore on 15 February 1942, the Japanese were faced with the reality of over 70000 Allied prisoners of war who, in Japanese eyes, had not had the decency to commit suicide after the shame of defeat. The Japanese were not keen to have large numbers of their troops guarding captured soldiers who couldn't go anywhere, so they marched the prisoners to the Changi peninsula on Singapore island and virtually left them to look after themselves. Senior officers above the rank of colonel were taken to separate camps in Manchuria, otherwise the Allied military command structure was left intact. This had advantages for both sides. The Japanese didn't have to worry about organising the internal running of the prisoner-of-war camps, which they would later use as a source of forced labour for projects like the Thai-Burma Railway, or building an aerodrome at Sandakan, in British North Borneo. The Allies, on the other hand, retained their group identity as a military entity—albeit captive—and mini-mised the contacts between Australian and British troops with their Japanese conquerors.

Changi, the biggest camp, and effectively the Allied POW head-quarters in Singapore, has become a buzzword in the public mind for deprivation and starvation. To the Australians forced to work on the construction of the Thai-Burma Railway in 1943, however, it was a home—almost like Australia—to which they longed to return. 'Changi was like heaven' was a phrase I was to hear more than once when talking to ex-prisoners of war. But it was heaven on short rations. Conditions in Changi deteriorated as the war went on: the skeletal frames of Australian prisoners of war are clearly seen in photographs taken at the war's end on Singapore island in 1945. Even so, there were far more brutal places than Changi.

# 1

# BETRAYED

Christian Neilson was a tough Queenslander from Cairns, not yet 30 years old when he arrived in Malaya. His grandfather, Neils Christian Frederick Neilson, a sea captain, came to Australia from his native Denmark. His father, Otto, had been born in Cooktown in 1885 and became a fisherman. His mother, Margaret Tate, was of Irish stock. The Neilsons had the sea in their blood, and Otto taught the young Chris how to mesh nets and splice rope and wire and all he needed to know about surviving at sea in prawn trawlers.

Neilson's younger brother, Gordon, suffered from a leaking valve in his heart and was allowed to attend school on the basis that the teachers would not chastise him, because it was believed he would not live very long. Inexplicably, one of the teachers decided to cane him for a minor mistake in his schoolwork. Chris, aged twelve, sprang to his brother's defence, and the teacher—unwisely—took Gordon into another room to cane him with Chris, who was to be caned as well for abusing the teacher. Neilson recalls, 'He locked the door, then hit me across the back with the cane and I spun around and left-hooked him—I was taught to fight very young—and I took the cane off him and belted the tripe out of him and then I hopped out the window.

He sent the bigger high school kids after me and I saw them coming up and hid around a corner before I jumped out and said, "Who's first?" They all headed back to school.'

Already a big kid for his age, Neilson left school at thirteen, and at fourteen was apprenticed as a saw miller before joining his father in the fishing trade. But, like many young men coming into adulthood through the Depression, he saw the army as a good prospect, particularly with the likelihood of a Pacific war close to Australian shores. He joined up in 1940. Always a handful for the military—his nickname was 'The Reb' (short for 'Rebel')—he soon got a reputation as a knuckle man. He joined the army in the Royal Australian Corps of Signals, for which he showed a natural aptitude, quickly picking up the basics of Morse code, radio work, setting up and operating field telephones and signalling by semaphore. He started in the 6th Division at Enoggera Barracks in Brisbane, and his skills were quickly noted. He was sent to Sydney as an instructor, somewhat to his dismay, as the months dragged on, and he couldn't see how he was ever going to get away overseas.

Quartered at Randwick Racecourse, the bored young signallers took any chance they could to get over to the conveniently situated Captain Cook pub. Neilson, then a corporal, had delegated a detail of soldiers to the cookhouse for potato peeling duties. The spud peelers had a better idea: they nicked off to the Captain Cook hostelry. This was noted by one of the officers, a captain, and he summoned Corporal Neilson.

'You posted those men, corporal?'

'Yessir.'

'Well, you'd better have another look.' Neilson noticed that they were all over at the pub, waving to the soldiers marching past.

'The captain turned to me and started upbraiding the Queenslanders. "You're nothing but an undisciplined rabble. You are all a disgrace to the army." I pointed, and said, "Look." As he did so, I gave him a classic left hook and flattened him. Almost cracked his jaw. Ron Richards [a noted Aboriginal boxer from Ipswich who won light-heavyweight and heavyweight Australian titles] reckoned I had one of the best left hooks in Australia.'

Striking an officer was a court-martial offence, but provocation was taken into account by one of the officers on the court martial board, a fellow Queenslander who was clearly unamused by the captain's handling of the matter. He reduced Neilson to the ranks (he never kept his stripes for long) and sent him to Bathurst. This enabled him to volunteer for the 8th Division, finally making it into the AIF (Australian Imperial Force).

Just after he arrived in Bathurst, and before he joined the AIF, Neilson and a mate, 'Berry' Arthur (later to be a fellow POW and a member of the Changi Concert Party), went down to the local RSL.

'There was a bloke in the bar—I didn't know whether he was drunk or half-drunk, but he wanted a fight. One of my mates there, Dicky Benson, wanted to fight, but I said, "No, he's drunk, leave him. We'll only get into trouble knocking anyone in the bar," and we left and went outside. This bloke followed us outside the RSL and said to me, "You're a yellow-gutted bastard. You're one of those choco bastards, aren't you," pointing to the insignias we wore on our shoulders. ["Choco" was a derogatory term meaning "chocolate soldier", as they were expected to melt under the heat of battle.]

'I said, "Put up now, come on!" He swung a punch, and I stepped out and went Whack! Whack! and all his teeth went everywhere. Then one of the RSL heads, the secretary, I think, called out, "You ought to be ashamed of yourself. You're not fit to wear that uniform." The other feller was out cold, and bleeding like a sieve. I said, "You cost him his teeth. I could have done that an hour ago, but didn't want to hit the poor bastard. You're next." But he took off and ran.'

It wasn't long before The Reb was in strife again. During training, a young officer organised a platoon to march up and down the parade ground saluting every time they went past him. Bored with this arrangement, the officer put his cap on a stick and sat in the shade while the pantomime continued. Chris Neilson was affronted, and left the marchers to sit in the shade too. He was accused of disobeying orders and refusing to salute a superior officer.

He was lucky that the matter was dealt with on the spot by one Major William French, an experienced officer, who had been awarded the Distinguished Service Order during World War I. French wasn't impressed by what had occurred. He asked Neilson for his side of the story. 'I said, "Sir, while you've got that hat on your head I'll salute you ten times a day, I'll salute those ribbons of yours—I'd be proud to. But I'm not going to salute that bloody hat on a stick while its owner is sitting in the shade." French tore a strip off [the] officer.'

Soldiers like Chris Neilson really needed a war. He was about to get one.

The disaster that was the Malayan campaign has been well covered by historians. The Australians of the 8th Division did not expect to become prisoners of war because, in their training, prejudice had replaced military intelligence. The Japanese soldiers were portrayed by instructors as near-sighted dwarfs, their equipment sub-standard and their fighting abilities poor. Chris Neilson had heard these stories too, but thought them fanciful: 'The north Queenslanders didn't believe that because in Cairns most of the hotels had Japanese cooks and there were some fairly solid, big blokes amongst them. We saw plenty of Japs on the luggers that pulled into Cairns and there were no weaklings amongst them—the best divers we had in the Torres Strait were Japanese.'

Racial stereotypes of the Japanese army were well and truly put to rest early in the retreat down the Malayan peninsula when the

Imperial Guards Division was encountered. Most were six footers and utterly ruthless. They were responsible for the massacre of wounded Allied troops on the banks of the Parit Sulong river after an initially successful action against the Japanese at Muar in late January 1942 by the 2/29th Battalion.

The British commander-in-chief, Lieutenant-General Arthur Percival, had 70 000 frontline troops at his disposal. They were made up of 38 infantry battalions—thirteen British, six Australian, seventeen Indian, and two Malayan—and three machine-gun battalions. They faced (as it turned out) an invasion force of only 30 000, but highly trained, well-equipped, jungle-savvy Japanese troops commanded by the pugnacious General Yamashita, known as 'The Tiger of Malaya'.

The Allies' obsolete aircraft were soon shot out of the skies and the fearless Japanese soldiers—for whom death in combat was a divine honour sanctioned by their emperor—streamed south on bicycles or any transport appropriate through the Malayan defences, brushing early opposition aside. The Indian troops first opposing them were well aware of moves for independence against the British Raj at home and were ambivalent about fighting for their colonial masters in Malaya. Although some fought bravely, other units just melted away. Realising this, the Japanese began signing the Indian troops over to their cause and many obliged, eventually to become the gaolers of their former rulers.

The Japanese advancing down the Malayan peninsula did not clash with the Australians before the middle of January. By then the Japanese were cocky and confident, and there were plenty of them. The cyclists, their rifles slung on their backs, rode into an ambush set for them by the 2/30th Battalion at Gemas.

Brief victories had been won by the Australians at Gemas, Muar and at Mersing in the west. These were positive moments in long days of preparing positions and retreating again.

General Yamashita later gave the Australians the ultimate compliment: 'In a week long, bloody battle, without heavy tank or air
support, they had held up the whole of my army.' Some two battalions of Australians had halted two divisions of advancing Japanese,
sustaining heavy casualties, but inflicting far more on the enemy.

Chris Neilson had been active in both the Muar and Gemas actions.
At last, 'The Reb' was earning his stripes in combat. Apart from his
bravery in keeping communications going under fire, with companions being killed around him, he was a skilled marksman and, with
one well-aimed bullet, brought down a Japanese sniper shooting down
from the top of a tall palm tree.

But none of the temporary victories could halt the Japanese
advance. The Allied forces had to retreat to the fortress island of
Singapore where, with the water cut off and civilian casualties from
bombing raids mounting, Lieutenant-General Percival had no alternative but to surrender all his troops on 15 February 1942.

Chris Neilson remembers that, somehow, in the chaos the day before
the surrender, he actually met the Australian commander, Lieutenant-
General Gordon Bennett, who told him that in the circumstances
he might as well try to escape. Bennett, of course, controversially
took his own advice and did get away by boat, eventually reaching
Australia.

'After the surrender, shame was the biggest thing I felt,' Neilson
says. 'I've never felt so isolated, so ashamed. I thought straight away,
"We'll go." A mate, Sergeant Frank Thomas, a New Guinea bloke,
came with me. We went looking for canoes to get out of the place,
because the surrender was to take place the following morning. I
buried two pistols I had in a latrine, and broke my good sniper's rifle
round a tree and threw it in a river. We went looking for canoes, but
the Malays had put holes in all of them.

'We were in a coconut plantation near a cemetery, and the Japs spotted us running out and began shooting. I called out, "Hit the ground," but a bullet hit Frank and he grabbed a coconut tree which was the worst thing he could have done, because they put a machine gun on him and cut him in half. I doubled back around the cemetery to where we were near the golf course and got away.'

That was the end of Neilson's first escape attempt. The following day, he joined the rest of his disconsolate fellow Australians for the march to Changi, where they would become prisoners of war. 'We were told to fill our packs with food because no one knew when the Japs would feed us, and sent on this long, forced march. Believe me, that's the saddest thing I ever saw in my life, all those blokes that were all dead keen and fit, marching along, and all those bloody Japs on the side of the road.'

Chris Neilson, bored with doing nothing, was at first pleased to be moved out of the Changi complex to a working party based at Adam Park—another partially wrecked former British military barracks about 50 kilometres from Changi. There, the job was to build a military shrine to the glorious Japanese dead. All Allied prisoners of war had been made honorary members of the Imperial Japanese Army—an honour that sat lightly on their shoulders. But moving away from Changi was a chance to scrounge for food and other useful material, like parts to build illegal radios. Security at Adam Park was comparatively loose, and there were many half-wrecked houses, formerly occupied by the British and wealthy Chinese, that yielded good contraband.

Building the shrine was hard work, the prisoners virtually acting as human pile-drivers while Japanese overseers shouted and screamed at them. The labouring Australians quietly did what they could to sabotage the construction by getting matchboxes of termites and inserting them in the wooden foundations of the Japanese memorial.

Neilson: 'I made up my mind that a man had to get out of there. But it wasn't to get home to Australia, because I knew that wasn't possible. At night, my mate Bob Green and I were able to get out scrounging for whatever we could find. Bob, who had a Marconi ticket for Morse code, said he could build a radio. One night I met a young Chinaman who asked me what we were looking for and I said, "wireless parts". But although there was the odd wireless to be found, the Japanese had been clever and taken out the master valve, so they couldn't be used. The Chinaman said that they were looking for wireless operators, and he told us about the guerrilla forces up in Malaya who were fighting the Japanese.'

They kept bumping into this young Chinese, who repeated the message that they needed technicians: 'Chinese up country want to fight on. We need wireless technicians, mechanical men. You come with us. Long way up country—plenty food.'

'I thought that suited me down to the ground—a chance to hit back,' Neilson recalls. 'We could get the Japs from behind and blow up their supply trains coming through and that sort of thing. He said there were not only Chinese, but some Indians, quite a few Australians and some British who had not been rounded up by the Japanese. They were working in the jungle between Malacca and Kuala Lumpur.'

The Chinese contact told Neilson that they needed two radio operators—Chris and Bob Green—and three truck drivers. Neilson asked how they were going to get there. 'Do not worry about that,' he was told. 'I will take you near Johor, then another man will take you over to the mainland. Just tell me when you want to go.'

Neilson and Green discussed this with three Motor Transport men they knew from South Australia, Ken Bird, Reg Morris and Bill Goodwin. Neilson began to make the arrangements in camp. He discussed the plan with his immediate senior officer, Captain Fred Stahl (arguing that it was the duty of every prisoner of war to try to escape), who provided him with quinine and a code to use if he was ever able to make contact by radio from the outside. They even had access to arms and ammunition, which had been buried in the area after the action. Equipped with a Tommy gun, pistols, a compass and the quinine, the five men made arrangements to leave. Their contact assured them there would be food provided at certain designated points along the way, and he had arranged some dark Chinese clothing for the escape. The Australians were taller than the average Chinese, but Chris Neilson gambled that the guards would be lax as they believed the prisoners were so exhausted after a day working on the shrine that they would just fall down and sleep.

'There were no guards as such, only on the main road coming in where the Japs were, so we just skirted around them. He was good, that Chinese boy, he took us on the main road in single file dressed as coolies. We were told to drop our heels as we walked and shuffle as the Chinese did. We bowed to every sentry along the road and walked right past the sentry near the ammunition dump—we had a Tommy gun, grenades, everything under our sarongs—and our guide walked in front and we weren't challenged once.'

The escapees were led through jungle paths and rubber plantations in almost total darkness for about ten miles and until they were about 400 yards from the Johor Strait, where they met the next Chinese who would take them over the strait to the mainland the following night. The plan was to wait until the regular Japanese patrol boats passed, and then set out, about 8 pm. 'But at 4 pm Bob Green came down with a bad attack of amoebic dysentery. The older Chinese man went into the village where he was known, but couldn't get any drugs at all—the Japs had everything. The only stuff you could get was Aquaflavine and stuff like that. We had to give poor Greenie an enema with a bike pump—a retention enema they called it, where you had to hold it in as long as you could. But nothing worked.'

This desperate situation went on for five days, and Green became delirious, screaming and raving. On the sixth day they actually discussed their alternatives. Ken Bird remembers it well: 'I said, "Christ, he's going to get us caught. What are we going to do, Neilson? He's your mate." He said, "Well, I don't want to get caught." "Neither do I, so what are we going to do with him?" Neilson said, "Well, there's only two things to choose from—knock him on the head and go on, or take him back." Up went a coin. Take him back.'

The Australians told their Chinese contacts what they planned to do with Green, and that they would get word to them when they were ready to leave again with another radio technician. Neilson says, 'Well, it took all that night until just on daylight to carry and drag him. The shortest way back was to follow the monsoon drains at the side of the road and we had to clobber him, hit him a few times to shut him up and carry him past Jap guards.'

They got into camp undetected by the Japanese—just before they went in Neilson cheekily stole a goose—and turned Green over to the medics, took the goose to the cookhouse and immediately started to make plans to leave again. They quickly arranged for another technician to replace Green, and decided to go out again that night. Their absence had been covered up for only three days, and then the Japanese were informed that five men were missing. The camp was paraded, the men counted, but no officers were physically beaten.

When the commanding officer of Adam Park, Lieutenant-Colonel Roland Oakes, heard that the escapees had returned, he ordered them all to parade before him. They were amazed and shocked to hear that their own commanding officer had decided to turn them over to the Japanese for punishment. Neilson remembers very clearly Colonel Oakes saying, as they stood to attention, 'The Japanese have been informed you have returned and have ordered you to be held here. They will be coming to take you away.' Oakes continued: 'I am not prepared to risk my life or the lives of the men in this camp for the sake of a few irresponsible men who try the impossible.'

Neilson said, 'You can't hand us over to the Japanese, they'll lop our heads off!' Oakes replied, 'I'll ask the Japanese if I can try you and I'll be severe.' Neilson argued, 'They won't take any notice of you. It's your duty to help us and it's our duty as POWs to escape.'

Ken Bird confirmed this in an interview in 1991, saying Oakes claimed he was 'building up confidence with the Japanese'. 'I said, "You silly bastard!" He was terrified of them, that's what it was.' Another of the escapees, Reg Morris, testified in a statutory declaration in 1946: 'Colonel Oakes saw fit to hand us over to the Japanese.'

The incredulous but exhausted men were then allowed to get some sleep while waiting for the Japanese response. Neilson: 'I was woken with a boot in the ribs. The people that picked us up were the *Kempeitai*, the military secret police. We knew they were important. Every Jap in the camp put his head down and started bowing when they came in, you could see they were frightened. They carried special brassards on both arms. You see, a corporal in the *Kempeitai* can belt the tripe out of, or arrest even a Japanese colonel who has a button undone! Even Hitler's Gestapo boys weren't that powerful.'

In the presence of Colonel Oakes and Captain Stahl, the five men were handcuffed, chained, tied together and pushed from the room, their legs locked with leg-irons. As they were being dragged into a truck, Neilson managed to speak to the adjutant, his signals officer, Captain Stahl: 'I said, "If they lop me, I've got three brothers in the Army, and if any of you make it out I want you to drum them that this bastard [Oakes] turned me in for doing my duty, and they'll fix him." And Stahl said, "I don't think you've got much chance. We've been reading orders from the Japanese twice a day for the last five days that anyone caught attempting to escape will be publicly executed."'

They were taken to *Kempeitai* headquarters, bizarrely situated in the former YMCA building in central Singapore. They were still handcuffed, but their hobbles were removed. There were about seventeen people in a big room, including one Chinese woman. Neilson was about to get a swift induction into his changed circumstances.

'I'll never forget the Chinese woman,' he said. 'Her son, a rather small slim fellow, had actually escaped by slipping through the bars, and they were holding her until he gave himself up. (When he did they topped them both anyway.) There was only one 20-gallon latrine bucket for the lot of us. I asked all the blokes whether they would turn their backs while the old girl got on the latrine bucket. While this was happening a young bloke—I think he was the *Kempeitai* commandant's son, or nephew—came in and asked in English why we were doing this.'

Neilson explained, and this man started to work him over and gave him a whack on the side of the head. Then he hit him again and Neilson was thrown across the room and onto a billiard table in the corner. 'It nearly crippled me! Turns out this bloke could kill with either hand. He was a first class karate expert, which I'd never seen before. Now, I'd always been fit and tough and pretty good with my mits. But I couldn't hit back—I'd have been beheaded if I did—and all I could do was roll with the punches as well as I could. Within twenty minutes I was bleeding from both ears, had a broken nose, and a tooth broken off at the gums. My head was spinning for weeks and I was black and blue. And that was just the start.'

Neilson was not to know, but he had just met the executioner from Outram Road Gaol, of whom he would see more later. 'That same afternoon the executioner hit a Chinaman called Song, who was a detective. He wouldn't give the names of the communists that the police had released from custody before the Japanese came in. Because he wouldn't give the names, this bloke hit him on the shoulder with one chop from his hand, and brought up a bruised swelling about as big as an orange. The next afternoon he busted that bruise with another chop, and Song was dead within 48 hours. He was a beauty. He used to skite how good he was and say, "One chop on the temple and that man's dead".'

At that point Neilson believed he and his companions would be executed. When their persecutor went out of the room, he was able to talk quickly to the other four Australians: 'That's a taste, we've only been here an hour. This is it—they're going to lop us all right. We've only got one chance, we've got to stick hard and fast to our story that we were lost and looking for food, we weren't trying to escape.'

The first impressions of interrogation were suspiciously benign. Neilson talked to a 'little bloke' at a desk, 'who seemed a quiet little chap'. He stuck to the script, saying they had been looking for food, not trying to escape, and was that very serious? The man at the desk said 'Oh no', and passed him a few boiled lollies. Then, one at a time, they were taken into another interrogation room. There was an interpreter and three muscle men. The interpreter said, 'You're the leader.' Neilson explained that there were no leaders, but he was a bushman at home, and was helping to look for some European food because they were worried about malnutrition from the rice diet they were getting in the camp. At that stage he was still sucking the little boiled lolly he had been given.

'The first thing was a whack across the mouth, and I lost the lolly. Then it started, the questions over and over again. They wouldn't believe anything you said. Then one of the muscle men would take over. They were very good at the karate chops you see on television these days. There's only a few that can do it. These blokes were experts.'

This interrogation and the beltings went on for ten hours a day, for five days. Everyone was exhausted at the end of each day. But the Australians more than the Japanese. Neilson stuck to his story of the

fear of beriberi (a condition caused by malnutrition and vitamin deficiency, where the body cannot rid itself of excess fluid) and hoped
the others were doing that too: "'We were just lost looking for food,"
I told them. "We know you Nipponese don't eat our sort of food and
you threw it away." (If you called them Japanese they belted you even
harder.) "We thought we'd look where the old dumps were and get
some food and save our lives.'"

All this time the Australians remained quartered in the old billiard
room at the YMCA. After five days, they were transferred to Outram
Road Gaol. Formerly known as Pearl's Hill Prison, it was probably
Singapore's earliest gaol. By 1912 it had well and truly outlived its
usefulness and was scheduled for demolition, but the British did not
get around to it. The Japanese took it over as a military prison not
only for serious offences committed by Allied prisoners of war, but
for Japanese soldiers as well. Executions were carried out there, by
decapitation with a samurai sword, shooting or hanging. As the gaol
had been specifically built for Asians, the Japanese certainly fitted in
better than the larger Caucasians. A six-foot European could touch
the walls of a cell on either side with outstretched arms, and there was
barely room to stretch out fully on the floor to sleep. The Japanese
inmates were certainly better fed, but subject to the same strict regime
of solitary confinement.

Chris Neilson never forgot his first impressions of Outram Road
Gaol. 'The whole front of it was three stories high, 68 cells to a floor.
At the end of it was a great big steel gate with about one-inch-diameter
steel all the way down. No way in the world could you get out of it.
Dynamite wouldn't have blown it up. We were in the bottom section,
in cells below ground level except for a tiny barred window at the top.
There were two steps up, and then a great wooden door with just a
little peep hole for [the guards] to look through, and another little
one down below where they shone a torch. The only things in the cell

were two to three six-feet-by-one-inch wooden boards to sleep on, and another shorter piece of wood with a groove cut in it for your neck, as a 'pillow', a *benki* [latrine] bucket and you. That was it.'

At first, Neilson and the other Australians were held in the 'black' punishment cells, so called because there was no light at all save for a glimmer in daylight hours coming from the tiny barred window high on the back wall. They were in those cells for 29 days waiting for their trial, and their latrine buckets were only emptied twice during that time, so conditions were unspeakable. For the first two days Chris Neilson was not even given a drink of water, and then only an occasional little bowl of rice.

The only variation in the diet was when the Japanese executed one of their own people: 'Then every one of us got a gift of a piece of banana, about an inch long, and a little cake in a paper cup with a few sultanas and things in them and a handful of those little boiled lollies that I'd been given at the YMCA before it was belted out of me. The man to be executed always had a holy man with him and, you have to give them full marks for this, not one of those Japs going out to be executed ever cried or asked for anything, they went out as if they expected it was their duty to go and get lopped. So did the Chinese.'

In the cell opposite was a young Chinese woman, also on death row. The symbol on her door was a white circle with a dot in the middle, meaning execution by samurai sword. She asked Neilson to tell her what was written on her door, but he pretended that his eyesight was poor and he couldn't see. 'She said, "Oh, please tell me. I think I'm due to be executed tomorrow." I said, "You've got a white circle with a dot in it." She thanked me, and I said I was sorry. She replied, "Oh, don't be sorry for me, I've been responsible for the death of hundreds of these little animals." She was charged with espionage, and had been working a wireless for the British. They took her out the next morning and she showed no apparent feeling at all, another brave face, certainly not crying and no sadness. Twenty minutes later the executioner came back and threw the shackles that she'd been in onto the floor, and said to me: "I'm very special, one chop and I took her head off.'"

Neilson always called him 'Very Special' from then on. At that time, before his trial, he fully expected to be beheaded himself. He did see one prisoner, a Dutchman, put to death by sword: 'I put the two bed boards up against the wall to look out of the window. And the way that blood gushed out of that bloke . . . he never moved. He didn't fall over straight away, he was on his knees with his hands behind him. Just a swish with the sword and his head was off as easily as you could cut a little carrot. The body just stayed motionless there, the blood squirting out the stump of his neck. That was enough for me. I got down, I didn't want to see any more.'

Very Special used to delight in giving Neilson a hard time. 'He could speak English, he'd been around the world in ships, and he used to try and get me to admit that my name was Nelson, not Neilson. I said, "No, my name is Neilson, it's Danish—Danska." "It doesn't matter, Nelson, I will do the honours for you, and you will be very happy, because I am very good. Just one chop." I thought, "Bugger him." So I'd say, "Well, thanks very much, I'm glad I'm getting you because you do a good job, so then it's straight up to heaven to my mother and father, grandma and grandad." He used to make me cranky, that beggar. He didn't know how bloody frightened I was!'

Then Chris Neilson had a lucky break—you certainly needed them in Outram Road Gaol. When he first went into the black cells, waiting for his trial, he had the same sign on his door as the Chinese woman, a white circle with a dot in the middle, indicating death by decapitation. At that time the Imperial Japanese Army was still running the gaol— the *Kempeitai* were not yet in charge. One morning, a senior Japanese officer came past Neilson's cell and noticed he was sentenced to death. Neilson saw he had some British campaign ribbons on his chest from earlier service when Japan had been Britain's ally in World War I, and he spoke good English. He asked Neilson what he had been charged with. He replied that he had been accused of attempting to escape, but in fact all he and his companions had been doing was looking for food. The officer nodded and continued on his way.

On 19 June 1942, the Australians were taken from Outram Road to the court for their trial. Near the Anderson Bridge, Ken Bird said to Reg Morris, 'Have a good look at that bridge, it's probably the last one you'll see.' He believed they were all going to be shot.

On their arrival they saw Bob Green already at the court. During the proceedings, the interpreter asked Bird, 'What family do you have?' Bird replied, 'Two brothers and one sister, mother and father.'

'Well, you won't see them again, we are bombing Darwin! What does your father do?' Bird said he was a pilot with New Guinea Airways. (Bird made this up to be cheeky because he knew his father hated aeroplanes.) The interpreter went on, 'Now you should learn Japanese, forget all about English, we will have all Australia soon.'

The prosecutor argued for the death penalty for all five men. To their surprise—and relief—the presiding judge, who spoke English, commuted their sentences to three years in Outram Road Gaol, adding, 'You sons of English criminal swine, you'll wish you had been beheaded during your three years' solitary confinement.'

Neilson said the only explanation he could think of was that the senior Japanese officer he had spoken to from the black cells must have made a submission to the court on their behalf. At least he could begin his sentence knowing that Very Special was not going to have the pleasure of cutting his head off. There wasn't much else to be happy about.

For prisoners in the tiny cells, every waking hour was organised, and if you disobeyed you were bashed. Every morning the two or three bed boards you lay on at night were leaned up against the wall, and you sat on the concrete at attention in a pre-ordained position facing the door. Every hour a bell would ring and you could change position. And so it went all day. The naked light bulb suspended from the curved ceiling remained on, day and night. With three more years of this ahead of him, Chris Neilson wondered whether he could retain his sanity.

When the Japanese said solitary confinement, they meant it.

# 2

# THE CHINESE GUERRILLAS

Chris Neilson and his four fellow escapees were not the first Australians to reach Outram Road Gaol. A month earlier, on 19 May 1942, Lieutenant Penrod Dean and Corporal John 'Mac' McGregor were incarcerated. They were both Western Australians from the 2/4th Machine Gun Battalion. They, too, had escaped early from Changi after the surrender in the chaos of those early few days, and had remained at large for some three months in the jungles of Malaya. Like Neilson's group, they were charged with escaping, but managed to convince the Japanese court martial that they were simply lost and looking for food.

Unfortunately, neither Dean nor McGregor were able to be interviewed for this book. During brief correspondence in the early 1980s, Dean expressed his unwillingness to answer questions while he was writing his own book. John McGregor, alas, had already died, but had written a self-published book, *Blood on the Rising Sun*, about his experiences during the escape and in Outram Road.

There are important discrepancies between the two accounts. In his book, *Singapore Samurai*, Dean described the last stages of the battle for Singapore and his part in it. He wrote of ignoble behaviour by soldiers and civilians alike, in an undignified rush to reach the waterfront and try to escape by ship:

> There were trucks, armoured cars, motorcycles, wheelbarrows, oxen and carts. In fact anything that would carry people or goods was trying to move on the [Pasir Panjang] road. And there were thousands of soldiers—Indians, English and Australians—all fleeing, pushing and jostling to try and reach Keppel harbour, with only one thought, escape . . . No-one could stop this flood of humanity as they made a bee-line for the harbour.

There is evidence that Dean, despite his own account of fighting to the last with his unit before being ordered to surrender, was among that flood of humanity. John McGregor's wife Nan, then in her late eighties, wrote to me on 4 August 1998:

> Now I will tell you all I know about that noble creature Penrod Dean. He was an officer in the 2/4th Machine Gunners. My husband was also in the 2/4th. Mac [her husband John] did tell me Dean proved no good in action. Threw his rifle in the air and cleared out leaving his men . . . [he was] down at the wharf trying to get on ships taking on women and children, at the last minute, to get away from Singapore.
>
> The British gave in and the deserters were put in Changi with the others. They were not made welcome. The men [2/4th Machine Gunners] were after Dean. Dean had to escape or else. That is when he asked Mac to go with him.

Chris Neilson (who grew to despise Dean for ingratiating himself with the Japanese in Outram Road Gaol) was also aware of Dean's desertion and that he had tried to get on the ships leaving Singapore with women and children and the wounded. He said Nan McGregor told him that, even after the war, Dean had to leave Western Australia for a time because some of the 2/4th Machine Gunners still wanted to kill him. 'Some of the blokes told me that Dr Bruce Hunt [a respected POW doctor] said that he should have been charged with bloody desertion,' Neilson recalls.

Nan McGregor knew her husband remained loyal to Dean long after the war because Dean had saved his life in Outram Road Gaol. But he also told her some of Dean's darker secrets, never mentioned in *Singapore Samurai*.

On 16 March 1942, the third week after the surrender, Penrod Dean approached John McGregor and asked him if he would escape with him. McGregor had considered the possibility of escaping, but had not thought it through. He knew that the Japanese would execute any prisoner of war who tried to escape. He told Dean he would need to think it over. In his memoir, McGregor wrote:

Pen assured me that he had given ample thought to the matter, provided we could reach the mainland safely. He considered the crossing of the Johor Strait to be the most difficult task, but once the mainland was reached there would be plenty of cover in the nature of rubber plantations and wild jungle. Pen Dean proved that he had gone into the matter thoroughly by making a reconnaissance of the area near the submarine naval depot. He had found a boat, which he had promptly submerged, and had prepared copies of maps covering the straits and the main arterial highways of southern Johor. Other essentials such as medical supplies, compasses, matches, food, clothing and equipment had been well taken care of and it was only a matter of my saying the word and we would be on our way.

But McGregor had his doubts. Why had Dean selected him to be the one to accompany him? Did he have sufficient confidence in him as a leader, or in himself as a mate, to ensure success? Should he, contrary to Dean's plans, approach his commanding officer for the purpose of seeking his opinion and advice? He slept on it, and awoke to the depressing reality of prisoner-of-war life, with its appalling food, soggy rice, and the humiliating and insufferable existence that had been imposed on him. But he also knew five men from Adam Park had been captured after only a few days out. Still, he told Dean he would go with him.

Dean was delighted and suggested they get out of the Changi camp that very night. McGregor's battalion commander, Captain Tom Bunning, wished McGregor good luck, saying he would cover up their disappearance for two days, but then would have to report there were two men missing. McGregor described their preparations:

> I bustled about gathering a change of clothing, traded my large groundsheet for a waterproof one, acquired a water bottle, and changed my slouch hat for an officer's. We had money, two compasses, two wristwatches, medical supplies, maps, a small quantity of tinned food, but no arms.

Carrying weapons was dismissed by both men because, in the event of being captured, this would be tantamount to signing their own death warrants. The darkness of the night quickly swallowed them up as they followed a track leading to a gate which was one of the very few official exits in the recently erected barbed wire perimeter. The gate was guarded by Indian soldiers, then working for the Japanese, and the escapees had planned to burrow under the fence. McGregor:

> But now that we were actually on the way we decided on a game of bluff with Nippon's new recruits. Standing orders regarding

the use of the gate by prisoners were rigid, but provided an officer could produce evidence to the guards on duty that he had been allocated to some specific duty beyond the prison area he was permitted, on production proof of his rank, to pass through unmolested. This did not apply at night, but we felt quietly confident of success as we approached the gate, our shirts boldly displaying the rank of an officer.

At the gate the guards halted them, demanded their business, and informed them quite politely that no soldier was allowed outside the perimeter at night. In a tone becoming an officer, Dean complimented the guards on their vigilance, but said that their business was private, that the gear on their backs was an essential part of that business, and they would both return when that business had been completed. The guards, perhaps imbued with an ingrained respect for British officers, seemed uncertain of what to do next, and the Australians strode purposefully past them and marched into the night.

Under cover of darkness, the two men reached the shores of Johor Strait in a couple of hours, and Dean recognised the jetty near which he had hidden the submerged boat, stolen some days before. They were not surprised to find it gone, and set off in search of another. But they ran into a Japanese patrol and hid in a large concrete pipe until the early morning light forced them to find a safer hiding place for another day. A deserted house, belonging to high-ranking British naval officers, provided an unexpectedly agreeable sanctuary and occasional naps on a comfortable settee. At 10 am, McGregor heard the unwelcome sound of marching feet, but they were astonished to find they were from a group of shirtless British prisoners of war on a scrounging party. McGregor and Dean locked themselves into their furnished room, but the closed door soon attracted the interest of the British prisoners of war. McGregor wrote:

When the onslaught on the door finally took place—and it was forceful—we quietly turned the key, stood back while the men entered the room, and then told them we were Australian provosts [military police] on duty seeking two prisoners of war who had left the camp area the night before. This tale earned its own reward, and the scroungers took off with surprising promptness, allowing us to enjoy the comfortable room for the rest of the day.

When night fell, the two men set out in different directions along the foreshore, looking for a boat. McGregor was lucky and stole a small canoe from under a local's house. He alerted Dean and they even managed to find a single paddle and a double paddle under the same house. The canoe was barely six-feet long, and was dangerously low in the water, but by balancing and paddling carefully, they managed to get to the mainland despite the strong, swirling tidal current. They pushed their canoe back out into the Johor Strait, hoping it would not be connected with them.

Their plan was to travel north for between 50 and 75 miles, remain under the cover of jungle or rubber plantations at all times, then cross a range of mountains and travel due west to the coast. There they hoped to locate a fishing village and get a boat for the sea crossing to the coast of Sumatra. From then on, they would have to play it by ear. McGregor wrote about Dean's prepared maps:

Before we set out from Changi camp, Lieutenant Dean had wisely prepared a series of maps, each in duplicate, and each covering a reasonable day's travelling. The purpose of the maps was two-fold. First, at the end of each day's journey, the section covering that day was to be destroyed, freeing us of any damning evidence of a connection with Changi prisoner-of-war camp.

Each of us now carried copies of the maps wrapped securely in waterproof cloth, with other items such as matches, cigarettes, and medical supplies.

The two men knew that the only help they could expect was from the Chinese, who had not only suffered great civilian casualties during the battle and indeed bombing of Singapore, but were hated by the Japanese—and the feeling was mutual. The Malays, on the other hand, were mainly pro-Japanese by that stage, enjoying their freedom from British colonial rule. Picking the different houses was easy. The Malays always built their huts on stilts, the Chinese on the ground.

The Chinese almost invariably fed and sheltered them as soon as they realised they weren't Japanese. But danger was never far away. The first time they slept in a Chinese house, they were preparing to leave in the morning when a Japanese truck pulled up outside to search the house. McGregor was packed and ready, so he climbed out a rear window and fled into a rubber plantation. Dean was caught in the house, but managed to climb out and underneath it. Dean recalled their escape in *Singapore Samurai*:

For some unknown reason one of the last of the soldiers bent down to look under the building. He got a terrific shock when he saw me and called out loudly to the others. I don't think he was sure what I was, but he soon realised that I was up to no good and the other soldiers started the engine of the truck. However I was well into the rubber by that time and Mac and I were running deeper into the plantation. For some reason the Japanese only fired a few shots and made no attempt to follow us. Perhaps they thought we were part of a larger group and didn't want to risk walking into an ambush.

Unfortunately the men had to leave their precious *kwalie* [wok] behind in their escape and planned to buy another in a Chinese shop if they could do so. They were also becoming savvy about local crops, like tapioca, almost invariably planted behind any Chinese or Malay house. Tapioca grows underground tubers like potato, and is nutritious, so they knew they would not starve.

A few days later, still heading north, they saw a large European-style house that seemed to be unoccupied. They checked it out and found the previous owners had left in a great hurry. Most of the furniture was still there, the crockery and even clothing in the bedroom. Dean wrote, 'Mac and I were like a couple of kids let loose in a lolly shop.'

There were four bedrooms with about eight beds, linen and mosquito nets, so we had a choice where we would sleep that night. We found a few odd things that had been overlooked when the owners fled, such as a jar of marmalade, a bottle of hot sauce and some very stale bread. There was even a gramophone and records but tempted as we were we didn't dare play them as we had no idea how far the music would carry. Exploring the house further, we found the bathroom equipped with both hot and cold taps so traced the waterline to a boiler. It didn't take us long to get a fire going and later after a good meal we soon had a steaming hot bath and then crawled into beds that had so recently been occupied by a planter and his family. This was not a night to be repeated for many years.

Cleaner than they had been for days, they risked walking into a village and into a shop, where they were greeted in English by the Chinese proprietor, treating them like normal shoppers in normal times. They bought another *kwalie* and some food. The shopkeeper asked them into the house behind his shop for a cup of tea. After some pleasantries, they asked him about making contact with the Chinese underground guerrilla forces. Dean described him as

> . . . very cagey, which was only to be expected, but when we were able to finally convince him that we had escaped from Singapore and showed him our pay books, he became more relaxed. We also assured him of our honesty and that we would not in any way jeopardise his position.

There were a number of guerrilla camps in the region, the Chinese shopkeeper said, but they were hidden deep in the jungle and only the guerrillas knew how to get to them. They were understandably cautious and distrusted everyone, even the villagers who supplied them with food, as there had been instances of Chinese spies helping the Japanese with information. No one from the village had ever been allowed into the camps, but there were some pickup points on the edge of the jungle for food and supplies. He offered to take them to a place that evening where they could make contact with the guerrillas.

At dusk the shopkeeper led them out behind his house, down to the edge of the jungle and through a well-disguised entrance to a small *atap* [thatched palm fronds] hut about 100 yards inside the jungle. There he quickly said goodbye and left them. Dean wrote:

> We didn't have long to wait. Suddenly, and very silently, three well-dressed Chinese soldiers appeared in front of us. They were wearing jungle green uniforms, with Japanese boots and puttees and peaked caps with a red star on the front. Each man had several grenades tied to his belt and the bandolier of cartridges slung across his shoulders. Their rifles were not ones we had seen before but there was no doubt the long bayonets on them were lethal.

The soldiers were not friendly. They did not speak, but two of them stood guard with their rifles trained on the two Australians while the third—putting his own weapon well out of reach—gestured for them to stand up and turn around while he checked for any weapons. Two of them remained, their weapons pointed at McGregor and Dean, while the man who had searched them disappeared into the jungle. The Australians began to wonder what they had got themselves into. Finally, several hours later, the two guards jumped to their feet as a young bespectacled Chinese officer with a pistol on his belt appeared. Dean:

He sent the guards out of the hut, sat down and started to interrogate us. During the next hour or so he questioned us carefully on a wide range of subjects trying to find holes in our story. At the same time we tried to get some information from him, but he was very evasive and we gleaned nothing. It was a totally one-sided conversation and his refusal to answer even the simplest question caused us deep concern.

When he was satisfied with their bona fides, the young officer apologised for the questioning but said he had to be absolutely certain that they were genuine escapees. He and his fellow guerrillas had already dealt with several traitors. As a dyed-in-the wool communist, the officer made no secret of his distrust of the British but felt that for the time being any help they could get to attack the Japanese would be welcome. He then told the Australians the camp was a long way off over a very rough and twisting track and it would be wise to stay with the Chinese shopkeeper for the night and set out early the following morning. Dean:

Now that we were on better terms with this young officer we felt he was a very interesting man. He told us that his name was Soon and that his parents were merchants in Kuala Lumpur. Soon was a founding member of the Communist Party in Malaya which was rapidly organising guerrilla forces all over the country. Their short-term objective was the defeat of the Japanese, followed eventually by the establishment of a Communist Malaya.

At dawn they set off, led by Soon. Every few hundred yards Soon gave a password to an unseen sentry beside the track. No one would be able to use this track without being seen. After some hours, Soon explained that Dean and McGregor would have to be blindfolded so that in the event of their being captured by the Japanese, they would be unable to lead them to the guerrilla camp. This made the journey slow, as they stumbled over roots and stones on the rough jungle track. They knew they were nearing the camp when they heard sounds of activity. Their blindfolds were removed and they were allowed time for their eyes to adjust to the light. McGregor wrote:

An amazing scene met our eyes. Dean and I gasped in wonderment as we stood and looked out upon the jungle headquarters of the Anti-Jap Movement. Stretched right across the clear area and fixed to the limbs of opposite trees by ropes was a huge calico banner: WELCOME INTERNATIONAL SOLDIERS—JOIN THE A[nti] J[apanese] TROOPS, revealing not only the true feelings of the Chinese towards us but also that our services were being sought. The banner, about 40 feet long and 4 feet wide, fluttered in the breeze directly above a double line of Chinese—men, women and children—who had been mustered for our welcome. Pen and I stepped forward to the head of the lines, halted, raised our right arms in salute, and began to march through. The cheering and handclapping affected us a great deal. But imagine our surprise when, at the very end of the lines, we found not Chinese—but Australians! Yes, nine khaki-clad Australians each holding mugs of steaming hot coffee in their left hands, and each with his right arm outstretched to shake our hands.

Dean wrote that he and McGregor were goggle-eyed at the extent of the camp:

It consisted of about 30 well built huts, including a hospital, all made of the usual *atap*. They were laid out in a square, beneath camouflage netting, which was regularly replaced with freshly cut foliage. There appeared to be several hundred people in the camp including a number of young women in uniform whose armbands signified their position—usually medical orderlies or volunteers—in this well-organised force. On the edge of the camp was an Australian 25-pounder artillery piece. How they got it in there I have no idea. There were also two Bofors guns and on the far side a large ammunition dump on which they had a constant guard.

The Chinese colonel in charge of the camp, Lieu Kim Bok, welcomed them in excellent English and invited them into his headquarters for biscuits, a cup of tea and a briefing. He first questioned them closely about their escape, the route they had taken north and what contacts they had with people along the way who might know which way they were heading. Dean and McGregor then told the colonel what they wanted to do—to go further north and then head to the west coast, where they hoped to get a boat and escape to Ceylon. The colonel explained that they would need a great deal of assistance from well-to-do Chinese to do this. The Japanese were in strength along the west coast and had the Straits of Malacca well covered with patrol boats.

However, if they could get to the Indian Ocean their chances would improve. In the meantime, he hoped they would stay with his camp and help train his troops, as they had a number of Vickers machine guns and Bren guns that they had picked up during the Malayan campaign.

Dean and McGregor agreed, but remained keen to get on with their own escape. For the moment, they had to join the group of Allied soldiers already with the guerrillas, who were doing similar work. A routine of daily training began, trying to teach raw recruits the basics of soldiering and weapons handling, while the guerrillas made daily forays out from the jungle, blowing up railway lines and performing other acts of sabotage. They had quite a few casualties on their night attacks, and the small hospital filled up with wounded, some of whom died. The colonel refused to let any of the Europeans join any of these parties, or indeed to leave the camp. All the Australians began to realise that they were effectively again prisoners in this situation. Clearly the guerrillas wouldn't feed them without expecting something in return. Perhaps it was better to escape while they were in reasonable health. Certainly life was cheap, even among the guerrillas themselves. Dean wrote:

> The Chinese tied up two of their own troops for some infringement of the camp rules. They executed them and, with much laughing and joking, tossed their bodies in graves that had already been dug. It frightened [the] hell out of us all, and brought home just how tenuous our position actually was.

Dean and McGregor had to think up a reason to get the colonel to let them all go. They cooked up a story that they would contact the Allies when they got to the coast and persuade them to drop arms and a good transmitter into a friendly village at the edge of the jungle. They offered to be blindfolded as they were led out of the camp. They managed to get the colonel to agree to provide them with a guide, and some rations, to help them on their way. They were ready to go the next morning, but, as Dean wrote, there was a delay:

All movements in and out of the camp were stopped when a number of traitors were brought into the camp for interrogation. The accused were marched onto the parade ground, two young Malays and an older Tamil man who had already been knocked about. From a distance we could see that each of those being questioned was being beaten with a rattan cane and that some of the inquisitors were using bayonets. The Malays were screaming for mercy saying they would tell their captors whatever they wanted to know, and the Tamil was already confessing. It appeared that the two Malays had told the Japanese who was sending in food to the camps, while the Tamil had apparently made his way to a nearby kampong to see if he could find out anything that merited a reward.

All three were tied to trees for the rest of the day and that night the political meeting was told what the traitors had confessed. It was agreed that all three would be executed the next morning and that our party could not leave until after lunch. The three condemned men were made to dig their own graves and then put to death. A rope was tied around their necks and gradually tightened. It took some time for each of them to die and we were expected to watch. When their bodies were eventually thrown into graves, all the guerrillas were happy and laughing. This only strengthened our urgent desire to quit the guerrilla forces forever.

To their great relief, all the Australians were blindfolded and led away from the camp and down out of the jungle until they reached a rubber plantation. Their blindfolds removed, Dean and McGregor parted company, as agreed, from the other Australians, who had joined them to get out of the camp and who intended to go north. Dean and McGregor planned to head towards the west coast. All were eventually captured. The five Australians who went north finished up in Pudu Gaol in Kuala Lumpur but managed to convince the Japanese that they were not escapees as they had never been prisoners of war, and had been wandering about lost since the end of the hostilities. They all got sent to Changi.

Dean and McGregor had one more week of freedom before their fortunes took a darker turn and, up to this point, descriptions of their experiences confirm each other's version of events. But for their last week on the run, Dean's account of their alleged sabotage is highly questionable. In a chapter of *Singapore Samurai*, starkly headed 'Sabotage', he recounts an action-packed week in which he led a personal campaign of sabotage against the Japanese.

On their first night away from the Chinese guerrilla camp, Dean claims he and McGregor set fire to a Japanese-run rubber factory and destroyed the whole complex. Two nights later he set fire to another rubber factory. Dean wrote:

Next morning we searched along the edge of the jungle to see if we could find a track. Suddenly Mac called out to me to come quickly. I made my way to Mac, who pointed to two Army boxes with rope handles. He had already opened the larger one that contained four mortar shells. We soon discovered that the smaller box had two-dozen hand-grenades.

We looked at each other, our brains surging with ideas, fumbling around for uses to which we could put this find. Our first thought was that the mortar shells were a dead loss, but then an idea came to me. We were going to cross the railway line before long. Maybe we could place the shells against the rails in such a manner that the train would detonate them. The grenades could be used to create problems in a multitude of ways.

This seems to have been an extraordinary and fortuitous find!

Dean claims they booby-trapped a train line with a grenade nestling next to two mortar bombs, its pin pulled but held by a twig, but they dared not stay around to judge the results. However, while sheltering with a friendly Chinese that night, they heard that there had been a derailment on the main line to Kuala Lumpur.

An engine and three wagons had gone down the embankment, quite a bit of rail was torn up and best of all, the wagons had caught fire as one of them had been carrying drums of fuel. The guerrillas were being blamed.

On their travels the next day, according to Dean, they saw a driver and one passenger in a small Japanese army truck travelling on a dirt road. The truck stopped, and the men walked away on some mission. Dean had told McGregor of a plan to use the grenades, to blow up a car or truck.

The plan was to remove the pin from a grenade and wedge it under the clutch pedal of a truck or van. When the driver started the engine the depressed clutch would dislodge the grenade. Four seconds later he would join his ancestors and the vehicle would be wrecked. This seemed like an ideal opportunity to test the plan as Mac could keep an eye on the two Japanese while I shot over to the vehicle and effectively booby-trapped it.

Everything went as planned. It was a soda to put the grenade in place and I was back with Mac very smartly. The two Japanese, who I think were from a construction unit, were still at the rise as we moved back deeper into the rubber, lay down and waited for their return. After about 20 minutes they slowly made their way back to the truck. The passenger got in first, and then the driver. They sat and talked for a while before the driver started the engine. A few seconds later there was a loud detonation and a lot of smoke, followed by a second explosion as the petrol tank blew up. The occupants didn't know what hit them, and Mac and I beat a very hasty retreat.

Later that day (Dean claimed), they burnt down another rubber factory for good measure. And the next day, they sabotaged another railway line with two grenades on a points junction, but again they could not stay around to see what happened. After having been shot at by two Japanese soldiers who saw them trying to cross a road, Dean thought he and McGregor would 'have to put their sabotage on hold'.

Now the curious thing about all this heroism is that McGregor didn't mention a single word about any of it in his parallel account of that momentous week. The obvious explanation is that Dean was big-noting himself half a century on, and that none of it ever happened.

What did happen (and was confirmed by the accounts of both men) was they were captured by a group of Malays and Tamils, dressed in blue Chinese-style clothes, whom they had mistakenly hailed thinking they were Chinese. The group was armed and hostile. They tied the two Australians up with rope, and looted their possessions, which had one blessing in that much incriminating material was scattered to the winds, or disposed of by the unaware mob. The Indians wanted to kill them on the spot, but the Malays thought there might be a reward if they handed them in to the police, who would notify the Japanese. Dean:

The crowd had grown as this discussion took place and we
were being kicked and punched, even urinated on. The crowd
was really enjoying the spectacle of the degradation of the two
Europeans and we were kicked along down the road to Pontian
Ketchil. Even the women spat on us and we were soon black
and blue from the kicks and the beatings we received. Someone
went off and alerted the local police who locked us up in a tiny
dirty cell.

At last the two men could talk to each other. They had to stick to
their cover story through thick and thin if they were to escape being
beheaded. Their story was that they were members of the 2/29th
Battalion who had been left behind in the fighting in Malaya. They
couldn't say that they belonged to the 2/4th Machine Gun Battalion
as they only fought on Singapore island. They would claim they had
been lost in the jungle since the action and had survived on pineapples
and tapioca roots and caught birds. Of course, no mention would be
made of any contact with the Chinese or that they had even heard of
the guerrilla forces.

Handed over to a Japanese officer (who did not mistreat them),
they were driven by car to Johor Bahru and put into a filthy dirt-
floored Malay police cell for several days, before being driven across
the causeway to Singapore. The faint hope surfaced that they might
be returning to Changi. Instead, they were put in the custody of their
former Allies, members of the Indian Army, who much enjoyed the
opportunity to humiliate their former 'white masters' by housing
them in squalid conditions, in an open compound without any shelter
from the sun or torrential rain.

McGregor felt that the commandant of the camp, an English-
educated officer, was not entirely ill-disposed towards them. Unfortunately, Dean complained through the barbed wire to a visiting Indian

officer (a friend of the commandant's) that they were being badly treated and asked if they could have some shelter. The commandant was humiliated by the approach to his friend, and angry that he had been put in such a position. The result was that, a week later, they were turned over to the Japanese and, worse, into the hands of the *Kempeitai*.

McGregor wondered until the day he died whether, if they had just put up with the conditions for a couple more weeks without complaining, there might have been a chance the Indians would have returned them to Changi—the best possible outcome. As it was, they got the worst outcome—delivered to *Kempeitai* headquarters in Singapore. There McGregor got off to a bad start because he smirked at a Japanese officer who was searching him—mindful that the Indians had just subjected him to a similar indignity:

> I earned myself two terrific smacks across the face for being so presumptuous and he then swung at me with all his strength, and connected fair and square with my unprotected jaw, then struck again. His authority had been insulted and belittled— that was more than evident—but after the second huge swing he restrained his arm and then attacked me verbally. I raised my hand-cuffed hands and gave him to understand that we resented such cowardly treatment.

This was just a curtain-raiser. Dean and McGregor were then interrogated for seventeen days, the *Kempeitai* officers playing their cards cunningly and well. At times they would shower the Australians with cigarettes and sweets, sit the men in comfortable chairs and supposedly regard them as their friends. When this velvet-glove approach failed, the iron fist emerged as they were bashed and hammered, forced to kneel on sharp wooden edges for lengthy periods and had lighted matches held under their elbows. When these extreme measures brought no satisfactory result, they would resort to the most dreaded torture of all—the water treatment. McGregor:

> The inhuman fiends would place a hose in my mouth, turn the tap on, and in this way force water down the throat and into the body. When I was still not prepared to talk I was pushed to the floor, held down on my back, and the water pressure increased. Then other intakes would be attacked, intake such as the ears, the nose and the anus. The body finally rebelled, having taken in as much water as was humanly possible, but the treatment didn't end there. The guards then got great pleasure from jumping on my stomach, holding my body upside down, or rolling it over and over to see how much fluid could be ejected. And so ended the interrogation for that day. Many natives who underwent the dreaded water treatment did not survive the ordeal and at times I wonder how I did.

McGregor and Dean were interviewed separately, but allowed to communicate with each other overnight. As a result of this break in security, they were able to co-ordinate their stories to a remarkable degree about their escape and capture, and sign statements to that effect. Dean had the water treatment too, but also electric shock treatment from his interrogator Sergeant Amura, who insisted that both men had been with the Chinese guerrilla forces, which, of course, they denied. Dean wrote:

> Sergeant Amura had some electric flex and what appeared to be a transformer, which he plugged into a power point. After I denied we even knew such guerrilla forces existed, he tied me to the chair, turned on the power and taking the bare ends of the electrical wires he held them against each side of my left

hand. I screamed, the pain in my body arching me in the chair. Deciding that this was not enough fun he pulled my pants down and applied the wires to my testicles. The agony was unbearable and I screamed and passed out.

At the YMCA, Dean vowed to himself that, come what may, he would learn Japanese so he could know what was being said. He had already learned quite a number of words and phrases.

The *Kempeitai* had remarkable power, even over the Japanese themselves. They were not subject to any civilian law, they had their own gaols, they tried people in military courts where there was no right of appeal, they conducted their enquiries within their own building and their own doctors provided death certificates as required. Their power was absolute in any area under Japanese control. They were brought in whenever a commander failed to obtain his objectives. Their methods of interrogation encompassed every form of torture known to man and they boasted that they always had a confession when they put a defender before an army court.

Furthermore, the *Kempeitai* were never in a hurry. The only important thing was to have a captive sign his own death warrant by finally confessing to whatever charges it suited them to bring against him. If they were short of work they would send out soldiers to round up any given group, put them through the grinder and come up with more impressive numbers of enemies of Japan. Dean and McGregor shared their YMCA accommodation with the Eurasian Anglican Archbishop of Singapore. The bishop told Dean he was charged with inciting rebellion. It was a trumped-up charge based on allegations from some Indian workers no doubt seeking favours from the Japanese.

After seventeen days of torture, their interrogators gave up on Dean and McGregor, who signed their 'confessions' before being taken to their court martial in the former Singapore Supreme Court building.

They understood nothing of the proceedings, but feared the worst when one of the guards drew his hand across his throat after the judge had left the court. One of the interpreters then told them they had been sentenced to two years' solitary confinement in Outram Road Gaol. By the standards of the *Kempeitai*, it was a remarkably light penalty.

It was evening when Dean and McGregor were taken to their cells in Outram Road Gaol. First, they were stripped of their clothes and issued with a Japanese army shirt and a pair of shorts. They realised their tiny cells were largely underground save for the window at ground level, but an earth wall outside kept any trace of sunlight from getting into the cell. A single globe—never turned off—hung from the ceiling. The thick wooden door had a small grill near its base and a peephole at shoulder height, both of which could be opened from the outside. The only items in the cell were three bed boards, each about eight-inches wide and seven-feet long, a curved wooden 'pillow' and a bucket for a toilet. That was it.

McGregor woke to his first full day at Outram Road on Anzac Day, 1942, roused by a Japanese guard who handed him some breakfast and suggested that he sit on the doorstep of the open cell door and eat. Dean was doing the same, as were several prisoners sitting on the other side, and conversation was allowed. After eating their meal the guard signalled that they could walk for exercise in the corridor. They were able to quickly glean what the other men were in gaol for, and for the first time where they were. McGregor wrote:

It was apparent that the Japanese had only recently set this place up as a military prison because of the small number of men being held in custody. Sandbags and tools strewn all over the ground floor area also were evidence of hasty preparation— nothing having as yet been done to remove whatever efforts the British had put into the resistance campaign.

For sixteen days there was no departure from the routine. After each meal the prisoners were allowed to mingle, and to stroll up and down the gaol corridor, with the one guard on duty being quite content to sit at a table near the gaol's entrance, either reading or writing letters. This guard was a frontline soldier, and, unlike the *Kempeitai*, who would eventually take over management of Outram Road Gaol, was not used to duties of this nature, so permitted liberties never to be experienced again. McGregor's gloomy comment written later—'The future was to prove to us that there is no situation in this world which cannot get worse'—was depressingly apt.

It was late in the afternoon of the sixteenth day that this relaxed regime came to a brutal halt. The meal was over and the prisoners were enjoying their usual stroll. Two Chinese were walking ahead of Dean and McGregor as they all walked towards the end of the corridor where the congenial guard was stationed, sitting at a table and, as usual, reading his letters. Suddenly, and without the slightest warning, one of the two Chinese in front of them headed towards one side of the corridor, grabbed a hammer lying there, then lunged forward at the unsuspecting guard, and struck him a sickening blow on the side of the head. A second blow was attempted, and would have succeeded had not Dean rushed at the Chinese and unbalanced him, causing the hammer to miss its mark. There was confusion everywhere. The guard's body lay slumped across the table, blood was streaming from the gaping wound, and his keys and letters lay on the blood-spattered floor. McGregor wrote:

Pen Dean, with the help of another Chinese, was holding down the would-be killer. Impulsively I rushed towards the entrance and shouted through the bars for help. In a matter of moments half a dozen uniformed men had reached the locked gates, one of them an officer, flourishing a revolver. They shouted and screamed rattling the gates as they pulled at the bars in their efforts to get inside. I picked up the key from where it had fallen and passed it through. The gates were unlocked and in rushed the half-dozen evil-looking guards.

What else could the Japanese officer do than assume, at first glance, that the prisoners had rioted, the guard had been brutally attacked and that a mass escape had been intended? For one tense moment he surveyed the scene, silently moving his head to and fro in order to take in all aspects of the scene before him. McGregor:

The Japanese officer thundered out some unintelligible oath or command and then started to shoot. One Chinese went down and others would have quickly followed had not the stricken guard suddenly shown signs of consciousness, a circumstance which, thank God, momentarily attracted the officer's attention. In a flash all the prisoners had gone, fleeing to their cells and slamming the doors behind them. What happened in the corridor after that I do not know, but I do know that, with the slamming of my door on that fateful occasion, I was destined to see the end of any form of freedom from my cell for the interminable period of sixteen unbroken months.

The stricken guard—who survived—was later shot for being so lax in his duties. McGregor wondered if the regime at the gaol five months later, once the *Kempeitai* took full control, would have been less bestial had this incident not occurred, but on balance thought it probably made little difference. Outram Road Gaol was a place of punishment and death, and the system made sure that the prisoners suffered for every second of their sentences.

# 3

# 'JUST TO GO INTO THAT PLACE . . .'

Chris Neilson's greatest fear in his first few months at Outram Road Gaol, in June 1942, was that he would go mad. 'Just to go into that place, it was something else, one of those old-fashioned British gaols. My sentence was three years' solitary confinement, and that's what it was. The guards didn't speak to you, and you had no one to speak to. As a matter of fact if you had a nightmare and yelled out in your sleep, the Jap guard would burst in the door and kick your ribs in.

'Twice a day you got a ball of rice the size of a cricket ball. There was a little bowl, about half the size of an ordinary cup, with what they called tea—it was mostly cherry leaves, and you only had two of those a day and that is all the water you had. You were thirsty all the time. Occasionally there might be a kind of soup, just the tops of pumpkin or sweet potato vines and a few leaves, never any real vegetables. But you wouldn't dare pick that up until they said you could eat. And if you were slow eating and hadn't finished by the time they said stop, they took it back. Sometimes you might only have thirty seconds. If you only had one chopstick, which was often the case, you just scoffed it as quick as you could.'

The diet was barely enough to sustain life. But that was another curious feature of Japanese thinking. Individually, they didn't care if prisoners lived or died, but the prisoners were supposed to serve out their full sentence, and if they died in their cells questions would be asked from higher echelons. So every now and then the prisoners would notice, say, a few soy beans in their soup, which would bring them back from the brink of utter starvation. 'But it didn't take long,' Neilson remembered, 'I'd say about six weeks, before you could see the first effects of the beriberi—the swelling of the ankles and then, later, of the testicles. They were the main two parts that were swollen, huge. Then the food might improve slightly, and the swelling would go down.'

Apart from being hungry all the time, the bugs and flesh-eating lice in the cells were tormenting and itching their ravaged bodies. Some simply couldn't take it and went mad. 'It's not just loneliness or fear, it's the isolation—there's nothing to turn to,' Neilson reflects. 'There's nothing you could pick up to read, you could only scratch on the stucco of the wall with a little sliver of bamboo, or a piece of fishbone salvaged from your food, about any event that happened that day, perhaps an execution and who did it. There was nothing else to do but just wait and sit around in that cell day after day.'

There were only a handful of Europeans in Outram Road Gaol when Neilson and his four fellow escapees arrived. They were three Free French civilians, who were later sent to Saigon, Penrod Dean, John McGregor and an older civilian Englishman they called 'Pop' Davies, who was dying when Neilson first saw him. 'They had the door of his cell open. He was lying there in his own excrement, his balls as big as footballs with beriberi. He kept yelling, "Oh my God, let me die." I bellowed out, "For Christ's sake, Davies, die quietly, you're giving these bastards the chance to laugh at you." And the bloody Japs that came past were joking about him. He got no medical attention and died not long after that.'

David Henry Davies was a civilian, a former rubber planter, who had been caught listening to a radio broadcast of light music, after the capitulation. As a civilian, he should have been interned, but the Japanese just did what they pleased. John McGregor thinks he was probably persecuted because of his name:

> The Japs could not—or would not—understand that the name David Davies was an authentic one. They claimed that Davies was lying to them and that perhaps he was a spy.

The guards were identified by nicknames. 'Cascara', named after a popular laxative of the day ('Just looking at him gave you the shits'), was one of the most brutal. Neilson's particular *bête noire* was 'The Groper', a six-foot Korean. One of Neilson's survival strategies was constant psychological warfare with the guards, who he always needled and goaded. He figured a bashing was preferable to the mind-numbing boredom of nothing happening at all.

Some prisoners did break down mentally, like the unfortunate Bob Green, who had been with Neilson on the attempted escape from the Adam Park work camp. 'I heard this great commotion and banging, and I knelt down on the floor of my cell and looked through the grate in the bottom of the door. There was poor Greenie running around outside his cell with his shit bucket upended over his head—he was covered in it. He was running around like Ned Kelly, banging his head against the walls. He'd dipped his hand into the bucket, with the piss and everything else, and said, "That's beer! It's me old man's supper, with sausages and gravy!" The Japanese couldn't cope with anyone with mental illness, it used to freak them out. The next day they put him in a car and took him back to the main POW camp at Changi. But if it hadn't been for Green going off his nut, I'd have been next. I thought, "This is it,

I'm going to go bloody hoopla." But strangely enough I was all right after that.'

In August, two months after Neilson had entered the grim portals of the gaol, John 'Mac' McGregor was moved into the cell next door. Neilson was desperate for some kind of contact with another Australian. At that stage of the gaol regime, a 'trusty' Chinese came into the cells occasionally to carry out the brimming *benki* buckets, by now thoughtfully provided with lids. One of Neilson's prized possessions was a precious half an inch of lead, split from a pencil he had managed to acquire. He wrote the basics of Morse code on a scrap of paper, bound it around a chopstick with a thread from his prison clothes, and asked the Chinese (who spoke Malay) to slip it to his next-door neighbour.

McGregor, who had a photographic memory, memorised the entire code during the day and got rid of the evidence. Neilson says, 'When we got into contact we used a tap with a fingernail on the wall for the dots, and a rap with our knuckles for the dashes.'

They had to be careful because in the silence of the gaol the tapping could be easily heard from the corridor outside. In that respect, the squalor and stench of their disgusting cells with the rarely emptied toilet buckets worked in their favour. The Japanese are a very fastidious people and hated entering any of the smelly cells. Even walking along the corridors was not free from unpleasant smells, and the guards used to drench themselves in perfume to ward off the stinking ambience of their workplace. The prisoners, although living in permanently malodorous surroundings, developed a sharp sense of smell to identify the guards' highly scented approach in time to stop transmission. Many of the guards failed to remove their swords, often with a chain rattling against them, which also gave away their approach.

Neilson and McGregor weren't the only Allied prisoners in Outram Road to communicate by Morse code. Others used buttons from their clothes and little chips of stone, which were more easily heard. One of the penalties for discovery was that all buttons were cut off every gaol garment. But Neilson and McGregor, their noses at the ready, got away with their daily chats for as long as they were in adjacent cells. McGregor quickly became proficient in Morse code. Neilson recalls, 'I'd say, "Well listen, today I'm going to take you for a trip north of Cooktown, fishing." It would take all day to tap through what you could say in half an hour. The next day Mac would say, "Come with me to the grape growing country, not far from Midland Junction," where he lived. I said, "Yeah, I've been there." He said, "But you people only went there to work, to pick the oranges and peaches and put them into bags. We were there in the school holidays, where the kids roll down one peach at a time at the market without being caught." This went on all the time, but you had to always be aware of the perfume of a guard sneaking up the corridor, wearing his split-toed rubber boots.'

There were other ways of getting news. When Flight-Lieutenant Jack Macalister came in to Outram Road in February 1943 (after plans to escape from Singapore using a captured aircraft were discovered by Japanese agents), he was put in a cell directly opposite Neilson. Using deaf-and-dumb sign language through the open food slots in their cell doors, Neilson learned from Macalister—via a Changi secret radio—about the bombing of Darwin, and the news quickly spread throughout the gaol through the Morse code and signing networks.

Neilson gave the news to his friend McGregor first, but was furious when he started to transmit the town name 'Wyndham', which Macalister told him had also been bombed. Every time he started to spell the name, McGregor 'erased' him, using the code for a mistake. After this happened three times, Neilson lost his temper and shouted through the slot in his door: '"Listen, you bloody smart university-educated bastard. It's your own state, Western Australia, it's W Y N D H A M." He thought I was misspelling it.'

Of course the guards were at his door in seconds, and he was severely belted for daring to shout through the door. Neilson, as he reasoned with all his bashings, thought it was worth it to get up the guards' noses.

John McGregor later wrote in *Blood on the Rising Sun* how Chris Neilson taught him Morse code and how grateful he was for this, and the communication and friendship that followed. Why McGregor's friend Penrod Dean found it necessary to write in *Singapore Samurai* that he had taught McGregor Morse code—when McGregor states in his own book that he didn't—is yet another example of self-aggrandisement from this curious character. Neilson claimed when interviewed that Dean didn't know Morse code.

It is difficult to be judgmental about those who live under such circumstances and who manage to survive. Chris Neilson and John McGregor found it essential to maintain a combative attitude to their gaolers, to try to take a rise out of them at some personal risk, and so maintain a psychological superiority over their tormentors who failed to break them. Dean, on the other hand, had different plans, which he expressed frankly in his memoir. After his first week in Outram Road, he concluded that those who were quick to learn the way the Japanese penal system worked would have the best chance of survival:

> I had worked out my options. I could refuse to co-operate with the gaol authorities and be as difficult as possible, or I could co-operate only as much as would be necessary to survive. A third option was to co-operate and learn Japanese as quickly as possible. Not only would I then know what was going on, but I would be able to present appeals for any urgent needs that arose. And I felt sure that speaking to the Japanese in their own language would ensure they would at least listen to me. Learning their difficult language also gave me a useful occupation to help pass the time.

Dean assessed his guards and only approached the ones he felt might be halfway reasonable. He began by memorising fifteen Japanese words a day, starting with parts of the body. Even though talking was forbidden, some of the guards took an interest in the foreigner who was trying to learn their language.

An unwelcome discovery was that the Japanese had a punitive attitude to illness. Their response to sickness, like beriberi or dysentery, was to withdraw all food until the men recovered—as though illness was a personal failure by the prisoner concerned. Of course, many did not recover in time to be fed again, and died.

Any break in routine was an event, no matter what it was. McGregor recalls one morning when a guard came round to each cell and asked each inmate if he could work a sewing machine:

> He came to me with the same question and I replied, 'Of course I can't you mad ape', figuring I was probably better off in my cell where I knew where I was. The guard kept getting knocked back until he reached Pen Dean's cell, after which he hurried away only to return pushing an old treadle sewing machine in front of him which he carried into Dean's cell. My first thought was, 'Pen working a sewing machine—I'd sure like to get a photograph'.

If Dean didn't know how to sew, he soon picked it up, and shortly was running up khaki prison uniforms. He was so productive that he was allowed to move out of his cell into the corridor to get better light. When the uniforms were done, he made himself popular with the guards by repairing rips in their clothes and sewing on buttons. When the sewing machine stint ended, he had won the best prize of all in Outram Road Gaol—being assigned as one of the 'trusties' to deliver food on a trolley to all the prisoners. For some reason, Dean did not mention the sewing machine breakthrough in his own memoir, but McGregor gave a full account.

Meanwhile, Dean's proficiency in the Japanese language was increasing steadily by the day. He realised that not all the guards were fiends in human form. He judged that there were some quite reasonable types who treated the prisoners decently when they were on their own but shouted and screamed as brutally as the others whenever anyone else was present. He also realised that, in the Japanese disciplinary system, their freedom was always on the line too. Dean worked on the ones he judged would co-operate. He found the best time for learning was always late at night, when everyone was asleep and the gaol was quiet. The friendly guards could then afford to lean in the recess of his door and talk to him without much chance of being caught by their superiors.

Finally I had five guards teaching me Japanese when they came on duty at night. They started by giving me the names of various items I pointed to, and as I sat the next day I repeated them over and over, hour by hour, until the words were stamped on my brain. It was a slow and laborious process but when I finally left the gaol I knew more Japanese words than English. After building a vocabulary, I gradually learnt verbs and adjectives and so on, until I could string sentences together—very badly at first, much to the amusement of my teachers. However by the latter stages of my incarceration I was quite fluent.

By his own account, Dean used his presence on the food trolley to make sure every prisoner got equal helpings. There had been cronyism before, he wrote, to such an extent that the Indian and Eurasian doing the job would run out of food when only 80 per cent of the prisoners had been fed, because they favoured their friends. Dean's reforms of the food distribution may well have been true, but Chris Neilson tells a different story when it came to how Dean looked after himself. Once, on a rare excursion out of his cell, Neilson came across Dean standing near the food trolley 'scoffing down a big meal of tinned fish and rice' that in Outram Road terms was a dreamed-of lavish banquet. Despite Dean's own assertion that he came out of gaol after his two-year sentence half his normal weight, Neilson and several others attest he came out at his normal weight, as fit as when he went in.

Neilson couldn't stand Dean, because he thought of him as a 'white Jap', a collaborator whose behaviour went against Neilson's personal philosophy of non co-operation and resistance. 'He was a cocky little bugger. Once when the *Kempeitai* cut our rations but allowed us to exercise out in the yard, we were so weak we couldn't do any exercises. Dean said, "I'm doing it as tough as you now." Geoff Shelley said, "Yes, you bastard, and you're three times my weight too".'

Ken Bird, one of Neilson's escape party, thought Dean 'a bastard' because he packed his and McGregor's food into the bowls so tightly 'you could barely push a chopstick into it', while everyone else's rice 'went in loose' so that you 'could have eaten ours [servings] with five teaspoons full'.

Private Bill Young thought Dean certainly looked after himself on the food trolley. He was also candid enough to think he probably would have done so too, had their positions been reversed. Young says, 'But I did take umbrage later when he said he was thin when he left Outram Road—he wasn't. When we went out he wasn't normal, he was fantastic! He used to bend down and do push-ups for the Japs to show off. I've seen it, myself. He was a pocket Mr Atlas [a famous bodybuilder] and that caught him out in a lie, a blatant lie. He was as fit as a fiddle and proud of that.'

McGregor, whose friendship and support of Dean never wavered, claimed Dean saved his life by smuggling him vitamin B pills obtained

from a sympathetic guard, which he managed to get to other prisoners as well, temporarily at least keeping beriberi at bay. The only time
their rice and soup diet was varied was when the Japanese executed
one of their own prisoners and then everyone got a little treat.

In his early months in Outram Road Gaol, McGregor joined enthu-
siastically with his Morse code mate Neilson in the sport of baiting
their guards. 'Jesse James'—so called because he always wore a mask
over his face to protect him from the stench of the cells—was a basher,
but not well endowed in the brains department. He knew McGregor
could count up to five in Japanese, so asked him one day to teach
him to count in English. McGregor kept Neilson informed by tapping
about what he was doing through the cell wall. After some time,
earnestly writing the English numbers in his notebook, Jesse proudly
told Neilson that he could count up to five in English. 'I said, "That's
not English, you bloody ape, that's Americano." It took me ten days to
teach him to count up to ten in Hindustani. Then he went to practise
on McGregor, and he said, "No, that's not Americano, that's Eskimo."'

McGregor told Jesse that Neilson was unreliable because he was
Norwegian and couldn't speak proper English.

After some days of this Jesse had had enough. He stepped back
a couple of paces to where he could view the two cell doors at
once, then took out his notebook [and] studied it for a minute
or two before ripping it to shreds, flinging the lot to the floor
and jumping on the offending fragments as if he was dealing
with a rattlesnake. Finally making up his mind both of us had
taken him for a ride, we each received a bashing which left us
sore for some days.

Each cell possessed four air vents, one in each lower corner. An
iron bar had been built into each of these vents to partly close up

the opening, but in the dim distant past one of those bars had been wrenched from its place and was now missing. However, the Japanese had not noticed that the bar was not in place—when they did, there was hell to pay. Unfortunately for McGregor, the missing bar was in his cell:

The commotion started with the arrival of the gaol captain. He tested the three remaining bars to see if they had been tampered with, then felt my muscles, measured my shoulders, and asked me if I'd pulled the bar away from its embedded place, wanting to know where it was, and was it my intention to use it on the head of some Japanese guard. The questions came quick and fast from the captain while half a dozen apes searched the cell.

A stepladder was rushed in, the ledge of the upper barred window was examined, I was searched, the hygiene bucket was tipped over, and the concrete walls and floor were tapped.

There was no trace of the missing 30-inch iron bar. The Japs even went so far as to peer into my ears and mouth! It was obvious that the bar had been wrenched out long before most of them had celebrated their first birthday. The fact that the bar couldn't be found didn't prove I was not in possession of it. Accordingly, for not handing it over when ordered, I was given a man-sized bashing, and placed in handcuffs for three months. Is it any wonder prisoners went mad when they were forced to exist in such a maniacal environment?

McGregor noticed that the food—what there was of it—was served in aluminium bowls that had been part of the prison equipment when the Japanese took Outram Road over. Realising that these bowls travelled all round the gaol, Mac started to scratch little drawings and messages on them. As the weeks went on, he realised that other

prisoners were using the dishes this way too. Of course it was too
good to last, and quite soon the eagle-eyed, paranoid Japanese guards
discovered the practice. By coincidence, McGregor, who had triggered
the whole affair, was the one chosen to take the rap. One day, just after
the midday meal, Mac was frog-marched out of his cell by a guard
and taken out into the courtyard to a heap of aluminium pannikins
stacked alongside a water hydrant and told to wash them. This was at
first a plus for McGregor:

> As the water gushed forth I managed to bring my stinking body
> into contact with the flow and commence washing away some
> of the filth which had been part of me for so long, but the Jap,
> damn him, soon made it clear it was the dishes which were to
> be washed. I apologised for my mistake but still managed to get
> myself mixed up with the terribly inviting stream of water.

To be out of the cell in the sunlight with cool fresh water, a gentle
breeze and the sense of freedom, was a fabulous bonus—except for
the guard prodding him with his sword to get on with washing the
dishes.

The real purpose of my outside visit was made clear when
the guard poked one of the washed dishes under my nose
and asked me to read aloud what was written on the bottom.
Lovingly I took the dish, turned it over and over in my hands,
all the time looking out for something new. I told the guard that
the scratchings referred to the prisoners' demand for extra food,
adding that they also wanted the rice dressed up a little with
green vegetables. He grunted and prodded me to go on with the
job of washing.

The end came when the guard tired of inventive translations, scattered the remaining dishes with his foot, told McGregor to turn off the hydrant, gave him several whacks across his back with his sword scabbard and pushed him back into his cell:

> When the tins next appeared they were gleaming with cleanliness, having been sanded to effectively delete the suspicious markings that had proved so baffling to [the] mighty Nippon.

And the clean surfaces were ready for more messages.

In the first five months before the *Kempeitai* took complete control of Outram Road Gaol, prisoners got out of their cells briefly, about once a week, to empty their toilet buckets, rinse them with water from a trough, and go back to their cells. Even though they were taken out in small groups, there was still time to exchange a few words, and swap the latest gossip. But the *Kempeitai* arranged for trusties to take the buckets in and out, and prisoners had to fester in their cells in unrelieved isolation. Part of the punishment of being in gaol was to endure the squalor of the never-cleaned cells. The only exception was if a prisoner were to die in his cell through suicide or disease—and many did. Then several prisoners would be escorted from their own cells to where the dead man lay to remove the body and clean up the detritus of death, flakes of skin, blood, vomit, faeces and often bodily fluids expressed from beriberi—ready for the next inmate.

While the Japanese may have taken some satisfaction in organising the squalor in the cells that their prisoners had to endure, an outbreak of scabies moved beyond the cells and into the clothes and skin of the gaolers. The biters were bit, and eventually had to take some action.

Malnutrition, boredom and bashings were one thing, but scabies dominated the lives of those affected. Lieutenant Rod Wells, who went to Outram Road from Borneo in March 1944, recounted a vivid description of enduring the scourge of scabies: 'My face and my whole body were covered in scabies. These get closer and closer together as the little mites bury themselves under your skin and lay their eggs and they hatch and then you get the pus-filled sores all over your skin and your whole body. There were not as many on my head and face because of the thinner skin, I suppose, I don't know why really.

'You would get the irresistible urge to scratch, knowing that by scratching you would only infect other parts of your body—not that there was much of the body left to be infected. There was a risk of re-infecting a part that had already been scratched to pieces where the skin was starting to grow tenderly over it again.

'And in the end, with these itchy periods gradually coming all over the body, during the day as these little things burrowed into you and the eggs moved or hatched, we would give way mentally to a complete abandonment of any desire to stop and one would scratch— and I mean really scratch and tear at our bodies. We always made sure when we peeled our fingernails back that we had a little bit of nail left so we would have something to scratch with, because without any good scratching we knew mentally it would be a most distressing situation to be in.

'So we would tear and tear at the skin all over from the toenails right to the neck over the head, tear at our hair or what hair there was left on our heads. Of course your fingernails would be covered with pus and blood and it was a sickening sort of mess at the end of it. One would finish this in about a quarter of an hour absolutely exhausted and deprived of all energy.

'After this period of scratching and exhaustion, you could then relax. You felt tender and sore all over, but at least there was no itching, and that was the most important thing. The tenderness was painful but you could put up with it. You would have maybe a couple of days without any further trouble. And then it would gradually begin again

as these mites were burying back further into the skin . . . it was just
one continual battle. You could do so little about it.'

Wells was comparatively late into Outram Road Gaol (his horrendous experiences in Borneo are described later). The Japanese had
begun to take the prisoners out into the gaol yard for scabies baths
the previous year. But these infrequent treatments were not enough to
control the scabies, which flourished in the unsanitary and unspeakable environment of the filthy cells and kept breaking out anew.

Bill Young recalled one of the early scabies' bath sessions, where
prisoners were taken out to the inner courtyard for treatment in
an old-fashioned high-backed Victorian hip-bath the Japanese had
found somewhere. He joined the skeletal group sitting in the yard;
they were a sorry sight. In his 1991 self-published memoir, *Return to
a Dark Age*, Young wrote: 'Eyes as big as saucers glistened from deep
skull sockets. Golf-ball sized Adams' apples rose up and down their
long necks, somewhat like a modern lift rising up and down outside
an ultra-modern office tower. Heaps of bones wrapped in skin. Little
piles of humanity, spread along the concrete floor of the "exercise
yard". Their shadows had more substance, and their skins—YUK!—
scabs and pus surrounded great ulcer pits, and even the palms of their
hands bubbled with pustules.'

Young was startled to hear a voice say 'G'day'. He looked around
to see who had spoken. Then he noticed a slight movement of the
jawbone of the skeleton sitting beside him. 'I'm Ken. Careful, don't let
the bastards see you talk—where are you from?' Ken Bird was from
South Australia, and had been one of Chris Neilson's escape party
from Adam Park. As they carefully swapped information, Young
realised everyone was doing the same:

What a deceptive landscape we were in, seemingly dead yet
full of life. From almost every pile of skin and bones some sort

of activity was taking place. Fluttering fingers semaphored messages from line to line. Blinking eyelids relayed information in Morse code. Fingers and palms combined in deaf and dumb signals. The place was alive with silent chatter of gaol-house gossip. All this activity was going on right in front of the alert, cruel eyes of the *Kempeitai* guard.

In stops and starts from ventriloquist-like lips, Young learned that others had been coming out for a disinfectant bath for some weeks:

One thing about scabies is they don't have any racial preferences at all. Aussies, Poms, Indians, Japs—they eat into the lot without discrimination, in fact they loved us all. The buggers were eating the Masters as well, so there was nothing left for it but to try and clean us up in the Bug Bath.

Ken Bird had more useful information for Young. The three Indians waiting in the yard all had venereal diseases, syphilis as well as gonorrhoea. It was important, Bird advised, to watch carefully when the chemicals were tipped into the bath, and get ahead of the Indians in the queue: 'Even though we had been forewarned, we weren't in the hunt with this mob, and found ourselves at the end of the line, behind the three untouchables. By the time our turn came round, the water was a black turgid swill of unspeakable filth—to which we had no option but to make our contribution.'

When they were back, sitting at their places, Bird reassured Young by saying he thought the stuff they put in it would kill any germs contributed by the venereal Indians. He whispered to Young that he was about to take a second plunge! Young was to find out that Bird was a superb practitioner of the art of mime. After getting permission from the surprised guard for a second round at the scabies bath, the show began: 'The guard, standing with his back to the tub, was unaware of the comedy about to unfold. Ken managed to wobble his way over to the bath. Then [he] proceeded to mime, first by taking off his dressing gown and hanging it on the back of the chair. We watched fascinated as the gown slid down from the rounded chair back, much to Ken's annoyance. Frowning, he put it back only to have it slide, again and again.

'Then at last one foot went into the water, only to be pulled up with a jerk—much too hot, so he turned on the cold tap and tried again. Then a look of peaceful contentment, as his long thin body snuggled down deep. Then a sudden movement of his arms as they reached out to the jacket on the chair for cigarettes, striking a match, lighting up, doing the drawback and sighing with content. For the finale, a series of "smoke rings" were blown swirling off above the guard's head.'

The guard, as if on cue, turned in time to see Bird rising with a flurry of splashing, bows and 'ah so's' from his ablutions. Leaving his jacket on the chair, he saluted, bowed again, and roared out his number, signalling he had finished with bath number two. For a suitable farewell, Bird saluted the guard with his thumb up under his nose and blew an audible raspberry.

Despite their desperate situation, the Australians—and indeed the British—found humour an indispensable morale booster. Neilson remembers a tough little Welshman, Topham-Brown, a former amateur boxer known as 'Topper'. In a throwback to primary school rules, the Japanese insisted that prisoners raised their hand if they wanted to use the toilet while out in the exercise yard: 'When the guard took notice, you were supposed to say, "I want to have a piss," in Japanese. Topper always had a grin on his face, and he was always taking the Japs on. He'd say, "Can I go for my gas mask, you silly bastard?" The Japs would say, "You speak terrible Nippon." It was a bloody cack. We'd start giggling.'

An Irish doctor, Major Jeremiah O'Neill, ex-British Indian Army, was permitted by the Japanese to enter the cells to help remove dead bodies, and on some other occasions too. On those visits he was not only handcuffed but hobbled as well while being marched to a new area, even though escape under the circumstances was wildly improbable. O'Neill was knock-kneed and pigeon-toed, and continually banged into his similarly tethered companion. Neilson remembers him saying in an exasperated voice, 'If you can't be after keeping step, I'll refuse to walk with you!' 'McGregor and I nearly died laughing.'

Neilson's combative attitude to his gaolers was an essential part of his personal survival strategy. 'You had to keep needling them, then they got a terrific respect for you. I've often said this, even to our psycho bloke [psychologist] later, when he asked me that question. He said, "Why do you do it?" I explained that it broke the monotony. On top of that they could have cut our heads off at any time when we first got to Outram Road—they were legally entitled to do that. But it would have been a greater feather in their cap to break you. No bastard in the world can break you but yourself. It's only if you lose charge of your nut. If you're in control of your head and your thinking, no one in the world can break you.

'Now, McGregor first worked that out, and it's true. You can be hurt, you can be tortured, but you can't be beaten. And McGregor would say, if you've got enough pride—McGregor with his [Scottish heritage] and me very proud of my Danish heritage—they'd walk away from you, shaking their heads. Every time they'd clobber you, you'd just grin and laugh at them, and tell them you've got a sister who is tougher than they are—oh Christ, that hurt them, they hated that. But at the same time you could see they respected you.'

The guard that Neilson most delighted in needling was The Groper, so named because the six-foot-tall Korean had a big mouth, 'a bloody great big gob like Joe E Brown' [the American comedian].

Their conversations took place in a mixture of Malay and broken English. The Groper had heard about the bombing of Darwin, and he told Neilson that Sydney would be their Japanese headquarters. He even produced a newspaper cutting of girls on Bondi Beach one day, and said that when he got there he would get a couple of these girls. 'I asked him if he was going to marry them, and he said, "Marry? No, just for sex purposes. Nippon only marry Nippon." For good measure he said he would buy a small car in Australia, and asked what was a good model. I said "Knackers" [testicles]. He tried this on Kenny Bird, just down the corridor from my cell. "Boom, boom, boom, Darwin finish. Boom, boom, boom, Alice Springs finish." Kenny said, "Oh bullshit. Bullshit boom, boom, finish too."'

Unfortunately for Neilson, The Groper asked an interpreter about the cars called 'knackers', and called back to the Queenslander's cell to give him a thorough bashing. Neilson didn't care.

The Groper became curious about his nickname, and questioned Neilson about it. He fenced about a bit, giving explanations The Groper clearly didn't believe. In the end, Neilson got sick of it, and shouted out as the guard was leaving the cell: '"You've got a bloody great mouth like an *ikan* [fish]." I pulled my mouth apart with my fingers to show him. "Like a groper with a bloody big gob."'

But this time Neilson had gone too far. The furious guard came back into his cell and stamped on his hands with his boots, breaking bones in both of them. He also hit him over the head with his heavy wooden baton, sheathed with latex, which gave Neilson a depressed fracture of the skull. Then he cupped his hands and simultaneously boxed Neilson's ears, causing them to bleed. As it happened, this was fortuitous, relieving the pressure on his brain caused by the fracture. Doctors in Changi told him later that had probably saved his life.

By this time even Neilson was near the end of his mental tether, but he could still communicate with McGregor in the cell next door using Morse code. McGregor knew his friend was at a low ebb. Neilson recalls: 'McGregor tapped through the wall to me, "What's your greatest gift?" I tapped back, "You're the smart bastard, you tell me." I was crook from a hiding, see. I said, "I'm bloody hungry and I'm bloody sick." He said, "I'll talk to you again tomorrow." Next morning he tapped through the wall, "Have you worked out your greatest gift?" I replied, "No, you're the smart bugger, you're the university man, you tell me." And he said, "Your brain, your memory." I said, "OK, there's a reason for everything, explain."

'McGregor said, "Can you remember three days ago?" I said, "No, I'm just bloody hungry and sick of getting the piss belted out of me." He said, "Well, hang on, just relax in a corner, and block out everything and just think. You can sit and enjoy a night with a good sort, [or] a Christmas party with your mother and family around, and you can re-live it in your memory—and you won't remember pain."'

A little later, McGregor tapped again: 'I can remember the first thing I asked you when we came in here.' That was the time prisoners were guarded by ordinary soldiers, before the *Kempeitai* took over. 'McGregor had asked me,' Neilson recalled, '"Where are you from?" I said, "North Queensland". "What age are you?" I told him I was born on the second of March 1913. Well, the next year, the second of March, I heard him tap through the wall, and I signalled for him to go ahead. He said, "Many happy returns of the day—March the second, 42, is the birthday I shall recall for you." [Laughs.] He was always making fun of you, that was his way.'

McGregor also said that if it hadn't been for the Morse code Neilson taught him, he would never have made it himself.

In April 1943, Neilson developed an ulcer on his right knee which became infected and blew up into a boil the size of an orange. Out in the exercise yard one day with McGregor, Neilson asked a Japanese guard to lance it with his sword to let the pus out. Jeremiah O'Neill happened to be in the yard at the same time, and the guard gave him a rusty razor blade and told him to get on with it. O'Neill at first refused until the guard threatened to shoot him. While Neilson's leg was held over a latrine bucket, O'Neill did the best he could and sliced the top off the swelling. 'It was the best thing actually, because it let all the muck out of it,' Neilson said.

Afterwards, O'Neill managed to get into Neilson's cell, where he saw the exposed bone of his knee-cap. As he said later, 'I intended to tell Neilson to make his peace with God, as I thought he would have no chance of living through the night.' Before he could speak, he was astounded to hear Neilson say, 'Look after yourself, Doc, we'll all be buggered if anything happens to you.' This broke O'Neill up, and he was unable to tell the Australian to prepare to meet his maker. Later he told Neilson he believed he had a 98 per cent chance of losing his leg, even had he been in Guy's Hospital in London. Neilson's theory was that their systems were too toxic to get poisoned!

With bodies being carted out of Outram Road at an increasing rate, both the commander of British forces in Changi, Colonel E B 'Eb' Holmes, and the Australian commander, Colonel Fred Galleghan, became concerned at the treatment of their soldiers. They wrote a polite but firm letter to be brought to the attention of the new Japanese head of all prisoners of war in Singapore, General Arimura (who had just taken over from General Fukuye), expressing their concerns and asking that an International Red Cross representative be permitted to visit Outram Road Gaol. This letter was given short shrift. Colonel Holmes was ordered to report to Conference House in Singapore, where he was given a dressing down by Captain Tazumi, an aide to Arimura. Tazumi said that although Japan was a signatory to the Geneva Convention, it also said that prisoners must obey their captors and that as prisoners they had no rights to protest on any matter. He then read extracts from Japanese law which confirmed that any Japanese soldiers taken prisoner would be shot on return to Japan.

Although no concessions were made formally by the Japanese command, from then on some prisoners who were so ill they were near death were returned to Changi for medical treatment, the rationale being that they be kept alive to finish their sentences, although the time spent at Changi being restored to health would be subtracted from their gaol terms. Those considered to be in a dire condition were unceremoniously loaded onto the tray of a flatbed truck, driven to the gates of Changi and dumped on the ground outside with no attempt to even alert anyone that they were there. This modest concession came just in time for Chris Neilson, who was so malnourished he had temporarily lost his sight. 'I'll never forget the doctor, Colonel Cotter Harvey. He said, "Can you sit up, lad?" I said, "I can bloody well walk if someone can guide me. I'm blind, I can't see." He said, "Christ, if we can save these blokes, we'll have to rewrite the medical books." And that's when we started to get all the attention.'

Another Changi doctor, Major John 'Glyn' White, recalled that the men could hardly move and were so emaciated he had no trouble in picking them up to carry them into a special ward which was isolated from the rest of the camp.

The medicos went into overdrive and they needed to. Neilson's heart stopped at one point: 'Dr Harvey gave me an adrenaline shot and got it going. He said, "You'd been dead for three minutes." I said I didn't remember it, but I hadn't seen any angels.'

There was considerable surprise that Neilson was there at all, because he had officially been reported executed in 1942!

McGregor and Neilson had four orderlies each, round the clock, watching these wrecks of human beings and looking after them constantly. They discovered several hundred scabies-infected wounds on Neilson's body alone, from his being regularly jabbed with bayonets and Japanese swords. The worst one was a cut from a whip, just above his kidneys, which was seething with scabies. 'They made me a night-gown and soaked me in red palm oil. I looked like a red Ku Klux Klanner, but it sure felt beautiful on me. When they took it off some weeks later my skin came off like a snake's, but underneath I had skin like a newborn baby.

'You see, [I] had nine major diseases for a start, including a perforation, bleeding haemorrhoids that had to be taken out, what they call a fistula, which is a crack in the lower bowel, my depressed fracture of the skull, scabies, scurvy, malaria and pellagra—and the only reason [most of us] hadn't died of septicaemia was that in that state of ill-health with malnutrition you can't die of blood poisoning—you haven't got enough blood left to poison!

'After the war, a British doctor, Sir Julian Taylor—he'd been knighted for brain surgery—said it was too dangerous to operate on my head until the fractures had healed, but said I would have head-aches every day for the rest of my life.' (Neilson did.)

Neilson had both his hands bandaged and he couldn't see very well, so Dr Harvey used to sit beside his bed and feed him. He was so hungry he used to bite on the spoon just as it entered his mouth. Harvey said, 'For Christ's sake, Neilson, wait till the spoon goes into your mouth and then close your lips.' Food was the priority in Changi, and a prized bonus was any leftover food from the evening meal known as *lagi makan* ('food again'). The POWs in Changi voted it should go to the Outram Road patients in the hospital. Prisoners allowed out of Changi on work parties would steal and bring in anything that would enhance their health. There was a little bit of Marmite left in the store that came in on the only Red Cross ship ever allowed in to Singapore, and the Outram Road men were given doses of Nutrene, a supplement normally provided to nursing mothers.

Vitamin C was manufactured from the local *lalang* grass that grew around the camp. The limbless men used to harvest it as one of their jobs. Neilson says, 'They had a big press, like the old wine presses used to squeeze grapes. They produced this horrible black juice that came out of the grass. We used to call it "panther's piss". But you had to be nearly blind to get an egg-cup full of it a day. It was vile, but oh, it did marvels for the sight and for scurvy.'

Sometimes Colonel 'Black Jack' Galleghan, the commander of the Changi camp, Major Phil Head and Captain Adrian Curlewis, all senior members of the intelligence network, came into the hospital to talk to Neilson about what was happening in Outram Road Gaol. As it happened, Neilson had some important information for them. One of the few friendly Japanese in Outram Road who befriended Neilson, the English- and French-speaking guard Neilson nicknamed 'The French-man', was a sensitive and cultured man who was appalled at what was going on in Outram Road, but could do nothing about it. Had he even been caught speaking in a friendly way to Neilson, he would have been severely punished, perhaps even executed. 'I asked Black Jack at one stage whether the Japanese were separating the Australian prisoners into smaller groups, and were they also putting machine guns in the turrets of the four corners of Changi gaol,' Neilson remembered. 'Black Jack said, "How do you know that?" Because The Frenchman told me that if the Allied forces invaded Singapore, there were orders that all the prisoners of war were to be massacred."'

According to Neilson, Galleghan said, 'Christ, we must warn the other camps.' He also drew up plans for a hit squad which, in the event of this happening, would take over the weakest of the towers and direct the machine gun in it on the other machine posts in the three remaining towers. Neilson says, 'We would have lost a hundred or so, but would have saved thousands.'

While the Outram Road prisoners were in Changi, the doctors did what they could to keep them there, and Japanese guards or occasionally doctors would visit unexpectedly to check if they were well enough to go back. Neilson explains, 'The reason for going back to Outram Road is that the Japs demanded you complete your sentence, and since I'd been given three years, three years you must do, and there's no remission. You do your three years to the day, right up to the hour.'

It took Chris Neilson eight months to get over his injuries, and build his weight to a comparatively healthy eight stone. He managed to stay in Changi for some fourteen months before being taken back to finish his sentence.

# 4

# 'I THOUGHT I'D GET A COUPLE OF THEM FIRST'

On first impression, Major John Wyett seemed to be a formidably patrician kind of chap with his straight-backed stance, rather English manner of speech and a wide paisley cravat around his throat. The cravat concealed a surgical neck support, following lifelong injuries sustained by a *Kempeitai* bashing during questioning in the notorious YMCA interrogation centre in Singapore on New Year's Eve, 1942. As reported in the foreword to Wyett's memoir *Staff Wallah: At the Fall of Singapore*, while stopped at a traffic light in Hobart:

> His appearance so enraged a car-load of hoons beside him that the young men began honking their horn and screaming obscene abuse at the surprised octogenarian. As the lights changed, they drove off still shouting and gesticulating. Wyatt was more amused than irritated. It is a pity the yobbos will never know why he presented that stiff-necked demeanour: John Wyett has not been without excruciating neck pain since the first of many brutal interrogations by the *Kempeitai*. During that early New Year's Eve encounter, several vertebrae in the base of his neck were crushed by savage blows from the flat of a Japanese officer's

Samurai sword. It was simply not possible to take pain-killing drugs all the time and retain mental agility, so he just put up with the pain.

Surely few inmates of Outram Road have walked a more curious path to that destination than John Wyett. It began when he was appointed to the staff of the Australian commander in Malaya, Lieutenant-General Gordon Bennett, at his Kuala Lumpur headquarters in May 1941. Bennett himself had only recently arrived from Australia and was already showing signs of the paranoid and autocratic behaviour that would make him a deeply flawed commander. Wyett, not then a staff officer, thought he was getting on well enough with Bennett until a garbled message arrived one night—which he had considerable difficulty in deciphering—saying that a couple of officers from the 2/18th Battalion had crossed the Siamese border and been arrested. Bennett had attended a large party that night and, as it was 11 pm, Wyett decided to wait till next morning before delivering the message. Unfortunately, the message was telephoned to Bennett by a senior officer before Wyett had a chance to send it, and he received a summons from Bennett. In *Staff Wallah*, Wyett wrote:

I marched into the general's office and chucked him a salute. He half rose out of his seat, almost white with fury, pointed his finger at me [and] said, 'You're hiding things from me, you're just another one, they're all against me. You're just another one that's against me, and you've joined the others . . .' and went on and raved like a madman.

I said, 'Well excuse me, sir, but I just don't know what you're talking about'.

'That telegram that came in last night you saved it up to show to the G1 you wouldn't show it to me—you hid it from me.'

Then it dawned on me about the message. I tried to explain that I intended to give the message to Colonel Henry Rourke, his G1 [second-in-command] and, if he thought it was something the general should deal with he would act accordingly.

He said, 'You don't go to the G1, you don't go to anyone—you come directly to me'. I said, 'That's not the way I have been trained I'm afraid, sir, and it's not really the way the army works or should work. You must know yourself that it's quite unworkable. If you've got every junior officer running into your door day and night, you'll never get anything done and no one will know where they are. And he said, 'I'll have none of that, I'm going to run this place ...' blah blah blah, and ranted on. Finally he kicked me out of his office. I thought, this man's a lunatic.

Wyett knew that spelling correct procedure out to Bennett was kindergarten stuff but felt he had to say it. The Siamese police released the two officers after a few hours. It was all an unnecessary flap, magnified in the minds of some into an international incident. Wyett:

After leaving the general I went to the latrines and was standing there when in came Colonel Rourke. I explained what had happened, showed him the message and told him of Bennett's reaction. Rourke's reply startled me somewhat. 'Don't take any notice of the silly bugger.' I felt that the conflicts of personality within the headquarters were about to break into the open and become a serious problem.

Even at that early stage, the British-run Malaya Command, headed by Lieutenant-General Arthur Percival, was already known in the trade as 'Confusion Castle'. Wyett was astonished to find out when he tried to contact officers in a British regiment after lunch that they

were all having their daily siestas in the hottest part of the day, arising
in time to dress formally for their mess dinners in the evening. The
Australians were out doing jungle training. It was now July and in a
few months Japanese forces would invade Malaya.

Another surprise was in store for Wyett when he was suddenly
told he had been selected to attend the Command and Staff College
in Quetta, India (now part of Pakistan), one of the most prestigious
senior military colleges in the world. Later he discovered that he was
the only non-regular soldier ever to have been selected for the Quetta
academy in its entire history.

Wyett had been nominated by Henry Rourke, who then shocked
him further by telling him that he was resigning and returning to
Australia. He said Bennett was impossible to work with, told him
nothing and made all the decisions himself without consultation.

Wyett went to India, passed his course with flying colours and
arrived back in Singapore on 4 January 1942. He immediately reported
to General Bennett's headquarters, now relocated from Kuala Lumpur
to Johor Bahru, just across the causeway from Singapore island.
Colonel Jim Thyer was now Bennett's G1, and another signals officer,
Major Clarence Dawkins, was acting as G2:

> I told Thyer that I had not seen the general—that I was reporting
> back to him as my senior officer. He became quite agitated at
> this, saying, 'Get in there at once, and for God's sake don't say
> you've seen me'. Things had not changed except for the worse.

When he did see Bennett, the general was uncharacteristically affable
and gave Wyett the unexpected news that he was to become his G2,
replacing Dawkins. By early January, Allied troops were retreating
down the Malay peninsula, and the Australians were putting up stiff
resistance where and when they were able. Wyett did what he could

to assist what was essentially a fight-and-retreat strategy against the Japanese onslaught. In six weeks' time, it would be all over.

By 1 February, all Allied forces had withdrawn across the causeway into Fortress Singapore. A week later, the storm clouds broke in earnest as Japanese troops came across the Straits of Johor in their thousands. The defenders' machine guns ran hot, but it was impossible to stop the onslaught. Unfortunately, Lieutenant-General Percival had anticipated the Japanese would attack from the northeast and had concentrated his main forces there. But the Japanese came across further west, to where the Australians had a very thin line indeed: their situation was strategically and practically desperate. Wyett went out to see for himself and was told to go and report to Bennett, who had just gone to a high-level meeting at Malaya Command Headquarters, now fully living up to its nick-name of Confusion Castle. Churchill had sent in Field Marshal Archibald Wavell, then the Supreme Commander of ABDA area (Australian British Dutch American), to see for himself. As he arrived, the Japanese bombed the headquarters. Wyett:

> Wavell insisted on driving around in a great big shiny motor car with the Union Jack flying from the bonnet. The Nips loved this of course, followed him around and began to drop eggs [bombs]. At this meeting with Wavell were Percival, Lieutenant-General Sir Lewis Heath, Bennett and other high ranking officers sitting around the table when the bombs fell. I arrived just at that moment. I remember the poor old signals operator had been literally blown out of his seat—he was lying dead in the driveway with his headphones still on.
>
> I walked into the conference room and one corner of the room was just crumbling to bits, the place was full of dust and debris and all senior men were flat on the floor and just picking

themselves up. Bennett was standing there with a supercilious grin on his face, he hadn't moved, he had that kind of bravado. He was utterly fearless from that point of view, but it was his sneering at all the others—at a man like Wavell for instance— which got my goat completely. I didn't mind so much about Percival [whom Wyett thought to be incompetent].

When things settled down a bit, Wyett reported to Jim Thyer, the G1, about the desperate situation of the Australians, and he said, 'Well, for God's sake, go and tell the general.' Bennett at this stage was with Major Dawkins dictating orders. Wyett recalled Bennett had a little one-inch scale map of the area and he just swept a pencil across the map and said, 'Dawkins, that will be the form-up line.' He then went about an inch further on and drew another semicircle, and said, 'Formations will be there by such and such a time, and that will be their line of attack, and that's the line that they will hold. Get the orders out.' Wyett:

I said, 'Look, excuse me, sir.' And he turned on me and said, 'What do you want Wyett?' I said, 'I've just been up there, at our old headquarters, but I only just managed to get out because the Japs dropped a smoke bomb on it and immediately afterwards there was machine-gun fire all around us.' I said, 'I don't know what happened to the chaps there, but I thought I'd better come back and report. I was a bit lucky to get back because the car was riddled with bullets as I came through.' Then I told him, 'You're asking men to form up there in a position which is already held by the Japanese.'

He turned to me absolutely furious. He said, 'You're frightened, Wyett, aren't you? You're another one of those lily-livered people.'

Look, I could have punched him on the bloody jaw. I'd had a pretty rigorous time and I wasn't really mentally in any state to get that kind of insult hurled at me. But I started to plead with him. I said, 'Look you've got to listen to me, you're sending men to their deaths by this kind of order.' And just at that moment Major Charles Moses, his liaison officer, strolled in, didn't salute the general or anything like that. I can see him now, he was stretching his arms above his head and said, 'Oh well everything is quiet up there.'

I said, 'Up where Charles?' And he said, 'Oh up where our old headquarters was.' I said, 'Charles, you're either mad or you're just a bloody liar. I've just this moment come from there.' And Bennett brushed me aside and said, 'Oh, well thanks for that Charles. Dawkins get the orders out.'

The inevitable result was that the battalion commander was killed, machine-gunned down by the Japanese as they were forming up. It was a shocking situation but Wyett said it gave some idea of the 'maniacal man' Bennett was. Although Bennett had done well in trench warfare in World War I, he had not adapted well to a different style of war. Wyett believed Bennett would have made a battalion commander but certainly should never have risen beyond. So he had no respect for him.

At the end, he exhibited very little leadership at all. His mind was completely set on getting out. Actually he'd made arrangements with the Sultan of Johor to take over his very luxurious and very powerful private launch. But the British Navy got in ahead of him and commandeered it, and he, Moses and others in his party had to find a sampan and get away to Sumatra in that. He seemed detached, not thinking of his division or his troops at all. The fiery Bennett who was querying things that Malaya Command ordered had disappeared completely.

Lieutenant-General Percival later described Bennett as, 'A man who had, without orders and of his own volition, deserted his post and abandoned his men.'

Major John Wyett joined the lugubrious cavalcade of defeated troops, and marched into Changi as a prisoner of war. Indeed, as the G2, he had to give the order for that march himself. Some weeks later when the Japanese decided to restrict movement in and around the camp, Wyett had to issue orders to the Australians to put up the barbed wire barriers which would enclose them. He commented wryly in his post-war memoir, 'The G2 is generally the one where the buck stops. That damned "staff wallah" again!'

As life in Changi settled down in the first year of captivity, Wyett, who had trained as an industrial chemist, began to work on ingenious ways to address shortages of needed materials, and the growing problems caused by malnutrition and the insufficient rice diet. The prisoners knew that the Japanese had tonnes and tonnes of palm oil in storage, now with no market to trade to. Palm oil was highly nutritious and rich in vitamin A, and they asked the Japanese for some, but were refused. Changi was also in need of soap—as were the Japanese. So the Australians offered to manufacture soap for them, and themselves. Wyett wasn't the only chemist in the camp, and a soap factory was set up to combine the essential ingredients of palm oil, soda and salt.

Production was surprisingly low as most of the palm oil was sidetracked to the kitchen for extra nutrition. The Japanese didn't know what the yield of palm oil to soap should be, and seemed happy with what they got.

Even so, with the poor and unbalanced diet, various medical deficiencies began to appear, and beriberi was the first and most urgent of these problems. If they could manufacture the right strain of yeast, vitamin B1 would help in combating beriberi. Wyett risked going through the wire to collect mangoes, wild berries and guava to prepare an experimental yeast culture. He needed wooden barrels, and somehow the resourceful Australians managed to produce a dozen large ones. Fermentation began and, analysed under a microscope, the yeast was found to have the right properties. Eventually, large-scale production supplied yeast broth not only to the hospital, but to the troops as well.

Nothing was wasted in Changi. As gastric problems were endemic, hydrochloric acid was sometimes suctioned out from patients' stomachs. This made excellent soldering flux, and was so used.

There were dentists as well as doctors in the camp but materials soon ran out, particularly amalgam, which was urgently required for fillings. Wyett:

We needed silver and mercury. The other metal required was copper, but there was plenty of telephone wire for that. One day a Gordon Highlander told me that one of their men had souvenired a huge silver cup from the Selangor Club during the retreat through Kuala Lumpur. It was indeed solid silver, and was coaxed away from its all-but-tearful owner. Mercury was obtained from thermometers 'acquired' from the Singapore Cool Stores and passed on to us.

The next problem was to organise an intense source of heat and a heat-resistant crucible to melt the silver and copper. Petrol was cleverly siphoned from the tank of the daily Changi food truck, and various clays were brought back to camp from *lalang* grass-cutting parties.

With an engineer's blow torch and a ceramic crucible, the dentists were soon back in business, and many soldiers returned to Australia with their Changi fillings intact and good for many more years.

Some of the pure white clay brought back to make the crucible was thought to be kaolin, and tests proved it was. Adding magnesium to the kaolin would provide treatment for a growing number of gastric ulcers. Sea water contains magnesium, and washing out the salt and adding kaolin—plus lye from wood ash—gave a cloudy precipitate of magnesia which gave immediate relief to victims of gastric ulcers.

With the secret radios—the most famous installed in a broom— keeping the prisoners well informed about the progress of the war, there was still concern about the expected invasion of Australia by the Japanese. Working parties on the docks were bringing information back to Changi about increased activity in shipping and troop movements, and John Wyett's next challenge was to find a way of getting this information back to Australia:

That was when I met Corporal Stan Elliman. He was an engineer corporal from Perth and an enthusiastic amateur radio fan. Clem Hill, a captain in the engineers, had told me about him and arranged a meeting. Elliman explained that he used to build and operate his own transmitters and felt that he could assemble one, given a few extra bits and pieces. Eventually, with the help of various working parties, we managed to collect all that he needed, and the transmitter was assembled. A risky undertaking if ever there was one, but considering the uncertain nature of our existence risks had to be taken and were accepted. This one was sheer dynamite and would endanger everyone if the radio was found by the Japs. Obviously we could not store it or operate it from the camp. Some other site would have to be found, but where?

Wyett decided to investigate the wrecked batteries of fifteen-inch guns, not far from the Changi camp. These massive naval guns were useless in the battle, not because they faced out to sea—they could be swivelled around to fire inland—but their ammunition was armour-piercing. Fine for attacking incoming ships, but ineffectual for general combat. The Japanese had blown them up and flooded the tunnels and ammunition storage chambers beneath them.

Wyett was of medium height, and Elliman somewhat taller, but they were both taller than the average Japanese who would have had to swim through the tunnels, and therefore paid them no attention. The water came up to Wyett's chin, but he was able to wade through to a chamber where they found a steel plate, above the water level, which when unscrewed revealed a chamber behind, large enough to house their transmitter and conveniently equipped with bags of silicon gel to combat the moisture. It seemed tailor-made for their purpose, and the transmitter was quickly installed.

While John Wyett had briefly been attached to the headquarters of the 3rd Indian Corps during the action in Malaya, several of the officers had been radio enthusiasts and had told Wyett they made arrangements before they left India for some of their ham radio colleagues to listen out at a particular time each Wednesday in case they managed to get in touch. He tracked down one of the Indian officers—who fortunately had not gone over to the Japanese—because he needed to know the time of day for the listening window and the radio frequency. That being known, they did transmit useful information on Wednesdays, but never knew if it was being picked up.

In the meantime, Wyett was hatching an escape plan. He had become friendly with an RAAF officer, Flight-Lieutenant Jack Macalister, a pilot, who had been shot down over Timor in a Hudson bomber by a couple of Japanese Zeros. He was the only member of the crew to survive, but had been betrayed to the Japanese by some Timorese who found him in the jungle. Wyett and Macalister hoped to steal a Hudson bomber from Seletar Airport, not too far away, and escape from Singapore. Wyett was in the process of making a sextant and taking navigation lessons. It was a fairly ambitious plan because all they had for a map was a page torn from a school atlas, and even if they became airborne with full tanks, they didn't have the range to reach Australia or even India. There was nothing closer than the Cocos Islands—a pinprick in the vastness of the Indian Ocean, which was held by the Japanese. In December, they continued to discuss the pros and cons of the plan which could only be described as foolhardy and would inevitably have got them killed. Meanwhile, their brother officers planned to celebrate New Year's Eve with a dinner, having saved some of their meagre rations for the occasion—hoping that the new year would not be as bad as the old. Wyett could not have known how mistaken that hope was.

Before going into a festive meal I stood casually chatting to Major Phil Head, our senior legal officer. Suddenly without warning, six armed Japanese *Kempeitai* secret police rushed into the room. Two of them came straight to me and pinioned my arms while the others began to search the room. They knew exactly where to come and what to do—Phil and all the rest were simply ignored.

The suddenness of it all confused Wyett, until he came to his senses with a jerk. He realised that lying on a packing case which he used as a desk was a most damning piece of evidence that would lead him to the chopping block if they found it, and it looked as though they soon would. It was no more than a small scrap of paper, but on it was a message that Wyett had been condensing into the shortest possible number of words, for sending out that night from the secret wireless transmitter. The information had been sent to him earlier in the day by Captain Adrian Curlewis, who was in charge of a working party on the Singapore docks.

Curlewis had noticed that a number of ships in the harbour, moored at the docks, had white bamboo blinds rolled up and fastened to the sides. Guns and other munitions were being loaded and from time to time Japanese troops arrived and were taken on board. One of the blinds unrolled by accident and was hastily rolled up again and re-fastened but not before it had revealed a huge red cross painted upon the white background. These were troopships preparing the disguise as hospital ships. The working party speculated they were part of a large convoy preparing to sail for Java and possibly Australia. This was the incriminating piece of paper that was now in imminent danger of being found by the *Kempeitai*. Wyett:

> I watched the search getting closer and closer to my desk, my mind working overtime to try and find a way of retrieving that scrap of paper.

They had found Wyett's tin trunk and were going carefully through it. The two guards holding him became intrigued and released their hold on his arms while they were watching the proceedings:

> Being momentarily free I strolled as nonchalantly as possible across the room to my desk, picked up the whole bundle of papers lying on it and handed them to Phil Head, saying quietly to him, 'Get rid of the top one.' As I did so my two guards rushed up and grabbed me again while others snatched the bundle of papers, but not before Phil had quietly crumpled that deadly scrap of paper into the palm of his hand, which now hung loosely at his side. He had the great good sense not to try to put

it in his pocket as that would certainly have aroused suspicion. As it was the Japs paid no further attention to him.

Wyett was not out of the woods by any means, but it was a great relief to be over that first hurdle. Even to have a wireless receiver was a capital offence—but to be caught with a transmitter? When the Japanese had finished their search he was hustled downstairs and into a waiting car together with his tin trunk and now harmless bundle of papers, leaving behind a small group of bewildered officers. The New Year's party had not begun well. Wyett:

> They bundled me into a staff car that they had standing by and whisked me off out of the camp. I'll never forget the guard's face when the car drove up to the gates and he naturally stepped forward to check it. One of these Nips just leaned out of the window, leered at him and said menacingly *Kempeitai*. And do you know that guard's face went absolutely white and he started to tremble. The *Kempeitai* had such a reputation, such a hold on all the troops, that they were terrified of them. This was the Nip discipline of course. Because they had *Kempeitai* people seeded right through every unit, nobody could do a thing without them knowing about it.

It was dark when they stopped at a building outside the city. Wyett was hauled from the car and taken into a brightly lit room, bare except for a desk and a few wooden chairs. One of these was placed in the centre of the room and he was made to sit down on it while they wound ropes around his body, tightly pinning his arms and torso to its straight wooden back:

> The Japanese officer who had been seated at the desk then came across to where I was, firmly bound and pinioned to my chair

and feeling completely helpless. He stood in front of me glaring into my face in the most ferocious manner and began shouting and gesticulating while accusing me in reasonably good English of being a spy. He reminded me of a mad ape and was soon to act like one.

When Wyett didn't reply to his questions and accusations, the officer gave a signal to the two guards, who immediately began punching Wyett in the face and head. This was followed by more questions and accusations interspersed with bashing by one or other of the guards, who were taking turns and obviously enjoying it. Being so firmly bound, there was no way Wyett could lessen the impact of their fists and the effect on his neck was extremely painful as their blows violently jerked his head this way and that:

My silence infuriated the officer who, after some time, unfastened his thick leather belt and began lashing me with it. As his blows became more vicious the chair tipped over several times and since I was so tightly bound there was nothing I could do to lessen the fall. My head often hit the floor first, and I must have fainted several times because on each occasion as I came to one of the guards was emptying a bucket of water over me. By this time the officer had worked himself up to a frenzy of rage and was inflicting painful cuts and bruises on my head and face with the heavy brass buckle under his belt.

Finally he drew his sword and it began to look as though my head would soon be rolling across the floor. It became apparent, however, that the purpose of the sword was to inflict more pain than to finish me off. The officer began using the flat of the blade as he danced around the chair dealing blows to any part of my body that his blind fury dictated. Suddenly one vicious blow, harder than any before, caught me across the shoulder and on the back and side of my neck. It sent me crashing and spinning across the bare wooden floor. There was a flash of stars within my head and then everything went black—I can recall nothing more of what happened in that room.

Wyett came to in a small cell in which there were about fourteen people. They had to sit in the cell all day with their backs against the wall and were touching each other as the cell was so full. Macalister wasn't there because they arrested another unfortunate English colonel with the same name, who was naturally a bit mystified, but quite early in the piece they let him go after Wyett convinced them they had the wrong man. A few days later, however, they brought in the real Macalister and put him in a separate cell to prevent contact between them.

And here we had a tremendous stroke of luck, really. They used to take people out every day from the room and bundle them upstairs, to the room immediately above my crowded cell, where they questioned people, and you'd hear the bumps and crashes and yells. I was the only European, the rest of them were all Malays, Tamils, Chinese, and a well-known Sikh businessman in Singapore, Ghian Singh. Sitting in the cell I noticed the Chinese were talking to one another across the room when the guard wasn't looking, using deaf and dumb sign language. I thought, this could be handy so I got one of these chaps to teach me. And by the greatest good fortune Macalister had done the same thing in his cell, which was across the other side of the passage along from where my cell was. Now the cell had a grating in the door and I found that by getting myself into a certain position I could look through the grating and just see the grating of Macalister's cell, and over the next few days we managed to swap information about what was happening to us.

Wyett's second day of questioning began somewhat ominously when wires were attached to his wrists. During these preparations, the officer seated at his desk remained impassive and no one spoke:

> Suddenly an electric shock shot through my whole body. I began to shake, with the pulsating current running through the wires on my arms. There was a knob on the major's desk, and as he turned it the current increased in intensity until it reached the point where every muscle in my body stiffened with searing, wracking pain. He watched me carefully and when this point was reached he suddenly flicked a switch—my jaw, clamped tightly shut by the current, now fell open, my head lolled forward and I collapsed in a heap as far as my bonds would allow. I was dazed and panting and no sooner had I started to recover than he began the process all over again.

As Wyett began to collect himself after a second bout of shock treatment, the accusations and questioning began. The Australian was confident that the Japanese would not know anything about the secret transmitter and thought the escape plan would be their focus. He was astonished when another charge was read out: 'Inciting revolt against the Imperial Japanese Army.' He realised by the questions being put to him that the *Kempeitai* somehow knew about secret plans the Australian command at Changi had discussed to combat the Japanese if they decided to massacre them in the event of the war going badly for the Japanese. Colonel Galleghan had told Wyett to make lists of the fittest men and form them into fighting units which could at least put up some resistance if this mass killing of prisoners was ordered. If the

*Kempeitai* knew about this, it had been a security breach of the highest order, and it was imperative that Wyett get word to Galleghan that their plans—and possibly other secret projects—had been compromised.

Back in his crowded cell later that afternoon, Wyett began to realise what might have happened. He had seen some Japanese wearing Indonesian officers' uniforms at the *Kempeitai* headquarters and the penny dropped. It was quite usual for the Indonesian officers in Changi to be around when sensitive matters were discussed. No one had noticed that several of these were English-speaking Japanese *Kempeitai* in sheep's clothing. It was impossible to know what information had been disclosed.

As John Wyett considered how on earth he could get word back to Changi, the Sikh businessman, Ghian Singh, was thrown back into his cell, dazed and bleeding from his latest *Kempeitai* interrogation, clothing torn, his turban missing and his usually contained long hair in disarray. He was a very different figure from the tall, dignified and imposing man who was so prominent a figure on the Singapore scene. He seemed in a bad way, panting for breath, and bleeding from his mouth:

> From where I was sitting I could see the Jap guard becoming more and more agitated. If Ghian Singh were to die, there on the floor, it would be a bad mark for the guard because the *Kempeitai* never like to see someone die in their hands in public. They killed thousands but always in secret. I felt it would not be long before the guard sent for a doctor and it suddenly dawned upon me that here at last was the opportunity I was looking for. If I were suddenly to develop an attack of appendicitis and could manage to bluff the doctor, there was an even chance I might be rushed to the hospital at Changi.

There was no time to be lost, and the first thing Wyett had to do before the doctor arrived was to get as hot and sweaty as he could to simulate running a temperature. On the floor in front of him was a small piece of matting which he managed to wrap around him before lying on his back on the floor clutching his stomach and tossing about as though in acute pain. In the warm humid climate of Singapore it was not long before beads of sweat covered his forehead and trickled down his face.

With so much activity going on in a normally still and silent cell, it was all becoming too much for the nervous guard. Singh seemed to be getting worse and that was no fake. It reached the point where the guard shot off and returned quickly with a Japanese medical officer, who went at once to examine Singh. Wyett continued his appendicitis act. He knew enough about symptoms of appendicitis from his pharmacy training days to lie on his back and draw up his right knee, leaving the left leg straight, apparently relieving the pressure on his inflamed appendix. Out of the corner of his eye he could see the doctor looking at him.

Then the doctor came over to me and going down on one knee he undid the buttons of my shorts. I simply pretended he wasn't there and continued my head rolling with occasional spasms and grimaces of pain while still clutching my right side. He laid a hand upon my brow and clearly thought I had a temperature.

He then set about exploring my abdomen. Every time those firm gently probing fingers touched the spot where my appendix was I winced and let out a groan. All this time he had one hand resting on my right knee and applied gentle pressure as he continued probing with the other. I let the knee sink until it was flat on the floor, and when he removed his hand to join the other in the examination I brought the leg slowly up again and I could see he was impressed although he pretended not to notice. However, his next move threw me off balance as it was a diagnostic test of which I was completely unaware. He dug his fingers into the left side of my abdomen, slowly and gently worming deep into my side. Suddenly with a quick, deft movement he lifted clear and the skin of my tummy shot back into place. The adrenaline was flowing freely that day.

Wyett let out a yell, grabbed his right side and continued to groan in agony, wondering all the time if he was overacting. Apparently not, because the doctor seemed convinced. He rapped out an order to a guard, who scuttled off and returned soon afterwards with two others. Wyett was assisted to his feet and dragged, stumbling and groaning, to a car.

They arrived at Changi in the evening and drove up to the hospital. Orders were shouted and a stretcher was laid on the ground next to the car. Wyett pretended to take no notice, too racked with non-existent pain as he was helped from the car and laid gently on the stretcher. A doctor arrived and to Wyett's great delight it was Colonel Charles Osborn, the surgeon-superintendent of the hospital and a good friend:

He knelt by the stretcher and loosened my shorts to feel around my abdomen. He then made a great show of taking my pulse. Apparently not satisfied he shook his head and, lifting my shirt he placed his ear on my chest, ostensibly to hear a better heart-beat. This brought his mouth close to my face so he was able to whisper without being heard by the two guards and the doctor standing nearby. 'John, is this real or is it fake?'

'It is a fake you fool.'

'I'll have to take it out.'

'Well take it out. It's no damn good anyway.'

Charles's only reply was, 'OK cock.'

The operation was performed, and fortunately the appendix looked a bit dodgy, satisfying the Japanese doctor, who then left. Wyett felt guilty because the doctor had been quite compassionate—the only Japanese he met in captivity who had been. Next morning he was able to pass on his revelation about the Japanese/Indonesian spies in the camp and after less than a week of convalescence was returned to the tender mercies of the *Kempeitai* torturers, who Wyett hoped wouldn't pay too much attention to his healing and tender abdomen. A forlorn hope, as it happened.

Knowing that the torture and interrogation would go on until the two Australians produced some kind of confession, Wyett began calculating the least damaging admissions they could make. Under the Geneva Convention (which the Japanese didn't recognise anyway) it was the duty of a prisoner of war to escape. He decided that he and Macalister would admit to their escape plan and hope that would satisfy the *Kempeitai*. But their stories would have to tally. Fortunately, they could converse, on occasions, using sign language. The plan was for Wyett to break down under extreme torture, and make a 'confession' that he and Macalister had decided to escape because they wanted to go home. It was a high-stakes gamble and the timing would have to be right, but they hoped that getting this confession would mean the interrogators would not push too hard on the other more serious charges. Wyett found out later that the Japanese commander in Singapore, General Fukuye (the Australian troops had their own pronunciation of his name), was pressing for quick results.

It seemed to Wyett that his interrogators were becoming more and more desperate for a result. One morning they began with what Wyett called 'Water Torture 2', where his hands were tied and he was laid out face-up on the floor. A funnel was then put in his mouth, with the spout rammed down far enough so he could not stop the flow of water into his stomach, which became swollen and distended. The funnel was then removed, and a guard stepped on his inflated, water-filled stomach. The pain was excruciating, but mercifully it did not burst his wound which was still slowly healing from the appendix operation. Wyett blacked out. When he came to, he found he was strapped in a chair with wires being attached to his wrists for the electric shock treatment, which began while he was still semi-conscious:

The current stopped suddenly and I slumped, only to be jerked upright and rigid with clamped jaws and staring eyes from the next surge as the officer flicked the switch on again. He was watching me closely as I managed to gasp out, 'For God's sake stop.' He did, and I slumped, letting my head fall forward on my chest. I needed a few moments to think about my next move. Looking, as I hoped, the picture of misery, I croaked out that I was ready to confess and I could stand no more. I had expected disbelief, suspicion and more questions—certainly not the delight and enthusiasm and air of relief that greeted my words.

The officer sprang to his feet and barked out a few words. The guards literally danced for joy, the interpreter looked dazed and uncertain and there were smiles all round. One of the guards rushed up and undid the ropes binding me to the chair, which he moved closer to the desk, the better for the officer and his scribe to hear me. The other guard returned a few moments later and gave me a glass of cold tea.

Wyett's 'confession' took some time to spell out, while the scribe worked assiduously and painstakingly with his brush, inking the bright red Japanese characters onto the tissue-thin paper of his now voluminous record book. When he thought the interrogator, interpreter and scribe were getting bored, he livened up proceedings by introducing the ploy that he was prepared to further co-operate with them and order Flight-Lieutenant Macalister to give up his useless resistance and tell the truth. The Japanese officer suddenly leapt to his feet and barked an order to the guards, who left the room. Wyett thought they had gone to fetch Macalister, but they returned and, each taking one of his arms, led him down to Macalister's cell followed by the officer and the interpreter:

They had taken him to a smaller cell and there, standing inside facing the grill door, was Mac, his hair now long and dishevelled, looking like the prince of all villains with his bushy ginger-coloured beard. To any onlooker we must have formed a weird tableau with Mac standing there like a caged gorilla and me facing him outside the bars with my scruffy beard and long, unkempt hair, a guard grasping my arms on either side.

I maintained a stern mien in spite of the whole Gilbertian nature of the charade, but nevertheless managed to give Mac a sly wink. Actually the whole show was deadly serious from our point of view because our lives depended upon its success, but it struck me as stupidly funny as I addressed him in my best parade ground manner: 'Flight-Lieutenant Macalister, I'm here to give you an order.'

Mac had obviously thought about how he would treat this, as he replied, 'You can go and get stuffed.'

Whether they understood what was said I don't know but the tone of the reply left no doubt as to its meaning and earned Mac a resounding slap across the face from one of the guards. I then continued, 'You will tell this officer all you know as I have done already, because he only wants to know the truth.'

Mac's acting was superb as he glared at me and said, 'I'm Air Force and am not taking orders from any damned Army officer. You can go to hell.'

This earned him a bashing until finally, with apparent great reluc-
tance, he agreed to obey. The Japanese were delighted and the men
were whisked off immediately—Macalister upstairs to the scribe
and Wyett back to his cell, where he was left to reflect upon the day's
happenings. He thought all had gone well. The next move was up to
the *Kempeitai*. They did not have long to wait because a few mornings
later they were taken out of their cells and put into a closed van. After
a short drive the van stopped and they were taken through a gateway
flanked by massive stone pillars and into a dimly lit hallway, stripped
naked and given a pair of shorts and a cotton shirt each.

We were then ushered into the gloomy interior of the gaol,
padding barefoot into the eerie silence of the great block of cells.
Mac was pushed into one cell line some distance farther on
from me and on the same side—no chance of communication
here. The heavy wooden doors were slammed shut and we now
found ourselves securely locked within the notorious Outram
Road Gaol.

Wyett and Macalister still had to face up to their trial, not yet
knowing their fate, or how successful their gameplay with the
*Kempeitai* had been. Several weeks after they entered Outram Road,
further humiliations awaited. The two men had not been officially
inducted into Outram Road, so their hair was long and matted, as
were their beards. They were driven from the gaol in a van to Singapore's main thoroughfare, where the two men realised they were to be
paraded before a large crowd as symbols of the defeat of the former
'British' white masters:

Barriers had been erected on either side of the roadway and
crowded behind them was a dense mass of people—men,

women and children of all ages and races. The whole populace had been ordered onto the streets to watch the spectacle. I was furious. The bashings and the ill-treatment I could understand. After all, I had been plotting and acting against the interests of his Imperial Majesty the Emperor and probably deserved it. Also, the Japanese were not much better in the way they treated their own people—that was the way they worked. I could forgive the physical abuse, I suppose, but not this public humiliation and disgrace which filled me with murderous thoughts of utter frustration. We were whipped and prodded into a trot down the centre of the road. I have been in a few public parades but nothing like this one. As I looked at that scene of solemn faces I saw more expressions of pity and anxiety than the gloating glee of the Japanese, which they, no doubt, had wished to arouse in the spectators.

The road swung around along the waterfront, past the green lawns of the Cricket Club *padang*, with views of the harbour. The Supreme Court Building towered above them, stone steps rising towards its imposing columns, their arrival watched by the crowd opposite, who were imported for the occasion. Inside the cool spacious court there were six small thrones, with a larger one in the middle, positioned on a dais:

A little while later the court came onto the dais led by General Fukuye who took his seat on the central, most imposing throne while the others ranged themselves on either side of him. I must say that they looked a rum bunch, more like something out of Gilbert and Sullivan than a military court. Without any preamble the interpreter began reading from his box below where the general was sitting. It was all in Japanese and I could see that he was using one of the fat dossiers prepared by the scribe during the long weeks of our interrogation. As there were two of these books I knew that it was going to be a lengthy trial.

The days dragged on, with the defendants understanding nothing of what was being said. At night they were returned to Outram Road Gaol. On the morning of the third day, Macalister threw a bombshell which completely disrupted the proceedings:

Looking squarely at Fukuye he said in a loud voice, 'I can't understand a word of what this stupid little monkey is saying.' In an instant all was chaos. The interpreter literally had a fit at such outlandish and unforgivable behaviour. He fell to the floor and lay there writhing and frothing at the mouth. The general sprang to his feet, livid with rage, and shouted something to the guards. They grabbed us, and Fukuye stormed furiously out of the court followed by the six other judges. I expected some dire punishment at any moment but none came. We were bustled roughly downstairs and into a van and taken immediately back to our cells. No food arrived that day or the next.

The following day, the charade started all over again with the president glowering and looking more menacing than ever. This time the defendants did get a smattering of English, so Mac's outburst must have had some effect. But Wyett learned from the little English they did hear that the *Kempeitai* were not convinced by their story, although the two men hoped they had at least weakened the case against them enough to save their heads. A vain hope as it turned out because that afternoon General Fukuye pronounced the death sentence.

Wyett and Macalister were to be beheaded.

Now locked in the condemned cells at Outram Road, the two Australians knew they could be executed at any time. Wyett did not see any way out of their dire situation. Certainly escape was impossible:

> I came to the conclusion that the only thing left was to put up some sort of a fight. If I had to go I was determined to take a couple of them with me. I had no idea at first how I would carry out such a plan but to do anything at all I would need to be a good deal fitter than I was. Muscles soon become flabby when they are not used and we had been leading a very sedentary life these last few months, as well as being knocked about and also severely undernourished. I decided I must exercise in my cell whenever I could.

A scenario started to form in Wyett's mind. He'd noticed that when his cell door was pulled shut, after the slop bucket had been replaced, it clicked to on the tongue and was quite secure. There was no means of opening it from the inside. Eventually, Wyett hit upon a solution. He tore the pocket out of his shorts and found, after several attempts, that if he was quick enough it was possible to insert this piece of rag folded in such a way that it was carried in to the lock when the door was pulled shut. After a while he found that by giving the rag a tug he was able to open the door at will. He was reasonably fit by that stage due to exercise, and if he could open the door when it was least expected, he thought he would at least have the advantage of surprise. With his own execution pending, Wyett worked out a plan to try and grab one of the guard's bayonets and have a go at him:

> It sounds far fetched now, but I seriously thought that if I could do that, I could cut out his liver and eat it raw to try and get me a bit more energy. I know it sounds a frightful thing, but it was all part of my plan. And I had noticed a drainpipe on the outer

wall which was covered in barbed wire and I thought that would give me a handhold. Even if I got a bit torn about I could climb that, and if they got me before I got over the top of that, at least I thought I'd get a couple of them first.

But one day when I thought all was safe I pulled my rag— which I purposely left in the lock to make sure I had not lost the knack of opening the door. Unfortunately it worked all too well. Before I could push it shut again, in rushed two guards who must've been watching me. All hell broke loose with the guards yelling and kicking and bashing and eventually leaving a very sorry, sick inmate, prone and bleeding on the cell floor. I was very sorry because I'd lost my precious rag.

All the inmates then had their pockets torn out and thrown away. In spite of all his careful planning, Wyett hadn't achieved anything.

On 29 April 1943, nearly one month after Macalister and Wyett's trial, a great change took place. It was the emperor's birthday and prisoners were each given a small rice cake as a gift from the emperor. Wyett had a good reason to remember the date because he had sailed from Sydney on that day two years before. Macalister and Wyett also had a rather special day—their death sentences had been changed to twenty years' solitary confinement courtesy of the emperor. They would not be beheaded after all. Wyett:

I had no feeling of gratitude towards that celestial monarch but I was quite elated that our carefully contrived plan had worked so well towards weakening the case against us. To complete that memorable day we were taken from our condemned cells and shorn like a couple of woolly sheep. They sat us in the wide passageway between the rows of cells and ran clippers over our heads thus removing the whole of that matted, dirty, three-month growth. I felt quite light-headed in every way. Also, joy of joys, we were allowed to wash under the tap in the yard and were then taken each to his new cell, unfortunately both again on the same side of the block. The door of my new cell closed behind me and so ended the most dramatic and intensely exciting period I've ever experienced. I was arrested on 31 December and it was then the end of April—after four months of suspense, torture, barbaric cruelty, and eternal repetitive questioning.

To John Wyett, solitary confinement was seen as something of an anti-climax by comparison, and his cell seemed quite friendly. He felt he needed a rest!

# 5

# SANDAKAN DEATH MARCHES

As early as mid 1942, the Japanese began moving large forces of Allied prisoners of war to unknown destinations. Most, bored with life in Changi, welcomed the chance for perhaps harder work, but hopefully more food and relative freedom. By the end of 1943, some 15 000 Australians had left Changi by ship or train as members of Japanese-controlled 'work forces'. The first to go, A Force, destined for the Burma end of the Thai-Burma Railway, had 3000 Australians in it, and there were wondrous rumours about their future. One of the most optimistic was that they were to be shipped to the neutral port of Mozambique, where they would be exchanged by the Japanese for bales of Australian wool!

Dunlop Force from Java left Changi in January 1943, followed by D Force, F Force, and H Force. Other smaller groups followed throughout the year. Unknowingly, they were bound for the Thai end of the railway, but hopes were still running high. Geoff O'Connor was on D Force: 'All we knew was that they wanted a work party to go to Thailand. It was going to be a land of milk and honey, plenty of food and very little to do.'

Dr Kevin Fagan followed on H Force with similar illusions, fostered by the Japanese: 'We were told we were going to a holiday camp, good food, "bring the old pianos and musical instruments".'

The reality was slave labour, disease, malnutrition and death. Only two out of three Australians sent to the Thai-Burma Railway would return alive.

But the shortest straw of all was drawn by those who were selected for B and E Forces. B Force left in May 1942, when 1500 Australians sailed for Borneo, followed by E Force with another 500 men in July. They were heading towards the worst atrocity committed by the Japanese against Allied prisoners of war in World War II—the Sandakan Death Marches. As with A Force, who were transported to Burma by sea, their journey to Borneo began in rust-bucket tramp ships, where they were crammed in 'like a stack of logs', as B Force member Lance-Corporal Herb Trackson, of 2/1st Motor Transport Company, described it. The *Ubi Maru* he sailed in was a typical 'hell ship', over-crowded and malodorous. It had been carrying coal, and black dust quickly invaded the pores of every prisoner on the ship. Signals officer Lieu-tenant Rod Wells remembers there were three small holds, with some 500 men—and their officers—divided into each space: 'We had to sit shoulder to shoulder, and you couldn't sleep or lie down. The holds were about fifteen feet below the deck above, and at the corner of each hold was a Japanese sentry with hand grenades and an automatic rifle. It was appallingly hot, of course, *Ubi Maru*'s last cargo had also been livestock, and the faeces from the cattle were still lying on the floor.'

For good measure, the captain had put the hold covers on, and although these were removed several days into the voyage, little or no fresh air managed to get down into the holds. Efforts were made to get groups of men on deck for one hour a day. The only toilet facili-ties for the serious business of 1500 men were four one-holer cubicles suspended over the side of the ship for direct access to the sea.

To add to the misery, the food provided for the journey was lime-impregnated rice, cooked on the deck in 44-gallon drums, which had been cut in half. Wells recalls: 'The green-coloured lime rice had been preserved in a sulphur compound to prevent the weevils getting in it. In those days, that would be done to preserve the rice for coolie work in remote areas. It was intended this rice would be then thoroughly washed, all the calcium sulphide removed from it plus any dead weevils, and then it would be cooked. But the Japanese on *Ubi Maru* didn't think that was necessary. They merely cooked the rice with all this in it, so while it was being boiled it emitted great fumes of hydrogen sulphide—rotten egg gas—and the stench was appalling. At least the weevils were cooked as well, so we got some protein we might not otherwise have had. By the second or third day we were eating it, because we were just so hungry. There were flies infesting the ship as well, so we all came down with extensive dysentery.'

With only four toilets for 1500 men—if they could get to them—the conditions in the holds, which were bad enough anyway, became horrendous. Desperate men with dysentery would queue for the one steel ladder that led to the deck. Mostly they could not hold on, and while still on the ladder let everything go, over those waiting behind them and back down onto the floor of the hold, which was being fouled anyway from those men who couldn't even get to the ladder.

Private Bill Young, then all of sixteen years old, managed to keep his quirky sense of humour despite all, and later wrote in his memoir:

I had always thought that the expression, 'To shit through the eye of a needle' an exaggerated impossibility. Not any more, believe me. All one could do was climb out of the hold up a ladder, and as it so often happened when only part way up, the 'bomb bays' would open prematurely. 'Be ye therefore sewers of men . . .'

To add to the misery, the ship had inadequate fresh water tanks, which ran out in four days. Private Keith Botterill came down with dengue fever as soon as he boarded the ship and couldn't eat anything at first, which was probably a good thing. But when the fresh water ran out he was in a bad way: 'When I got on deck I used to go along to the winches and catch the rusty steam water as it was dripping out of the winch to quench my thirst. I survived on that for the whole trip.'

Rod Wells remembered that some prisoners died. The Japanese refused to have anything to do with the bodies and ordered the Australians to get rid of them. The dead were wrapped in a blanket or pieces of hessian and dropped over the side of the moving ship. Wells recalls: 'The ship didn't even pull up as you might have expected. There was a reverence though—just silence and a meditation without a word being spoken. When something like that happened, people did what they were supposed to do and kept their thoughts. I think it was the silence that indicated the respect.'

B Force endured nine days of this floating hell before disembarking in the disarmingly beautiful surrounds of Sandakan, with its turquoise water, harbourside cliffs and former British bungalows situated among the vivid green rainforest on the surrounding hills.

The 1500 Australians were in poor shape after their voyage as they assembled on the green grass of the *padang* in Sandakan. Some had joined *Ubi Maru* straight out of Changi's improvised hospital, like Bombardier Dick Braithwaite, after having had his appendix removed. To their collective dismay they were served more of the execrable 'limed' rice that had been inflicted on them during the voyage, and marched up a hill to a deserted convent where they dossed down as best they could.

Next morning they were assembled and marched back to the *padang*, counted, given breakfast—the leftovers from their previous encounter with the putrid rice—and force-marched eight miles inland to a former internment camp built by the British to house 300. It was surrounded by barbed wire and had seven wooden watchtowers for the guards. Twenty sick men who could not walk were taken by truck. The slowest of the marchers were tormented by the guards, who jabbed stragglers with bayonets and rifle butts and hit them with sticks. Powerful electric lights illuminated the double-barbed wire fence around the camp. A savage afternoon thunderstorm broke as they reached their new home, drenching the exhausted marchers.

The 1500 men of B Force wondered why they were there. They were housed in bamboo huts, with walls and roofs made from *atap*. Some had been hastily put together by local labour and were flimsy, to say the least. Dick Braithwaite recalled that his group had just started to settle in to their allocated hut when some other prisoners moved further up the hill to do the same: 'I just happened to look out and I shouted, "Hey, go for your lives!" And the hut further up the slope just collapsed and rolled down on us. No one was hurt, fortunately. There might have been a few bruises, but nothing serious.'

There were no beds and the men had to lie on wooden benches in their huts, which had been built on wooden stilts and contained three small rooms. Seventy-five men were crammed into each. The Australians' sodden kitbags arrived during the afternoon, but had been looted of cigarettes and other valuables. There was no work for the first few days.

(Later, in April 1943, another 500 Australians of E Force were to join them as well as a contingent of 750 British prisoners of war. Two extra camps would be built to accommodate them, with no fraternisation allowed between the three camps. Eventually, some 2500 Allied prisoners of war were housed at the Sandakan camp.)

At the end of July 1942, the camp commandant, Captain Susumi Hoshijima—a man they would come to know and fear—told them they had been brought to Sandakan to construct an airfield for the

Japanese air force, on land originally set aside for an airfield by the Royal Air Force. Keith Botterill recalls: 'Captain Hoshijima was almost six foot and could be kind or vicious, depending on his mood. He gave our officers permission to build a vegetable garden outside the camp, and then he'd turn around and gouge a man's eye out.'

The prisoners were relieved when they saw him in the distance, riding on an old white (former Australian) racehorse, and reacted with fear when he came to give an order. Gunner Owen Campbell says: 'One day he decided he'd put on a sports day. I think it was just a ruse to see how many fit men were in the camp. And of course a lot of blokes fell for it. They had boxing matches, wrestling and foot races. They had a race round the camp and back again, and a lot of them went in for that like fools. The winners got a big basket of fruit—but the next day they were on working parties.'

In the early period of building the aerodrome, Sunday was a rest day. On Sunday, there was an unexpected bonus when a wandering goat—from a flock tended by an old Indian shepherd—unwisely ambled into the camp. Frank Martin says: 'Some of us had seen it coming in, and while one bloke was milking it, another was cutting its throat, and in no time they had it all done—into the dixies and down onto the fires, and all the guts and head and everything was thrown into the swamp out of sight. Well the old Indian made the Japs understand that his goat had come in, and the guards came looking for it. Everyone shook their heads, but as soon as they got down past the first two or three huts, some bright spark bleated "Maaaa . . . Maaaa", and thinking they'd found the goat the Japs would run back to the first hut, when another "Maaaa" would have them running somewhere else. It was like one of those comedies you see on the TV these days. The poor old Indian was screaming for his lost goat, the Japs were screaming because everyone was making fools of them, and at the same time the poor bloody goat was simmering in our dixies down at the end of the camp.'

Hoshijima stayed in command of the Sandakan camp until April 1945. At first, the guards were Japanese, but for the last two years they were young Formosans, who, like the Korean guards on the Thai-Burma Railway, were treated with contempt by the Japanese. They did their best to curry favour with their masters by the intensity of their hatred for the emperor's enemies and cruelty toward them.

The aerodrome, with two runways and its service roads, had to be built from scratch. First, the jungle had to be cleared, and the runways carved out of undulating hills. Although the work was hard, with workers beaten and bashed to encourage their efforts, the supply of food in the camp improved with a three-weekly ration of fish, and a reasonable quantity of rice and local vegetables. Keith Botterill (who would be one of the six survivors of the death marches in 1945) recalls the first twelve months as reasonable, in prisoner-of-war terms: 'Sure, we had to work on the drome, we used to get flogged, but we had plenty of food and cigarettes—roll your own, you know. We actually had a canteen in the prison camp. We were getting ten cents a day, about eight cents because you'd give two cents for the sick. I think a coconut was about one cent, and a turtle's egg one cent. Cigarette papers without glue were about one cent a packet. Tobacco was three cents an ounce. And a fair-sized banana went for a cent. Yeah, we had it pretty easy. We had a two-up game. We had lights on in the huts, boxing every Saturday night, and concerts.'

Early in captivity the prisoners staged two musical reviews, 'Radio Rubbish' and 'Let's Boong It On'. Captain Claude Pickford, with his fine tenor voice, trained a choir among the officers. Performed on a wooden stage in a natural amphitheatre, the shows were a memorable extension of the Changi concerts in Singapore. But from the end of 1943 the Japanese raised successive petty objections—they refused rehearsal time, they allowed a show to be planned and then suddenly cancelled it, and they objected to all the scripts shown to them for censorship. Nelson Short recalls: 'But there were also impromptu shows from men who were fit enough to try to put on acts. I had an improvised ukulele, which I'd made out of 3-ply, signal wire and part of a comb for the frets. The pegs were whittled out of glass. When you're put to the test you can make anything, I think.'

Men recited their own poems and Short wrote songs, accompanied on his ukulele:

> If that Harbour Bridge was spanned across the causeway,
> And old Fremantle came to Singapore,
> If Adelaide bells rang out at Bukit Timah,
> And Bondi Beach was lined around these shores,
> If the River Yarra flowed into the harbour
> And old Rockhampton on this island did appear,
> Then we wouldn't want to roam,
> We would always feel at home,
> If we only had Australia over here.

In spite of the barbed wire that circled the camp, the men at Sandakan had better contact with the outside world than other prisoners. Some of the civilians in the town had not been interned, including Dr James Taylor, an Australian working at the Sandakan hospital. Many of the British North Borneo Constabulary were loyal to their old colonial masters and, as elsewhere, the Chinese took risks to help the prisoners.

Taking advantage of the comparative ease of movement, Captain Lionel Matthews, B Force's intelligence officer, arranged for the Borneo policeman to collect medicines from Dr Taylor and bring them to the camp. Major Oxley, a British police officer held on Berhala Island in Sandakan Harbour, also arranged for his former Borneo police to work for Matthews. Lieutenant Rod Wells, out on wood-collecting parties, picked up the life-saving B1, iodine, M&B tablets and surgical instruments. The police also delivered the basic parts for a radio. Lieutenants Gordon Weynton and Wells, using aluminium foil and other makeshift components, soon had a radio receiver working.

To pick up BBC news broadcasts on the headphones of the primitive radio took fine co-ordination. The electricity for the camp came from a generator driven by a wood-fuelled steam engine controlled by a Chinese engineer, Ah Ping. But the power that gave a dull glow to the light globes was insufficient for the radio. On the promise of being given news of his homeland, Ah Ping agreed to build up the revolutions of his ancient engine each night at about 10 pm to produce extra power. The first attempt to hear the international news was unsuccessful. Wells and Weynton found the BBC frequency, but heard over 30 minutes of a documentary on hop-growing in Kent. Also, Ah Ping fired his boilers with such enthusiasm that he blew nearly all the lights in the camp! The enthusiastic engineer was persuaded to increase the revolutions gradually, and Wells and Weynton soon discovered the news schedules. The wireless gave service for nearly a year, from August 1942 until July 1943.

A secret group among the prisoners began working on a more ambitious scheme. The same team that built the radio receiver now made a transmitter, which they developed to the point that they made test broadcasts. Matthews hoped that through Chinese Filipino traders he could pass messages through the Sulu chain of islands to the American guerrilla forces in the Philippines. Given time, he hoped to be able to send information to and receive it from Australia. But the number of people now involved on the outside made these operations increasingly risky and the network was ultimately betrayed.

Rod Wells: 'Sometime in the early part of July 1943, an Indian blackmailed a Chinese who was helping us in our general intelligence work. The Chinese refused to help the Indian—I think he wanted money—and the Indian told the Japanese. As a result, two or three of our trusted Asian helpers were arrested. During the interrogations, unknown to us, Lionel Matthews' name was mentioned. Japanese troops arrived suddenly in the camp. Most of the prisoners were working at the aerodrome, and the sick and those engaged on camp duties were driven outside the wire while the inside of the huts were torn apart and gear scattered in a frantic search.'

The Japanese found neither radio nor transmitter, well concealed under the odorous seats of latrine boreholes, but they did find evidence of communications—some notes that Wells was to take to a police-man, Corporal Arbin, the next morning, were hidden in some of his socks. The Japanese called for Lionel Matthews and took him away. Wells and Weynton were arrested soon afterwards and all three men were taken to the *Kempeitai* headquarters in Sandakan. The list of those thought to be involved began to grow, including the courageous Dr Taylor, their Asian helpers in Sandakan and some Australian prisoners who had absolutely nothing to do with the underground network, like Signalman Frank Martin and Private Stan Davis. Stan Davis's name had been confused with another suspect, Sapper Roy Davis, but he was arrested nevertheless. Both Davises and Frank Martin ended up at Outram Road Gaol.

The Japanese were furious at the underground network that had been operating under their noses—despite the habit of Captain Nagai, Hoshijima's second-in-command, who lurked under the Australian huts at night to eavesdrop on conversations. This was a watershed in the treatment of the prisoners of war in Borneo who, from then on, would be given no quarter at all. There were more bashings, less food and bestial punishments. Early in October 1943, the Japanese suddenly announced that 200 officers were to be transferred by ship to Kuching, in present day Sarawak, leaving only five Australian officers in Sandakan, including three doctors.

Eyewitness accounts of events at Sandakan after the bulk of the officers were shipped out have come from the only six survivors of the death marches, four of whom were alive in the early 1980s when I recorded them for my ABC Radio documentary series *Prisoners of War: Australians Under Nippon*. They were Bombardier Dick Braithwaite, Privates Nelson Short and Keith Botterill, and Gunner Owen Campbell (Lance Bombardier William Moxham and Warrant Officer Williaw Sticpewich were the other two survivors). Everyone else died at the Sandakan camp or on the two death marches in 1945.

It is no wonder that the story of the greatest atrocity committed against Allied prisoners of war by the Japanese during World War II —the unnecessary deaths of 1787 Australians and 641 British soldiers—received less attention than other major slave-labour projects like the Thai-Burma Railway, on which some 30 000 Australians worked in 1943. In round figures, 20 000 returned to Changi able to report what had occurred. But in Borneo the details of the death marches could only be told by the six Australians who survived them, and some local Borneo people who witnessed what went on.

The Japanese reacted to the underground network vindictively. Guards around the perimeter of the camp were doubled. Savage dogs were tethered around the wire as well. (Some were not so savage and were coaxed into contact with prisoners, killed and eaten.) Rations and medical supplies were cut. Work on the aerodrome was intensified and so were the bashings, which went on from dawn till dusk. The lack of food was the most serious deprivation and innovative and desperate alternatives were sought.

Going out under the wire to scrounge for food was no laughing matter. All the sewage from the camp ran into a swamp nearby, which also fertilised a small tapioca plantation. Owen Campbell recalls: 'We used to go over and "bandicoot" the tapioca—dig up the roots away from the main tree, and leave it standing. One night one of the blokes went out, and he must have been betrayed for sure, because he'd only just got through the wire when a Jap appeared and shot him. We used to scrounge anything that moved. I've eaten snakes and snails and grasshoppers. I couldn't come at rats, but some blokes ate them. And we used to eat berries. [We] just watched the monkeys when we were out on working parties and what they ate, we ate.'

Nelson Short: 'Some of the blokes ate the swamp rats, but their skin turned scaly and they died, so I didn't. You'd lay green leaves out on the ground and the slugs would get under them, and you'd thread them on a bit of wire and toast them over the fire. At least they were clean because they only ate greens, and when the slime was off them they tasted just like pork. We ate frogs too—anything we could eat we did.'

As the death rate started to increase, so did the burial parties, but the prisoners couldn't keep up with making coffins. The existing ones were fitted with sliding bottoms so the corpse could be carried to the grave, and the coffin used again. Owen Campbell says: 'On a few occasions we carried live blokes out so they could escape. But the silly galahs never went away, they hung around outside the camp and got caught again. When the Japs found out about that, they used to jab their bayonets into the soles of the feet to make sure the corpse was dead.'

Bombardier Braithwaite was concerned that the wooden crosses marking the graves of dead comrades would eventually rot away, so he began making little aluminium disks to put on them, engraved with the names and regimental numbers of the dead, which might be a permanent record—until there were so many deaths he simply could not continue.

The slightest misdemeanour on the aerodrome or in the camp was punished by confinement in specially built cages. Constructed of slats of wood, the cages stood about a metre above the ground, but were so low that a man could not stand up and it was too crowded to ever lie down. An added indignity was that they had to urinate and defecate where they were. Each man was taken out once a day for a bashing, and then returned. Nelson Short recalled that if any prisoner passed by and even looked at the caged men, he would be grabbed and put in to join them. 'As you went past the Japanese headquarters they were watching you. You just had to keep your head and eyes straight ahead. I missed the cages luckily, but Keith Botterill was in them. No clothes or anything and malarial mosquitos—it was alive with them there. I saw one chap go in there, and later come back into the camp. He was bent over and walking on a stick, and he died about five hours after that. He was like an old man. He was only about 25 years old. That's what the cage could do to you.'

That consummate survivor, Keith Botterill, endured 40 days straight in a cage: 'There were 17 others in the cages. No water for the first three days. On the third night they'd force you to drink water till you were sick. For the first seven days you got no food. On the seventh day they started feeding you half camp rations. I was just in a G-string, never had a wash, and covered in lice and scabies. We were not allowed to talk, but we used to whisper. We had to kneel down all day. There wasn't really room to lie down at night, but we all lay side-by-side, squashed up, and had to sit up again at dawn and kneel. Every evening we would get a bashing, which they used to call physical exercise.

'They'd bring us out at a set time, at 5 o'clock every night. They had English cooks working for them because they wouldn't trust the Australians anywhere near the cookhouse. The Englishmen knew that we got out at 5, so they'd come down then to feed the [guard] dogs with swill, the kitchen rubbish. They'd pour it into this trough. We'd all hit it together, the dogs and all of us, and we'd fight the dogs for the scraps. If you've ever tried to pull a bone out of the starving dog's mouth you'll know what it was like. The dog would fasten onto your wrist to take the bone off you, and you'd still be putting the bone into your mouth. And you'd finish up the better.'

Meanwhile, starving men still had to put in a long day's work building the aerodrome. There was little mechanical help, with men having to carry baskets of earth and clay to fill in the valleys, having levelled the hills first. The Japanese had managed to find an ancient wood-fired steamroller but some of the filled areas were so spongy that the steamroller got bogged, and could not be retrieved, eventually sinking down so far—to the secret joy of the Australians—that they were ordered to fill in rubble over the top of it.

'The guards were watching you all the time,' Nelson Short remembered, 'walking around with sticks like swords, and if you weren't working hard enough you'd get whacked. Or you stood for an hour or two, holding up weights and looking into the sun, which I did and got solar burns in both eyes. The beatings never stopped.'

Dick Braithwaite recalled that 'One man [was] bashed for an unknown misdemeanour, had his eye knocked clean out of its socket. There was no sympathy given for that at all. He was kept standing there and he didn't get any treatment until about six or seven hours later. There were numerous incidents of that nature. You tended to live with them, and they didn't stick in your memory because they were commonplace—as with the deaths. It was a way of life that you learned to accept, and expected.'

The prisoners of war at Sandakan began to wonder if they could survive for much longer but, with the war going badly for the Japanese, they continued to hope that an Allied landing would save them.

They could not know of secret Japanese orders that the prisoners of war in all the South-East Asian camps were to be killed in the event of an Allied landing—in Changi, Java, Hainan, Thailand, Saigon, and anywhere prisoners of war were held. The dropping of the atomic bombs on Hiroshima and Nagasaki in August 1945, and the emperor's personal directive for an unconditional surrender, meant this order was not carried out, and guaranteed the survival of most of the POWs still alive at that time. Early in 1945, the prisoners of war in Changi were made to dig trenches outside the camp that they suspected were to be their own mass graves.

Unfortunately for the Borneo POWs, Allied attacks began to impinge on the Sandakan camp as early as October 1944, with bombing raids on the Japanese infrastructure and even on the Sandakan POW camp itself. Nelson Short says: 'The Japanese allowed us to put a big POW sign in black and white on the highest point. But the planes continued to bomb and strafe the camp. So the Japanese made us take down the POW sign and give them an open go. Bombs left craters right in the camp, and one bomb went right under a hut and killed twenty or thirty blokes. I can't understand it. When we had the POW sign there and everybody could see it, they just continued to strafe and bomb. The Japanese opened up on us as well. They were putting rifle fire into the camp. They were having a go too. They wanted to get rid of as many of us as they could.'

Perhaps anticipating invasion, the Japanese started shifting prisoners out of the Sandakan camps in January 1945 and marching them into the jungle-covered interior of Borneo. By then the deaths in the camps had reached epidemic proportions. Short: 'You saw the men every day when you were getting treated for ulcers. The dead were lying there, naked skeletons. They were all ready to be buried. Day after day they were just dying like flies in the camp of malaria or malnutrition. And you thought to yourself, well, how can I possibly get out of a place like this?'

After the death marches began, only Short and five others were able to escape. However, there were other survivors too—the 33 prisoners in Sandakan who had been tried and sent to serve sentences at Outram Road Gaol, Singapore, for various crimes against the Imperial

Japanese Army from 1942 till 1944, before the death marches began. Lieutenant Rod Wells was one of them.

Suspected of being a member of the underground network betrayed to the Japanese in July 1943, Wells was pulled out of an aerodrome working party several days after the leader of the network, Captain Lionel Matthews, had been detained. Wells says: 'The next two nights weren't very happy for me. On the third day they stopped all work parties outside the camp, Hoshijima got up on the back of the vehicle, and I thought he was about to address everybody. He just called out those two words I'll never forget, "Lieutenant Wells".'

Hoshijima ordered Wells to come forward and accused him of having a radio. When Wells denied the accusation, Hoshijima hit him twice under the chin, then grasped the rag around Wells's neck and began to throttle him. Eventually, Wells decided it was better to give up part of the non-functional transmitter and leave the radio intact. He gambled correctly that the Japanese wouldn't realise that they were holding the valves of a transmitter rather than that of the receiver. Hoshijima called a parade: 'He took me to the top of the platform where the morning parades were held. He asked the whole camp to look at me and said they would not see me again. And that was the last time I saw my lovely friends who went on the death marches.'

Sitting on the back of a truck with two silent guards, Wells was driven off into the night. In the town of Sandakan, he was forced into cells under what had been a beautiful old bungalow. It was now the headquarters of the *Kempeitai*. 'It was a horrifying place because you would hear the groans and the cries from people being interrogated. Every morning the *Kempeitai* had their meeting for the day, and always there was a quietness. Then all the chairs were pulled back. You'd know the meeting was over, and you'd think, who's [in] for it now? You'd hear the clumping down the stairs and then in would come one of the *Kempeitai*. He would just signal with a gesture and you knew that you were in the box that day. That was horrible. And this went on for months, from July to November 1943.'

Wells, who had started out as an electrical trade apprentice and as a student teacher before he enlisted, was 23 at the time of his arrest. Isolated from all other prisoners in the first weeks of his imprisonment, and untrained in intelligence, he could only guess what the Japanese already knew and what points he could concede without further incriminating himself and others. The *Kempeitai* were excruciatingly professional. They used the standard interrogation techniques of reward and punishment. He was offered a cigarette and then he was belted. His crisply dressed and pomaded captors pleaded, then screamed. And when the *Kempeitai* chief lost patience, he turned to tougher methods.

'He asked whether I was hungry and I said I was,' Wells remembered. 'With that they brought in a container of raw rice. I thought it was cooked rice. He said, "Eat," and I thought he was joking because he smiled when he said it. I said I would, but only ate a little bit because it was raw rice. With that, two of their bullies came in, held my hands behind my back, opened my mouth, poured it in by spoon, and kept tapping my head until I swallowed it. I don't know how much of it I had. Probably three or four cupfuls got down my throat. Then they brought a garden hose in, held me, pushed the hose down my neck and turned it on. They kept going until the water came gushing up.

'Then they threw me back in my cell. You can imagine the rest. About three or four hours later the pain became excruciating as the rice swelled within the stomach. I didn't know much about human anatomy then, but the rice must have somehow gone through the pylorus, the output from the stomach into the small intestine, and the pain for about a day and a half was intense. Part of the bowel came out, but there was no medical attention. It bled for a while, it was very painful and gradually got better. I managed to push it back by hand. Then the interrogation continued.

'On another occasion the interviewer produced a small piece of wood like a meat skewer, pushed that into my left ear and tapped it in with a small hammer. I think I fainted sometime after it went through the ear drum. I remember the most excruciating pain, and I must have gone out to it for some time because I was revived with a bucket of water. I was put back in the cell again after that. The ear was very painful, it bled for a couple of days. But fortunately for me it didn't become infected. Eventually it healed but of course I couldn't hear with it, and I have never been able to hear with that ear since.'

Wells later found out a most curious thing. At the very instant his torturer punctured his ear drum with the skewer, a picture of him in a glass frame in his parents' living room at their Victorian farm fell from the mantelpiece for no explicable reason, and shattered on the floor: 'It happened to be my mother's birthday in August, and she cried out, and my father said, "What's wrong?" My mother was very distressed and said, "Rod is being hurt."'

Wells checked on the timing of this later, and found it was indeed about the time of his torture by the *Kempeitai*. He thinks he may have called out to his mother as he passed out, either consciously or unconsciously. After he returned home, Wells never mentioned anything about his treatment by the *Kempeitai*, as he didn't want to upset her. But she told the story to him! 'It was a most remarkable coincidence and it shocked me when she told me about it.'

At that time, Wells thought he had little chance of getting home alive. He thought it was a case of getting whatever nourishment he could, keeping out of as much trouble as possible, and hoping that there wouldn't be any more interrogations until the following day. After the first weeks of questioning, Wells was sometimes held in the same room as Lionel Matthews and Gordon Weynton. As signallers, they all had an advantage.

*Left:* Fifteen-year-old Bill Young is accepted into the AIF in September 1941. (Courtesy Bill Young, Anthony Hill) *Right:* Sandakan veterans (from left) Nelson Short, Bill Young and Keith Botterill. Short and Botterill were two of the six men who survived the Borneo Death Marches. (Courtesy Bill Young, Anthony Hill)

*Left:* A young Chris Neilson shortly after joining the AIF as a signaller in Brisbane in 1940. (Courtesy Chris Neilson) *Right:* Chris Neilson in later life. (Courtesy Chris Neilson)

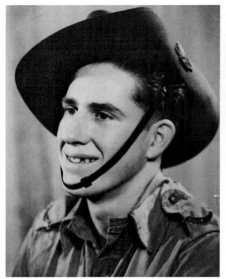
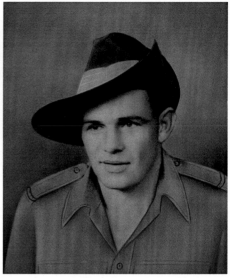

*Left:* MP 'Jimmy' Brown tried to escape from the Sandakan Camp with Bill Young and finished up in Outram Road Gaol. (Courtesy Judith Gee and Majella Gee)
*Right:* Aboriginal boxer Jimmy Darlington, survivor of torture in Sandakan and incarceration in Outram Road Gaol. (Courtesy Anthony Hill and Robert Sweeney)

Jimmy Darlington being trussed and tortured in the Sandakan camp after striking a guard. (Courtesy Bill Young)

A Japanese punishment cage in the Sandakan camp, Borneo. Inside Allied POWs sat hunched, unable to stretch out or stand up. (Courtesy Bill Young)

Cell 72, Outram Road Gaol. (Courtesy Bill Young)

A cramped, three-tiered cell block at Outram Road Gaol. Allied POWs were housed on the ground floor. (Courtesy Bill Young)

'The Postman' cometh with his heavy keys. (Courtesy Bill Young)

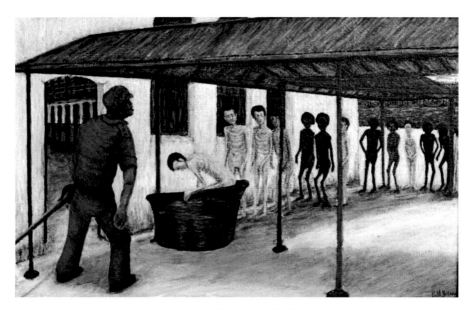

A scabies bath in the yard of the gaol. (Courtesy Bill Young)

*Left:* John McGregor, author of *Blood on the Rising Sun*. (Courtesy John McGregor)
*Right:* Outram Road survivor Penrod Dean, author of *Singapore Samurai*, pictured immediately post-war. (Courtesy Penrod Dean)

*Left:* Thai–Burma Railway survivor, Herbert James 'Ringer' Edwards, as a cattleman in the Northern Territory post-war. (Courtesy Chris Neilson) *Right:* A cheerful Rod Wells before being discharged from the army in 1945 after his experiences in Sandakan and Outram Road Gaol. (Courtesy Pam Wells)

Rod Wells (right) and Tim Bowden in December 1984. (Courtesy Pam Wells)

John Wyett (left) and Tim Bowden in the early 1990s. (Photo Tim Bowden)

*Left:* Ken Bird (right), perpetrator of the wondrous mime during the Outram Road scabbies bath routine, in the 1980s. (Photo Tim Bowden) *Right:* Bert Rollason on Anzac Day 2008. He celebrated his 92nd birthday in 2013. (Courtesy Bert Rollason)

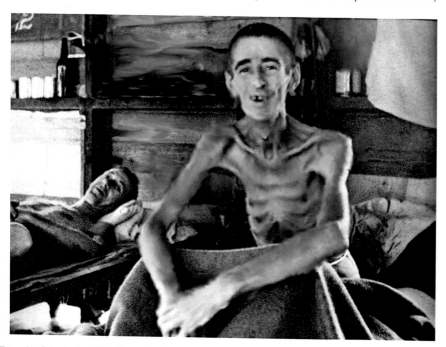

Despite his skeletal body, British soldier John 'Becky' Sharpe smiles at the camera on his release from Outram Road Gaol to the hospital in Changi. (*Illustrated London News*)

Japanese prisoners paraded at their cell doors on the second level at Outram Road Gaol, 1945. (*Illustrated London News*)

In the grounds of Outram Road Gaol, Captain Francis paraded four of the war criminals who inflicted so much suffering on Australian and British troops. From left: Mastochi Saito (Malaya), Mikizawa (commandant of the civilians Outram Road), Tominago (Changi) and Ogata (Inspector of Japan Police). (*Illustrated London News*)

The hated Kempeitai officer and sometimes commandant of Changi, Tominago, behind bars at Outram Road. He was later hanged for war crimes. (*Illustrated London News*)

'We were placed in a triangular formation, all facing the sentry whose instructions were to watch and make sure there was no talking. Matthews commenced using Morse [code],' Wells recalled. 'He would come back from interrogation, sit down, cross his legs as we were instructed to, and tap his fingers on his chest. I could read the message. It was a laborious way of communicating, but anything is better than nothing. He would go through the topics on which he'd been interrogated that morning and the answers he had given.'

These exchanges not only enabled the prisoners to avoid accidental incrimination, but they boosted confidence. One sentry, noticing the persistent tapping, indicated to the relieving guard that Matthews had gone a little crazy and might turn dangerous.

After what seemed a very long four months, the three signallers were suddenly put in a car, transported to the Sandakan wharf and put on board a small ship, in the company of eighteen other prisoners including Australians, Europeans, Chinese, Malays, Filipinos and a couple of Indians. They were handcuffed and kept on the upper deck, but they could move a little. They arrived in Kuching on Melbourne Cup Day, 2 November, and were locked in the Kuching Gaol. There were six to eight men in each cell, and although they weren't supposed to talk to each other there was not enough supervision to prevent it. Wells thought that the interrogations were now over and they were to attend court. Matthews, Wells and Weynton were not court-martialled until 29 February 1944—a leap year.

The day before the trial, Major Suga, the commander of all the POWs in Borneo, came to their cell and took them to an adjoining room where he gave them all some fruit, bananas and papaya, and conversed amicably with them. Suga, an older man, spoke reasonable English, but the three Australians did not think this gesture boded well for their future.

On the morning of 29 February 1944, Matthews, Weynton and Wells were taken down to the courtroom situated in the Cathedral School at Kuching. Wells was struck by the irony of the proceedings being held in the science room: 'The court was assembled, and the President was a lieutenant colonel in full uniform, polished leggings, boots, gloves, white gloves—immaculately turned out. We were led into the court and stood at the foot of the judges' area. A series of questions was put to us, some true and some false. Eventually we were sentenced—Lionel Matthews and I were to be executed and Gordon Weynton was to spend ten years in Outram Road Gaol—all sentences subject to confirmation.'

All those sentenced were then taken back to their cells. On 2 March, eight Asians who had not been sentenced were taken to the courtroom, followed by the three Australians, who were escorted from the gaol to the court in handcuffs, after being marched barefoot down the main street of Kuching. Wells says: 'We found our eight Asian friends tied together and absolutely distraught, and one passed his hand across his throat to indicate that they were all to be executed. Then we went back into the courtroom and the court confirmed our sentences. For Lionel Matthews—capital punishment was the word they used that day—and for myself, twelve years' penal servitude and solitary confinement in Outram Road Gaol, and Gordon Weynton, ten years. The other sentences were passed on the rest, and that completed the court martial. Before Lionel was taken away, we were allowed to have a few words with each other and later I was able to pass on his love to his wife and son when I returned to Australia.'

Matthews was executed immediately after his sentence was confirmed, followed shortly afterwards by the eight local Asians. Affectionately known as 'The Duke' by his men, Matthews defied the Japanese by refusing to be blindfolded and his last words to the firing squad were, 'My God and King forever.' He was an exceptionally brave man, who had won a Military Cross during the Malayan campaign, and in 1947 was awarded the George Cross posthumously for 'his gallant and distinguished services while a prisoner of war'.

Wells, who had expected to be executed with Matthews, was astounded that his sentence had been commuted to twelve years at Outram Road Gaol. He did not learn why until after the war. He was the fortunate recipient of a bungle in the Japanese bureaucracy: 'It came out during the war crimes trials that the whole of Borneo was administered by the Japanese area headquarters in Saigon. Apparently a request from the court through the official channels to Saigon some weeks before had requested authority to execute two Europeans and eight Asians. Due to an administrative foul up, the authority in writing— which was retrieved by the war crimes people—indicated the authority to execute only one European but not two. As Lionel was a captain and I was a lieutenant, the death sentence was confirmed on him and the penal servitude in solitary confinement sentence was passed on me. I couldn't believe my ears. At first I thought I was dreaming. This may seem strange, but I didn't want to be, sort of, separated from Lionel. I felt that wherever he went, I should go too. But there it was.'

On 4 March, Wells, Weynton and some European civilians, including the exceedingly courageous Dr Taylor from Sandakan, were taken to the Kuching wharves and put in a crate which was lifted by crane into the hold of a small coastal ship. To Wells's surprise, they shared their new quarters with a bevy of Japanese prostitutes on their way to Singapore to join the regiment they were currently servicing. The girls enjoyed better rations than the European prisoners for the four days and nights of the voyage. They shared the sleeping quarters too, but Wells said they were too exhausted to even think of taking advantage of this unique opportunity in prisoner-of-war life.

In Singapore they were taken by truck to Outram Road Gaol, which Wells remembers as an utterly forbidding place reminding him of the penitentiary built for convicts at Port Arthur in Tasmania—except that he was soon to find out the convicts there undoubtedly had bigger and better cells. He was stripped and issued with his prison shirt and shorts and given his number, 641.

Wells was a comparative latecomer to Outram Road when he was admitted in March 1944. The regime was still strict, with starvation rations of rice and soup, and he also suffered the torments of scabies that still infected all the prisoners in those filthy cells. To Wells's misery was added the curse of tapeworms. The brimming toilet buckets, by then emptied once a week, had to be used for an additional purpose. 'The body's way of rejecting these long tapeworms we had in us was that you would feel sick, and then you would vomit into the toilet bucket, bringing up these great long tapeworms out of your throat. That was horrible enough, but also demoralising to think that this loathsome thing was getting the nourishment you should have. It would be dead by the time it got into the bucket—they come off as segments I believe—and then they would stay in the bucket for the rest of the week until it was emptied.'

Getting out of the cell to empty the toilet bucket—or better still being drafted on toilet bucket duties for other sections of the gaol—was a prized opportunity to venture into the yard, where a prisoner might have access to more food. If Wells walked past a hibiscus plant he would pluck some leaves and cram them into his mouth for some hoped-for extra nourishment, or crunch up a snail and eat it raw: 'Hunger is a bad thing. During the emptying of these toilet buckets, the buckets of Japanese prisoners were emptied also. And the Japanese, of course, had better rations, but like us they had to eat them quickly. They were given lots of lovely cooked rice with big black beans in it, high-protein beans. They swallowed these whole and of course they passed through—they were in the buckets. And I've seen our chaps, if the opportunity came, grab a handful of excrement, rinse it away from the beans when they were washing their buckets, and eat it. It was extra protein, and that just gives you some idea of how hungry we were. I didn't quite do it. I nearly did the day I was out, but some of the other chaps had been doing this job more regularly and one or two of them were indulging in this when the sentries weren't looking.'

To combat the utter boredom of sitting in his cell in the designated position for each hour, Wells kept his mind occupied in a number of ways. To keep track of the days, he memorised each day's date—and was spot on when he was eventually released back into Changi a year after he entered Outram Road.

However, concerned about his deteriorating health, Wells devoted considerable mental energy to thinking how he could measure his possibly slowing pulse rate. But that needed some practical equipment. 'To take my pulse I needed a time reference. I managed to smuggle a strand of hemp about 18-inches long back into my cell by putting it around the cheeks of my anus and hoping I would get through the inspection. A piece of stone was the next thing to bring in, as the weight for a pendulum. My plan was to make a pendulum with a known period of oscillation.

'I had to put the stone up my anus to get it into the cell. It wasn't a very smooth stone either, but neither was my anus then so it probably didn't matter. That wasn't detected either. And then I was fortunate one day when some of the shorts we were issued with, which all had numbers on them, were lying in a heap on the corridor floor. Across them was lying a tape measure—the Japanese had been doing some mending or alterations to them. I noticed that the number stamped on all the trousers was on a piece of cloth and was one and three-quarter inches long, because of the position of the tape measure. Having got some means of measuring the hemp, and with the stone already smuggled into the cell, I then made up a pendulum of the correct length to have an oscillation of one second as accurately as I could do it.'

The arithmetic was complicated as Wells had to do it in his head. Choosing a period of one second simplified the sums required. Taking gravity to be 32 foot/second/second, the length of the pendulum becomes 8/pi2 = 8/3.142/3.142 foot = 0.8106 foot = 9.73 inches. He was lucky that the length of the pendulum gave him some leeway. If he rounded the length to 9¾ inches, the period would have been 1.000 seconds, allowing for the actual gravity in Singapore. But if his measuring inaccuracy gave an actual length of say 9½ inches, the period would have been 0.987 seconds—an insignificant difference. His difficulty would have been deciding what to measure. The length required is the distance from the pivot (the point where the string is secured) to the centre of mass of the pendulum. He knew where the pivot was, but where was the centre of mass? Fortunately, he could use a slender fibre of hemp which would have an insignificant weight compared with the rock. Now he could assume the centre of mass to be the centre of the rock and measure from the pivot to that point. Having no measuring tape, he would have used a bit more than five and a half times the size of the number on his prison shorts (5½ × 1¾ inches = 9.6 inches plus a bit). This was enough to get him very close to a one-second oscillation.

Wells concludes: 'Then merely by finding the pulse in my wrist and doing a juggling act of counting two things at the same time—that is, the pulse and the pendulum—I could time the number of pulses for 60 swings of the pendulum. And I did this for some time. In fact, the bit of stone was with me for months in the cell and was never found. It was pushed into a corner where there were a couple of cracks in the cell wall and it was probably seen, but no significance placed on it. The distressing part, of course, was the fact that, over some months my pulse rate was getting appreciably slower, which was worrying. I can't remember the exact numbers but I think my pulse was down to about three quarters of the rate that it should have been, but medical evidence may have contradicted this. It was certainly slower than it should have been and was gradually getting more so. I don't think it was a great thing to discover anyway because there was nothing I could do about it. The main reason for doing it, really, was the mental exercise. I just assumed probably, rightly, that one's metabolism was merely slowing down with a low intake of food and less physical activity.'

Towards the end of 1944, so many prisoners came in to Outram Road Gaol that the rule of solitary confinement had to be scrapped, and two—sometimes three—prisoners shared each tiny cell. Talking was forbidden, but was impossible to police. At least there was some social contact rather than the loneliness of a solitary existence. The extra prisoners tended to be moved about quite soon, probably to prevent friendships developing. But sharing a cell in such a confined space created tension.

Rod Wells says: 'It's surprising when two people are put together— unless they can work out some compatibility, the individual habits of one person can irritate another person intensely. And the best way to have this difficulty was in food. The bowls of rice were placed in the cell, through the slots in the door, and there would always have to be some kind of agreement with your friend in the cell before the bowls arrived about which one was going to be whose, whether it would be the left or the right one. It sounds silly now, but it was very impor- tant for harmony, particularly if one bowl had a teaspoon more of rice than the other.

'I remember once not liking the way someone scratched his scabies. But my scratching probably was just as ugly to look at. Unnecessary time sitting on the toilet bucket was also an irritation. Or if the chap that you were with had no conversation except driving a truck and the food he would eat if he could. That was a minus as a whole, because you didn't have shared interests to keep both of you mentally active and you would have been better off alone.

'There were two chaps, one Australian and one from the United Kingdom, who both committed suicide through thinking too much about eating. One was a Tasmanian, and his educational background and ability to think abstractly were limited. He could only think and talk about big plates of steak and eggs and in the end this just got the better of him. The cell walls were made of thick concrete. I heard a "thud" and he had just thrown himself against the wall and committed suicide.'

One very rewarding experience was when Wells shared a cell with a civilian, Englishman Robert Scott, later Sir Robert Scott, a well-known public servant, and later Commissioner General to South-East Asia in the 1950s. He and Wells became close friends at Outram Road and after the war.

'He was a very wise and well-educated man,' Wells remembered, 'some fifteen years older than I was and I found my time with him very stimulating because he regarded my body, and I regarded his, as being of no consequence. He inspired me tremendously and gave me the will to go on. At the end of the war he had asked me to write to him. He had become the British Ambassador in Washington and I told him I was just finishing my university course—which he had encouraged me to do.

'When his wife, Lady Scott, remarked some years later that we seemed to get on very well after long absences, Rob's reply was, "Well, we got to know each other fairly well during those days in every way possible." He was a remarkable man and our conversations in the cell ranged widely. Once he went through part of Milton's *Paradise Lost* almost word for word—he was a most fantastic and fascinating man.'

Herb Trackson shared his cell, for a time, with a young man who never spoke. At night when they were permitted to put their bed boards down on the cell floor to sleep, he would just lie down and pull his tattered blanket over him and not even say goodnight. 'After quite some time, this kept nagging at me and one night I really flared up and I said to him, "Look, there's only the two of us in the cell and we are in the same predicament. If you won't even say goodnight to me I'll fix you up good and proper. I'll bloody kill you. Then I'll have the cell to myself." That was an example of a typical nervous upset. After that he did say goodnight to me. But he never even told me where he came from or anything. I think he was English but I'm not sure. After that I had a fellow named Shelley from New South Wales. He was an ex-wheat lumper, but a very nice sort of bloke and we got on well. He taught me a piece of poetry, a love poem [*Lasca*, by Frank Desprez], that I can recite word for word right to this day:

> *I want free life, and I want fresh air;*
> *And I sigh for the canter after the cattle,*
> *The crack of the whips like shots in battle,*
> *The medley of horns and hoofs and heads*
> *That wars and wrangles and scatters and spreads;*
> *The green beneath and the blue above,*
> *And dash and danger, and life and love . . .*

# 6

# JUST ONE DAY AT OUTRAM ROAD GAOL

As punishment was a top priority at Outram Road Gaol, being in permanent solitary confinement was not considered, in itself, to be sufficient deprivation. Mention has been made of prisoners having to sit to attention at all times during their waking hours in their tiny stone cells and that they had a skimpy blanket/sheet, a pair of shorts and nothing else. Rod Wells outlines a typical day at Outram Road: 'All prisoners were woken about 6 am—if you were not already awake— and we had to stand to attention, after getting up from lying on our bed planks. The light, which had been on all night, was switched off. We stood to attention for the roll call, which was organised in a book in which cards were fixed like an album, with each prisoner's number— mine was 641. When your number was called out in Japanese, you had to answer *hai* ("yes"). If you didn't—perhaps you hadn't woken up—the cell door opened and you were knocked and hit. This would happen even if you were just slow in answering. You were bashed across the back or across your shoulders with a wooden sword.'

That ritual took about half an hour, during which every prisoner had to stand rigidly to attention while a guard peeked through the spy-hole in the door to make sure the inmate was not only standing to attention properly but was also the person he was supposed to be, although the alternative was unlikely. Routine was routine nevertheless. After that prisoners were supposed to sit in the cross-legged position—roughly the lotus position favoured by the Buddha—which most Europeans found awkward to maintain. The next break in monotony took place three-quarters of an hour later with the arrival of breakfast, if it could be dignified by that name. This was pushed through a little cubby hole, about two or three inches by five inches, that had been cut in all the cell doors to deliver meals. There was a wooden flap hanging down which was opened from the outside while a small bowl was pushed in.

'You couldn't eat anything immediately,' Wells recalled, 'but you left it there until all the distribution in your corridor had been made, when they gave you the order to start eating. The first meal of the day was just a sort of gruel, a watery rice soup which was probably warm when it arrived, but stone cold by the time you were allowed to eat it. You only had about ten seconds, until they yelled "stop!" Not that it was a great achievement to finish it in that time, you could do that in about two seconds, so the meal was over pretty quickly.'

The plates were pushed back into the slot straight away and were usually picked up by some Japanese prisoners, who had more luxurious conditions and food than the Allied prisoners, but who also had to work on gaol jobs. That completed the morning meal. There was no bed to make except to fold up the small blanket, which was always hard to fold after long periods of continuous use. It wasn't much, but provided some warmth when the body metabolism was very low at night and particularly in the early morning. Wells continued: 'Except that using the blanket did tend to make you scratch more and tear your scabies-infected skin away, even though our skin by this time was very sensitive and raw. It would be difficult to fold up—without being too crude about it—all these blankets became as though they were starched, because they were so rarely washed, if you could call it that. They were probably just thrown in some water without soap and then re-distributed randomly. They would then re-infect your body with somebody else's scabies.'

Next the prisoners sat, facing the door and the day ahead. They could only amuse themselves inside their heads, without any physical movement. Even walking up and down was against the rules. Permission had to be sought to use the toilet bucket, but Wells said, 'Once you were on the toilet bucket they didn't hurry you off it.' I often sat there virtually all morning. I think half the time I was in a kind of semi-coma, deliberately brought about to put oneself into some kind of fantasy land, to try and divorce the brain from the body. I think I did that because the body was then a useless sort of appendage, covered in scabies, ringworm or bedbug bites with a tapeworm in your stomach and tinea all over you. Your body was something that you couldn't do much about, so diving into the realm of fantasy was a good way to pass the time.

'I would take myself back to my boyhood on a farm—not so much the sentimentalism of parents and so forth, but just schoolboy activities, getting birds' eggs out of the trees, playing football or cricket and riding a horse about. I thought of the winter mornings with the spider webs covered in a sort of dew on the ground and the freedom to be able to walk around on the grass and in the paddocks and thinking, well, will one ever be able to do that again? I think that enabled me to forget the present and re-think part of the past.'

Asked if he ever thought about sex at all, Wells replied: 'Yes and no. We thought about it, but not seriously. Some wit once said that if Mae West—who was the glamour girl in those days, of course—was on one side of him and a bowl of rice on the other, he'd smack Mae West on the bottom and turn around to eat the bowl of rice. If we did think about sex it wasn't seriously. Most of us had a strong sexual urge during the first twelve months of captivity—not that one could do anything about it—but after that it was of no importance. You know, sex is a fantasy, imagining it, and we had lost the idea, really, of what a beautiful European girl would actually look like!

'I stopped having erections after a year of captivity, when the food supply went down and the will to live was uppermost. It was considered a complete waste of energy—if one had any urges that way. We needed all the strength and vitality we could muster to keep alive. That was the same for most of us, I think.'

At least once a week Wells had to attend to unwelcome bodily functions while seated on his *benki*, before heading into fantasy land. Because of the sparse food, lack of roughage and so little water, constipation was inevitable, and most prisoners only had one bowel motion a week. But passing his impacted stools was an agonising affair for Wells—particularly because his lower bowel had been badly damaged by *Kempeitai* torture in Sandakan when he was being forced to eat raw rice and ingest water: 'So having a motion was a painful event. I would sit on the bucket with two conflicting desires. One was to save the pain by not straining, and the other was you had to do it for your health. So I would tear at the scabies infected skin on my legs with my fingernails to ease the itching and at the same time distract me from the pain of what I was trying to do.'

On other less fraught days, Wells used to sit on his toilet bucket imagining that he was in a big bath with lovely hot water and big, clean fluffy towels. It was a mistake to start thinking about food, because that simply demoralised him. Sometimes he would think of something practical, like inventing or engineering various devices: 'Calculus was another interest I had, mainly as a mental occupation. I really hadn't done any differential calculus. I touched on it at Leaving Standard in those days, but one didn't go into calculus in the detail that they do now, nor that I later had to do at university. But I did think there must be a way of finding out the area of spaces with curved boundaries and I was able to do this by a sort of data method—which we would call it now—in other words, sectionalising the irregularity, or constancy, between sections, and I was able to derive a simple differential equation ultimately, after lots and lots of thinking.

'As I couldn't write anything down, every time I stopped a session, I would have to go through the whole exercise again from the beginning. But because I was so run-down I had to ration this kind of thinking and could not really go longer than one hour at a time.' He later discovered that he had mentally worked his way up to the fifth differential!

About noon he would hear the rattle of plates again, signalling lunch in about an hour. Unlike the watery rice soup, this would at least be some solid food, but not much of it—a level bowl of between two and three ounces of cooked rice, occasionally with some salt or dried fish with some small bones in it. Even before the food arrived he would imagine how he might eat each mouthful, chewing it and chewing it before letting it go down. And when the bowls were pushed through the door again, he would have about twenty seconds to realise these gastronomic dreams before the command to stop eating was shouted out.

After the midday meal, Wells and everyone else would be told to get up and walk around to get some exercise to shouted numbers and orders, indicating arms up, or extended sideways—the same sort of exercises done in a primary school playground: 'The afternoon was filled with the same kind of meditation I practised in the morning, until the reflected light of the setting sun would throw the shadows of the bars on the cell wall. You'd realise that it was getting towards evening. Time had no real significance except for the light and dark periods. The feeding procedure would begin again, the plates would be rattled and a small bowl of rice would be placed inside the cell door.

In the evening we also had tea, a small bowl of brownish coloured water I'll call very weak tea that was normally cold by the time it got to you. It didn't have any nourishing value in it, but it was the only liquid you were allowed. You couldn't have water, there was no free water supply, so that was your liquid ration and that was all you had. Not that thirst ever worried me very much, I suppose, because our metabolism was so slow. The perspiration rate wasn't very high because the cells had thick stone walls and our body temperatures were probably a bit below normal anyway.'

The cell light was switched on as dusk approached. Each cell had one unshielded 50 watt light globe. The inmates had the rest of the evening to fill until 10.30 pm when the guards would call out the command to sleep. Everyone then had to lie down on their bed planks, and they weren't allowed to walk around in their cells after that. Guards would patrol the corridors and look through the peep-holes to make sure everyone was lying down. The prisoners weren't disturbed during the night, apart from the sentries doing their rounds to check they were all horizontal until morning: 'The light was on all night from dusk till dawn for the whole eighteen months I was there, and I didn't know what darkness during that time was, other than closing my eyes.'

The only variation from this routine was the weekly wash, combined with a change of gaol shorts every two weeks. The shorts, issued by the Japanese, were like jockey underpants, although not so tight. Wells said they were so flimsy and small they barely provided the covering expected in civilised life—which was in short supply at Outram Road in any case. On occasions, communal exercises would accompany the weekly wash or changing of shorts.

'About once a fortnight the cell door was flung open. There wasn't any order given, you were expected to know the routine, which was to drop your shorts to the ground—by then so stiff you could stand them up on the floor by themselves—and stand there naked. They did have additional guards who were posted outside when that happened. Then you would be told to come out with the shorts or without the shorts. If you were to come out with the shorts you knew they were going to be changed. Then they would give an order to step outside your cell. You would take a couple of paces down the steps into the hallway, and stand waiting for another order to file out of the prison block into a courtyard. There you would each be placed in front of a little tin bucket with about two gallons of water in it. You would stand to attention until all the prisoners were behind their buckets.'

The washing happened once a week in the late afternoon. There was no soap, just the bucket, and when the order was given to start washing, the prisoners knew they only had twenty seconds. They cupped their hands, throwing as much water as they could over their heads and bodies for about eight to ten seconds, then rubbed their wet bodies furiously with their hands. Just before their time ran out, they would pick up the bucket and throw what water was left over themselves. Sometimes a little piece of rag was provided for a primitive towel but, if not, the prisoners used their hands again to remove what excess water they could from their ravaged bodies. Then the order to stop was shouted, and anyone rash enough to keep washing would be bashed.

'We came out of the cells naked and sometimes after the wash we would have to exercise by numbers. If you didn't bend the right way a guard would walk behind with a wooden sword and give you a good crack across the back to make sure you did exactly what you were supposed to do. Then we were taken back to our cells and stood up outside the doors again in the same position as when we first came out. With legs apart and our arms in the air we were then physically searched—still naked. And if it was a shorts changing day, a clean pair of shorts—clean is hardly the operative word—so-called washed shorts, would be there at the cell door and you would pick them up as you were ordered back in. You put them on, they came round and closed the doors and that completed the activity.'

Wells said the toilet buckets were not emptied at that stage but in a separate operation, once a week when the toilet bucket had to be placed near the door. When the cell doors were opened, prisoners had to put their buckets on the step outside the door then stand back while the buckets were collected and taken away and replaced shortly afterwards with empty ones. The washing and shorts-changing routine was the only time the prisoners were allowed out of their fetid cells.

So passed the dreary, dispiriting days at Outram Road Gaol.

# 7

# YOUNGIE

Bill Young and his mate Don Miller were both fifteen years old and stoney motherless broke—literally—when they fronted up to a recruiting office in Melbourne to enlist in the Australian Imperial Force on 27 July 1941. They were both big lads and looked more mature than their age. Both were orphans, so parental permission could be bypassed. The recruiting officer asked if they had any aunts, and they said they had. Taking the forms away, they made up names of mythical aunts, and each forged a signature on the other's form.

The recruiting officer could see their forms were shonky, but didn't care. The war was going badly for the Allies at the time. Germany had invaded Russia, London was being bombed, Greece and Crete had fallen in the Middle East, and the Japanese were also showing signs of belligerence.

The medical examination was also high farce. Bill Young wrote:

A tall thin fellow dressed in a long white coat peered across at me through glasses so thick they must have been the last resort before a seeing eye dog, and asked me to read the top line of a chart big enough to lead off a May Day procession. Then, counting my eyes, and finding I had two, he passed me as having all the prerequisites for shooting anyone legally shootable.

I can still remember the smell of whisky coming at me as he belched. 'Right lad, strip off and hop on the scales. Good, turn round and bend over, good. Now turn around and face me. Breathe in, breathe out, mouth wide open. Say ah-h-h. Very good.' Then he grabbed me balls and, weighing one against the other, told me to cough. 'Now sit down and cross your legs', and he whacked my knee and almost took a bow for the reaction it achieved. With a final 'Good, good, excellent, excellent', I was allowed to get dressed and that was that. I was passed with flying colours and declared medically A1, fit to be a soldier in the King's army.

So they were in the army, but for the first two weeks they didn't have any uniforms, nor rifles. Young:

Finally we got a rifle but we didn't have bullets. Then they came out with great ceremony and gave us a couple of bullets and said, 'Look after 'em'. Then they took us out to a paddock and we fired them. I think that's the only time I fired, other than in a little rifle competition we had. And then they sent us out to Bacchus Marsh to a training camp. We were there for a couple of weeks and then they put us on a boat for Malaya—we were fully trained! We had one fellow who was only fourteen.

They boarded a little Dutch ship, the SS *Sibajak*. Young was only five months away from combat as a member of the 2/30th Battalion. The following year, as a prisoner of war, he was sent on B Force to Sandakan in Borneo. By August 1943, he was at Outram Road Gaol, serving a three-year term for attempting to escape. When the war ended in 1945 he was still a teenager—not quite eighteen!

Bill Young was born in the front room of his grandmother's house in New Town, Hobart, on 4 November 1927 at 11.50 pm. He was always disappointed that his mother 'didn't hang on for another ten minutes so I'd have been a Guy Fawkes boy'. He certainly saw plenty of explosions. His mother, Adora Shaw, died when he was a baby and he was then in the care of his father, 'Big' Bill Young, a six-foot-three knockabout bloke who took his son to Sydney and gave him a bumpy start in life. 'He boxed in [Jimmy] Sharman's tents. He ran a snooker parlour. He rouseabouted around the place, one thing and another, until he joined the Communist Party. That more or less became his religion and, like all converts, he became a fanatic. He gave up drinking, gave up being a hooligan and he went off to Spain to fight in the civil war against General Franco's fascists and got killed in Spain, never thinking about the little boy he left behind—and he was my law and my life and everything.'

Young was barely four years old when he was placed in a Catholic orphanage at Seven Hills: 'I remember being bullied, mainly by the big boys. The orphanage was a Queensland-like house, on big stilts, and then the surround underneath was latticework. At lunchtime you'd sit on stools around the edges of the latticework, making a quadrangle, and the big boys would come with a baby bath, I can remember that vividly, carried by two boys holding a handle at each end, and in it would be all these big dodgers of bread and treacle, and everyone was allowed two slices. The big boys would come around as we sat on these stools and they'd give you a clout if you tried to take three dodgers or something like that.'

At that stage his father was cutting cane in Queensland. The sectarian divide was vast and Big Bill was a staunch Protestant. He had heard his son was in a Catholic orphanage and he wrote to friends, the Jepsons, to take the child into their care and rescue him from the Papists.

'On that delightful day one of the Catholic Sisters in her black habit that used to frighten the life out of me came to me and said, "William, there's a lady who wants to meet you." And this little old lady, I can always remember, had this fox fur around her neck and this fox had two beady eyes and it was looking straight at me and I was thinking, "The moment that lady comes towards me I'm off out of this." We used to talk about it later. And Christina Jepson, "Ma" as I got to know her, said, "Keithy"—my first name is Keith—"Your Daddy wants you to come home with me, and he's asked me to come and get you." I can remember she grabbed my hand and off we went, up this steep hill, to the station and all the while she was talking to me. It started to open up the world for me really. We sat on the railway station and she said, "Would you like a drink of cordial? I'd like a cup of tea." I said, "Yes," and we sat in the tea shop at the Seven Hills Railway Station and waited for the steam train to come along. I had a raspberry drink and a Chester cake, a lovely big square of Chester cake. It was like a Christmas pudding slice [with] icing on it. It lasted for ages, it was beautiful. When I was a prisoner of war I used to tell people about that Chester cake slice. And we talked, and she took me home to her place in Ultimo.'

George 'Pop' Jepson was born a Cockney and had been a jockey in London in the late-nineteenth century. In those days the racing game wasn't too clean, and he was often injured, suffering broken legs and arms. Young remembers him as a bent-up old fellow. He retired from racing and became an animal trainer in a circus. The circus came out to Australia, where he met Christina, an Australian girl who was a trapeze artist, and they married. It was Depression time by then, the circus went broke and all the cast were left marooned in Australia.

When Young went to the Jepsons from the orphanage, they lived in a big house in Ultimo, with a yard which had stables all the way around it making a quadrangle. At the rear of the property an archway led into the yard. Around the yards were a number of carts, all standing on their ends with their shafts pointing up in the air. Harness and reins were draped over the front ends of the carts. Pop Jepson used to hire carts out with their horses, but his timing wasn't good. By the late 1920s there were two factors running against the Jepsons' horse and cart hire business. Not only was the Depression biting, but cars were coming in, taking work away from horses. Young noticed that every now and then Pop Jepson would sell a horse and cart to make ends meet. Eventually he lost not only the business but his house as well, and the Jepsons moved into a smaller place nearby in Bulwara Lane. They let out some of the rooms in their terrace house and Young slept out on the balcony on the first floor.

'Just down from the balcony was the street light. Of course the house only had one gas mantle in the kitchen, no other electric light, nothing, and I don't think any of the houses in those days had electric light, not the kids I knew at any rate. And there was a canvas blind that separated me from the outside—you'd pull the canvas down if it was raining. I'd pull the canvas up a bit and the light from the street lamp would come in and I could read. And I used to read everything and anything I could get. And that was the one little thing, the salvation of me in that place there. That was my school, that outside electric street light.'

Before Big Bill took off to fight the fascists in Spain, he did take some interest in his young son's education. 'He used to have books and he'd always bring picture books home for me, and he'd sit down with me and we'd talk—usually about Comrade Lenin, Comrade Stalin and all the comrades rah rah rah. So I used to think, when I went to the Catholic orphanage, that they'd be Comrade Jesus and Comrade God and I'd put them in a row and didn't know which was which. Even the apostles were all comrades to me.'

The boy's education remained patchy. Pop Jepson was reduced to running a barrow at Paddy's Markets, but he couldn't afford a licence.

By the time Young was eight, he was Pop's 'cockatoo' at the market: 'He'd position his barrow and I'd stand down near the corner. If I saw an inspector come, I'd tell Pop. So long as your cart was moving they couldn't do anything. People took it for granted, I think. Quite often you'd see a lady getting served, and say she wanted a dozen oranges, he'd get to about seven, and I'd say, "Pop", and he'd pick the barrow up and say to the lady, "Follow me love, come on," and the lady would follow him to get her dozen oranges.'

Young did get some schooling at the Ultimo Public School and completed First and Second Grade, but his cockatoo duties for Pop at Paddy's Markets sabotaged Third Grade. 'The truant inspectors used to come about a bit and that was one of the things I had to watch out for, when I was at the market. I knew nearly every truant inspector in Sydney by the end of that time.'

He eventually made it to Sixth Grade when he moved briefly to the South Coast, but that was the end of his formal education. At fifteen, he and his mate Don Miller bumped their ages up to nineteen to get work as bicycle couriers for the Eastern Extension Company in Bent Street, Sydney. When they saved some money they decided to ride pushbikes all the way around Australia. They rode over 1000 miles to Mt Gambier, South Australia, before both their second-hand bikes packed it in completely. An amiable truck driver gave them some money out of his own pocket for the bikes and a lift to Melbourne. It was winter, they were broke and starving, and joining the army seemed an immediate solution. They arrived at the recruiting office at 4 am and waited, shivering, until the doors opened at 9 am.

Bill Young has always considered himself a lucky man. In 2013, Young had just turned 87. He was in reasonable health, cheerful and outgoing as always, and a bit bemused by the amount of interest still being taken in him and his experiences. (Anthony Hill recently published a biography of Bill, *The Story of Billy Young: A teenager in Changi, Sandakan and Outram Road.*) Even though Young enlisted at fifteen years of age, he is eyeing off his ninth decade. Most surviving World War II veterans are already nonagenarians. Bill Young is one of two veterans of Outram Road Gaol still alive.

Although scoring a sentence at Outram Road Gaol would not normally be considered lucky, in the case of the men of B Force sent to Sandakan, it was a chance at survival. It is worth mentioning again that, apart from the six men who escaped the actual death marches, and the 200 officers removed to Kuching, 33 other Australians missed the death marches by being sentenced to Outram Road for various misdemeanours. Not all of them survived their imprisonment there, but most did. The combined force of 1787 Australian and 641 British soldiers who marched to their deaths in Borneo had no chance.

Bill Young's luck began in the immediate aftermath of the action in Malaya, and the battle for Singapore. He was only sixteen when the Allied surrender was declared on 15 February 1942, but the days before that were extremely volatile. His unit, the 2/29th Battalion, had fought bravely at the Battle of Muar. But during the retreat to Singapore island, Bill Young's feet were badly infected with tinea and in the fighting at Bukit Timah he was wounded in the leg by shrapnel. To compound his foot problems, he lost his boots and cut his feet rather badly getting back to the Allied lines. He managed to purloin some more boots, but couldn't put them on as both feet were too swollen with a combination of tinea and lacerations. One of the doctors at the Regimental Aid Post said he had to go to hospital. 'And he said, "Now, if you can't walk, we'll carry you over to the ambulance." He went on, "Or if you can walk, take the ambulance on the left." I can remember quite distinctly lying down there thinking, "Will I make the bludgers carry me? Or will I be a hero and walk?" I thought, I'll be a hero. So I got up and I walked across.'

It was a fateful decision. The stretcher cases were driven to the Alexandra Hospital, and were all massacred by the Japanese after they arrived. Young was taken to the 2/13th Australian General Hospital: 'I was laying down on a stretcher thinking, "Oh this is alright, I'm out of the war," and quite happy with myself and along came these lovely nursing sisters, and one of them bent down and kissed me and cried and cuddled me, and I'm thinking, "Gee whizz, this is good." But they had come to tell us they had been ordered to leave Singapore—and of course they were the ones that were machine-gunned and killed later in Sumatra by the Japs.'

Not long afterwards, some Japanese soldiers came into the ward, and Young feared the worst. But all they did was steal watches and a few other items, otherwise the wounded were left alone. Bill Young's 'heroic' decision to walk to his transport had saved his life.

Similarly, after having endured the Sandakan camp in Borneo for a year, building the aerodrome along with receiving bashings and sadistic punishments, his decision to escape in July 1943—with a friend, MP 'Jimmy' Brown—saved him again. Their sentence to four years at Outram Road Gaol meant they missed the death marches in early 1945. When Brown complained later about his folly in joining the escape bid, Young replied truthfully, 'I saved your life.' Brown, typically, replied, 'Inadvertently.'

But Young and Brown timed their escape badly. They had buried a small haversack of bits and pieces, including two knives, just outside the camp. Their escape plan was optimistic, to say the least. 'All we had to do was to travel over a few hundred miles of unexplored mountainous jungle country, and cross a vast expanse of ocean. Then pass through the lines of three or four Jap armies and who knows what else. It didn't look all that difficult going by the little pencilled copy of the map we had—no more than six inches from Borneo to Australia. Rambo had nothing on us.'

Bill Young and some of the other young reprobates from the hut in the Sandakan camp, known to house 'The Dead End Kids', had made several journeys outside the wire and back scrounging for food. But when they did make their serious break for freedom they were quickly sprung. A standing reward had been posted for the nearby villagers, who would get $25 for every prisoner attempting to escape. The would-be escapees had not even reached the spot where their haversack was buried when all hell broke loose.

'There were six or so villagers with the Japs when they came yelling and screaming at us, hitting out with rifle butts, sword scabbards and an assortment of canes, so we decided to surrender,' Young remembers. 'Our hands were tied behind our backs, the rope then looped around our throats with about four or five feet of slack between us. Aided by the liberal application of boots, fists and sticks, we were "assisted" along the track to where a truck stood waiting. The guards then picked us up like so much garbage and threw us into the back of the truck.'

Back inside the camp, a hit squad of six young Formosan guards, a corporal and a sergeant each picked out a suitable length of split firewood from a stack standing outside the boiler shed. The pieces were about the size of a large mattock handle, but much rougher. They swung these with great gusto over and across the two escapees' bare backs. Because of the ropes around their necks, whenever one man fell, the other would come tumbling down too. Then some Japanese NCOs weighed in with their steel sword scabbards, after which Young and Brown were dragged along by the ropes around their necks, choking and spluttering, trying desperately to get on their feet, fighting to stay alive.

With some parting kicks and stomps, they were left lying in the afternoon sun, in the middle of the gravel road between the gates and the guardhouse. They were still lying there when the men came back from work at the aerodrome. As he went past, Corporal Bob Ship-sides stopped beside Young and poured some water down his dry and aching throat. 'After all these years, I can still hear and see him as he bent over me saying over and over again, "The dirty rotten bludgers", until the guards came rushing up and smashed him away with their sticks. That was the last time I ever saw Shippy, as he was being beaten for helping one of his men. I wouldn't have traded Lance-Corporal Bob Shipsides for twenty bloody generals. My arm was broken, some of my ribs didn't seem to be too hot, one of my ankles was kaput and the rest of me was, to put it mildly, as my old uncle would say, "Up to shit bonzer."'

Jimmy Brown was in much worse shape. The flesh had been peeled off his forehead, back and legs. One of his hands had taken the full force of a blow and was swollen and smashed. Bill Young said that the 25-year-old was never again to be the man he had been, his body broken, his health spent, with the few remaining years of his life full of suffering: 'MP was a man of many talents, a linguist and fine musician. Many a night back at the camp we had all sat together outside the hut and listened while Jimmy played his harmonica. Now he lay a crumpled, smashed wreck on a dusty road in North Borneo.'

Being unconscious, Brown missed his interview with the camp commandant, Captain Hoshijima. Young was dragged into his office, where Hoshijima was sitting behind his desk—a bottle and glass on his desk indicating he'd been drinking heavily. He jumped to his feet and raved at Young in a confusing mix of English, Malay and Japanese.

'The last I remember of that creep was of his distorted face coming towards me, the wooden-holstered Italian revolver he almost always wore flapping at his side, and him screaming, "You bad man, you no honour." Then he lashed out and hit me fair in the face and I landed outside—out like a light. When I came to, it was to find both MP and me tied up together being loaded into the back of the truck. Bound up as we were and unable to move without too much pain, our last impressions of the Sandakan camp were the beautiful star-blazed sky, a silver crescent moon and the shadowy outline of the great rainforest tree that dominated the entrance to the camp. Its branches waved farewell, right up until the bend in the road erased from our view, this last tie with our friends and comrades, the men of B Force.'

After a great deal of bouncing and bumping and being flung from side to side, the truck finally came to a stop. In total darkness the two Australians were unloaded and dragged along to a group of small wooden box-like cells. 'Holy cow, that was a night that was,' Young recalls. 'We were curled up with our pain, waiting, afraid to move, in fear of reawakening resting aches. Unable to move because of the limited space, we were hemmed in by the pressure of the unknown that hovered all around.'

Bill Young heard a low moan coming out of the dark close by, and he realised that a friend, Jimmy Darlington, was sharing his accommodation. Darlington was in a terrible mess. His wrists and ankles, where tightening cords had cut into him, were angry with proud flesh, his eyes black and blue in a grossly swollen face. His eyes were just slits. He'd been lying there for the best part of two weeks in a mess of urine and faeces.

Darlington, a feisty Aboriginal boxer, had committed what was a grievous crime in the eyes of the Japanese at the Sandakan camp, a week before Young and Brown's escape—he had punched a guard. The camp cook, an Australian, had become outraged when one of the Japanese guards started to wash his dirty underwear in a rice-cooking bucket. When the cook, an older man, started to complain, the guard knocked him to the ground and started kicking him. Darlington went to his aid and the guard swung a round-armed punch at his head. Instinct took over: Darlington came up with a right hook that knocked the Japanese out cold. It was a wonder he wasn't shot right then and there.

Instead, the Japanese rushed up and beat him with their rifle butts before torturing him by making him kneel on rough splintered timbers, then wedging a piece of timber behind his knees, and another between his arms which were pulled around and tied behind his back. They took special care to truss him up with wet ropes around his neck, then down about his ankles, on to his wrists and criss-crossed across his body. Bill Young noticed that the blazing tropical sun burning into Darlington's back and head was also drying out the cords, which began to cut into his flesh. A diversion was created by other prisoners nearby, who started screaming and yelling: 'This distracted the guards, and one of our first aid blokes from the 10th Field Ambulance darted in and cut the cords. There is no doubt this brave action saved Jimmy's life. Unfortunately they also spotted the Good Samaritan, who was badly beaten.'

The last Young had seen of Darlington was being thrown into a truck and driven away. He now knew where he had been taken. Despite everything, Darlington had not lost his sense of humour. Through swollen lips he could barely open, his greeting to Young was, 'Welcome to the honeymoon suite of the Sandakan Branch of the Japanese *Kempeitai* Hotel.' For the first few days he had been unable to move at all, but when Young arrived he had managed to crawl over for their reunion.

There were five cells, about five-by-four-feet high, with wooden bars. Their occupants could see some timber steps leading down to what proved to be the *Kempeitai* interrogation room, which they would come to know too well. 'Room service consisted of some meagre meals that sometimes didn't come at all, and being hosed down like animals by a little old bow-legged yardman who obviously enjoyed his work: he laughed as he aimed his hose at our faces, or sometimes our more tender parts.'

One day there was an unexpected bonus. After a more restrained hosing down, they were visited by a Japanese medic who seemed to know his job and did it well. 'It was our first and only experience of a gentle Jap. He went over us completely and when he had finished, we looked like the final night of a first-aid disaster demonstration, with bandages, slings and masses of cotton wool over red antiseptic, covering our cuts and bruises. As for myself, with an arm in a sling, my ankle nicely strapped and a bandage around my head holding my ear back in place, I could have gone another five rounds—well, not really. Even Jimmy [Darlington] and MP were looking better, that is the parts of them I could see other than the bandaged bits. It was Darlo we were most concerned about over the weeks to come. His hands were still a horrible black colour with no life in them. We weren't sure if it was just us [worrying], or gangrene. Fortunately it was mostly us.'

The day after they were patched up, the interrogations began. Either Young or Brown would go into the interrogation room and be made to kneel in front of a desk, where a Japanese dressed in civilian clothes and with thick glasses would begin the questioning. During the two-hour sessions both Australians would be bashed with rifle butts interspersed with lashes from a knotted rope. This continued for eight days. What puzzled both men was the line of questioning: 'What did you do with all the guns? Who did you give them to? What were their names?'; or, 'How did you contact the submarines? How many civilians were in your group?'

It was not until months later in Kuching that they learned of the breaking of the underground network which had coincided with their arrest. Clearly the Japanese thought they must be connected with Lionel Matthews' organisation which, Young thought later, might have been the only reason they were not shot out of hand for escaping, as they were wanted for later questioning. It eventually became clear to the Japanese that neither escapee knew anything about the network, no matter how much they belted them.

Five weeks later, Brown, Young and Darlington were taken out of their cages and transported by truck to the docks, to a rather stylish motor cruiser they found out later had once belonged to the Rajah of Sarawak. They were dumped on its upper deck and, just before they sailed, they heard the distinctive sound of Australian voices, which came from five men who had attempted to escape from the Sandakan camp some months before they had. Allen Minty, Bruce McWilliams, Bill Fairy, Norm Morris and Fred New were all handcuffed together. In their escape attempt, they had nearly got away in a Chinese junk but unfortunately ran aground on a mud bank close to Sandakan Harbour, where they were spotted by a Japanese patrol boat.

The voyage to Kuching was a pleasant interlude compared with what they had just been through. The boat called in to Labuan to take on supplies, and the guards decided to have a night on the town. They handcuffed the Australians to a cable on the wharf and took off, leaving the prisoners to enjoy a period of comparative freedom. It was an experience that resonated deeply with the teenage soldier.

'Soon we were caught up, spellbound, as we sat and watched the last act of the play of day. I had never seen its like, before or since. A symphony of clouds, land and sea, in crescendo. Orchestrated shafts of colour speared up and down every which way. Such a magnitude of changing colours were being duplicated and reflected so faithfully into the bay as to make it difficult to decide which way was up. We sat entranced by this entanglement of hues placed in the battle line of encroaching night and retreating day.

'Across from where we sat we heard gentle laughter wafting femininity over and around us. A caress of sound, from a group of Malay girls, enjoying their evening *tong* [bath]. We watched, tantalised and teased by the graceful shadowy subtlety of movement within the confines of their sarongs displayed by this lovely, modest bathing party. Soon only the voices remained. Soothed by the moment we settled into our separate thoughts, cocooned in the blackness, as the moon rose.

'I had never had what you would call a regular home environment, certainly nothing like most of us take for granted today. That night filled me with a desperate longing, as in the poet's words, "A feeling fer I dunno wot". I'd come down with my first dose of homesickness. It was there in the dark on a faraway tropical island chained to a cable that I came to have a feeling for my home, Australia. I realised that being an Aussie was much different than anything else, especially when measured against the bestiality shown by our enemy. Never having thought on it before—I had taken for granted my country's freedoms, the wide open spaces, its give-and-take, the way it shapes the character of its people, giving them a rugged individuality and the sense of giving and receiving a fair go. Never again would I take those essential freedom-loving qualities for granted.'

Yet another tough time lay ahead. Upon landing at Kuching, the Australians were taken to their new prison, which looked to Young as though it had once been a warehouse. It had two floors and the Japanese had run cyclone wire around the supporting columns and the timbers in between to create about 24 cages. It reminded Young of a gigantic aviary, filled, in place of birds, with men of all kinds, shapes and sizes: 'Whenever I see chooks sitting on a perch near our house, I see us at Kuching, perched on a platform in a cage waiting, too weak and weary to even bother to hatch a plan of escape.'

Each cage had a timber bench, about three feet off the floor and running its full width, on which the prisoners slept at night, from 9 pm until 5.30 am. It was also where they sat to attention with crossed legs, every day, waiting to go to court and discover their fates. The Europeans in particular found this crossed-leg pose not only difficult, but excruciatingly painful. Adding to the discomfort was the indignity and torment of bed bugs, literally in their thousands.

'They'd come rushing out at night in open attack formation, literally thirsting for battle—almost like the Battle of Singapore over again with much the same results, for we would fight a desperate losing action every night,' Young remembered. 'As we squished and squashed the bugs, our shirts and shorts became red with our own blood. Bleary eyed we would show the results of the fight to the guards in the mornings, pleading for some bug killer. Finally they gave us some of the magic potion, together with a spray can. The great and terrible day of reckoning had come. We were about to bugger the bugs.'

The first spraying produced four heaped shovelfuls of bed bugs and the men were allowed to keep spraying for a week. That particular scourge was finally fixed. But the guard on duty would patrol around and around the cages, making sure that every prisoner was sitting to attention until the officer in charge left for the day—then, like soldiers the world over, they would retreat into the guardroom for a sit-down and smoke. That was a respite for all the Chinese and Malay prisoners shielded from immediate view by the Australians, who happened to be in the front row facing the archway in front of the guardhouse. They still had to keep watch for an approaching guard—and cough a signal to those behind.

Of course the guards could see they were being watched by their quarry and they got their carpenters to build a timber screen between the Australians' front facing cages and the archway. The game of cat and mouse went on, but this time in the prisoners' favour. Using a precious bit of sharpened wire, they managed to make a small hole through a join in the screen, just big enough to show when the light was broken by a guard walking towards them.

'Now we could also enjoy the siestas too. We drew up a roster to decide whose turn it was to watch the peephole. Often a guard, after he finished his smoke, would come sneaking up on tippy-toes, hoping to catch us doing something we shouldn't. The enjoyment we got each time we saw a Jap jumping out from behind the screen only to find us models of straight-backed, cross-legged propriety, never diminished. They never, ever tumbled to the tiny hole in the screen caper.'

After three dreary months in Kuching, their day in court finally arrived. The courtroom had originally been a main hall of the Catholic convent. Seated up the front on a raised platform were the Japanese trial officers, and at the centre and on a raised chair sat the presiding field officer. Along the front sat six or seven minor officials. All the proceedings were conducted in Japanese so the accused stayed in linguistic darkness right to the end.

Young explains: 'The moment of understanding came when at long last the interpreter rose and began to read out to us the findings of the court, and the sentences. Our original eight had been increased with the addition of five Chinese civilians, thirteen of us taking the curtain call. For some it was to be their final curtain call. In clear public school English the sentences of the court were read. The five Chinese, each found guilty of espionage, would be taken outside and beheaded. MP standing on my right was the next to be sentenced, I felt the tremor from his hands pass along the handcuffs to me while mine also transmitted down the line, and I guess, the shockwave went right on down to Jimmy Darlington, who was at the end. Such was the effect when we heard those dreaded words, "To be executed". In the presence of death everyone became aware. Every sound came clear to the ear. Every movement was noticed, instantly.

'The clear voice of the interpreter came down at us. "Myles Pierce Brown you have been found guilty of escaping from a Japanese prison. Your sentence is"—we waited tensely—"to serve eight years"—oh happy days—"hard labour in Outram Road Gaol, Singapore."

'Our part of the line relaxed, such is the desire for life when death stands so close and beckons. "William Young"—I'd stopped shaking, the air tasted so much sweeter—"because of your youth the court in its mercy has decided to reduce your sentence to four years' hard labour in Outram Road Gaol, Singapore."'

The sentencing went on down the line. The Australians who had escaped before Young and Brown all received five years, and 'J Darlington, for daring to hit a Japanese guard, six months' hard labour'. No allowance was made for time already spent in prison.

The five Chinese, accused of subversive activities, had taken the news of their sentence with a remarkable degree of calmness and showed no outward emotion. They were taken outside, where their graves were already dug, and decapitated immediately. The Australians, who had been so much more leniently dealt with, were greatly impressed by their brave exit from the courtroom. That day, Bill Young reflected, he had learned a valuable lesson: 'When death is the alternative, all other choices grow more desirable by the second.'

After so much inaction for nearly a year, the pace of events quickened. The eight Australians sentenced to Outram Road were taken immediately to the wharves at Kuching, placed in a horse box—with straw and dung still thick on the floor—and lowered into the hold of what they soon discovered was a troop ship. When the top of their horse box was lifted off, they realised the hold was full of Japanese soldiers packed in like sardines. Their isolation in the horse box prevented eye contact, but one bonus for the perpetually hungry prisoners was extra food scraps from the troops, many of whom were too seasick to eat.

At the end of their journey, and within an hour of being dumped on the wharf in Singapore in their horse box, the Australians were bundled into a truck and driven away. Shortly afterwards, at the end of a road, they saw for the first time the menacing and brooding bulk of the old British penitentiary, Outram Road Gaol.

# 8

# PATHWAYS TO OUTRAM ROAD

Outram Road Gaol was a 'glasshouse', as service parlance has it, a military prison, always a tougher establishment than a civilian institution. Most of the Allied prisoners at Outram Road were on the ground floor of the nineteenth-century penitentiary. On the second floor were the Japanese wrong-doers, many of whom were quite high-ranking military commanders deemed not to have achieved their objectives in battle. The Imperial Japanese Army had a rigid and unforgiving policy of disciplinary severity. The *Kempeitai* were a symbol of this rigour, and their powers extended up to the most senior ranks of the army.

While the Japanese inmates got better food than the Allied prisoners, that was about all. They were subjected to the same brutal regime of solitary confinement, and bashings and punishments were de rigueur. Many Japanese officers were executed there and went stoically to their deaths, usually by firing squad or decapitation. Hanging was considered the most ignominious way to die. The executioners were kept busy from 1942 to 1945.

One of the most improbable inmates of Outram Road Gaol was a westernised Japanese, known as 'Hank the Yank' by Allied prisoners of war. He was a Japanese American from California who had been sent by his parents to Japan in 1937 to improve his Japanese language skills and pay his respects to his grandparents. The timing was bad, because he was conscripted into the Imperial Japanese Army and eventually got to Singapore, where he came to the notice of some of the Australian prisoners of war. Dick Armstrong met him on the Singapore docks, early in the captivity, and became intrigued with him. Although of Japanese descent, he considered himself an American.

Armstrong recalls: 'He said to us, "I didn't want to go to goddamned bloody Japan, but Mom and Dad wanted it." He got off the boat in Japan, and they promptly grabbed him and shot him off to China. Before he could scratch himself, he was conscripted into the Japanese army although he was an American-born Japanese, and an American citizen. He told us his sad life story. He had been three years in China, then went back to Japan, and was drafted into the forces for the Pacific invasion. He did keep himself out of the fighting troops by claiming to be a top transport driver, and he was a good driver. He also told us that what he did to keep himself out of the infantry was to deliberately bugger up his firing: "Couldn't hit a barn. If these little yellow bastards knew that I go hunting a lot back home in the States and I can hit a squirrel at a couple of hundred yards with no trouble," he said, "goddammit, they'll shoot me." But he did keep himself out of the fighting troops. He said he had no wish and desire to serve Japan, nor to die for Japan. He considered himself an American citizen and a prisoner of the Japanese system.'

Armstrong thought he was too good to be true, possibly a *Kempeitai* plant, and told his fellow Australians working on the docks to keep clear of him. Hank the Yank kept offering Armstrong to help them all 'make a fast buck' by knocking off some of the goodies stored in the bulging godowns on the waterfront. He was so persistent that Armstrong decided to try him out, in a way that only he would be compromised if Hank was a plant. Armstrong knew where there were cases of food and liquor and slipped them into the back of Hank's truck. Hank returned an hour or so later and gave Armstrong 600 Singapore dollars. So began a profitable partnership between the Japanese American and the Australians.

Armstrong says: 'He was one of the funniest men I have known. He never spoke of the Japanese, particularly the Japanese authorities, by any expression in my hearing except to say "Those goddamn little yellow bastards". He helped us steal the place blind. Hank the Yank hated the Japanese hierarchy system as much as we did, so we just joined forces. It was as simple as that, he being a transport driver. The Jap guarding the wharves never checked the loads going out, they wouldn't know, he'd just show his paperwork and drive in and out.'

After about a month of this happy partnership, one of the Japanese officers began to suspect that Hank was being a bit too sympathetic to the prisoners of war. He told Armstrong he was going to have to put on a show: 'So Hank lined a digger up and told him that he had to really belt him one. Before he did, he said to the soldier, "When I whack you, digger, just duck and go arse-over-head." Anyway, he hauled off and went whack!—but he used a cupped hand, the way people did in the years gone by to box a kid's ear. It makes a great noise but does no harm. The digger threw his head back and went down onto his knees, staggered and reeled, and dragged himself back to his feet—a beautiful bit of acting which would have put Clark Gable to shame in *Gone with the Wind*. Then he straightened up and bowed low to Hank the Yank, who gave a perfunctory sort of bow, and then he bowed to his officer, and the officer bowed too and walked away, thoroughly satisfied that Hank the Yank had proved himself to be a good Jap.'

Donald Wise, a British officer captured on Singapore island, also ran into Hank at the Adam Park work camp in the early days. Wise got to know the Australians there, who told him of the petrol-stealing racket they were running. The diggers would milk the Japanese lorries of petrol inside the camp, put it into hidden 44-gallon drums, and at night put a hosepipe through the wire and pump it out to Chinese entrepreneurs on the outside who paid in Singapore dollars.

Wise says: 'This went on very successfully, and it meant that the Australians could buy more food and they were getting one over the Japs. It was a very good operation, until one day a Japanese officer came in a car with his blue flag flying—he was a lieutenant or captain—and ordered all the prisoners paraded. And the interpreter, Hank the Yank, got up on the tabletop in the middle of all these prisoners, and the officer started bellowing and shouting as the Japanese officers used to do, speaking from the base of their stomachs. And Hank would say, "Oh Jesus, you guys, he's really mad at you this time—you've been flogging the petrol," and so on. And this Japanese officer laid the law down. He said, "If there's any more petrol stealing I'll take out one or two prisoners a day and behead them until it stops." And he really meant it.

'There were a lot of long faces—I happened to be in the camp that day. Anyway, finally the Japanese officer stepped off the table down onto a chair onto the ground. And Hank said, "Well, he really means it guys, take my tip he really means it, so watch it." The officer then got in his car, the guard saluted, and he drove off but not very far. About thirty yards on his car halted because there was no petrol in the tank. The Australians had siphoned it out while he was speaking.

'The officer did get very mad and started beating up the guards, his own guards, with the flat of his sword, because they were supposed to have been looking after the car. At the same time, even he realised it would be difficult to pin it on any of the prisoners because they were all on parade! But he made life very difficult for the Australians after that. They had to pull back a bit.'

The most ambitious partnership between Hank the Yank and the Australians took place shortly after the Japanese officer's humiliation.

Dick Armstrong knew where there was plenty of petrol, buried in rubber plantations over the causeway in the Johor Bahru area, where it had been stored for use during the fighting. Armstrong himself had helped to bury the cache of petrol in 44-gallon drums: 'I asked Hank if he could get transport orders for shifting petrol from Johor Bahru to Singapore that would get him across the causeway through the *Kempeitai* checkpoint. And Hank said he would look into it. A couple of days later, he said, "I've got those goddamn transport orders." I said, "Do you think they'll stand up?" He said, "Well, it's my head if they don't. I've got the Japanese lieutenant's chop—a stamp." So Hank stamped all the papers, sneaked them out and forged the Japanese lieutenant's signature, but the important thing was the chop on them, the official stamp. We went across the causeway and he gave his transport movement order to the *Kempeitai* guard. They checked the four prisoners of war on the truck and one driver, and waved us through.

'We went and got the petrol and came back, and Hank dropped us at the godown on the wharf where we were supposed to be working. He came back an hour later with 1000 Singapore dollars for each drum of petrol. I sent the money back to mates in Changi who were in need of a bit of help.'

Perhaps it was only a matter of time before Hank got rumbled. His crimes were heinous, not only fraternising with the enemy, but also robbing his own people. Private Bert Rollason, who was early in to Outram Road in January 1943 after escaping from Changi, thinks he met him in the Japanese section of the gaol when he was emptying toilet buckets. He was in the cells on death row. It is likely his last friendly gesture to his Australian fellow inmates, following his execution, was to provide them with some lollies and ritual cupcakes.

If a tough childhood was a good training ground for surviving Outram Road Gaol, Bert Rollason is a fine example. Born at Maldon,

Victoria, not far from Bendigo, Rollason says he was an unwanted child who, he believes, was traded for a sheep to another family. There was never any formal adoption: 'It was the way it was done in the country then. I wasn't wanted. In them days families were big, and they traded you up. I was never legally adopted, and I never found that out until I was in my forties, because I wanted an overdraft in the business I was in and they wouldn't come at it when they found I had no birth certificate.'

Rollason knew enough to trace his origins, and had taken the name 'Rollason' from the family who had adopted him. His family name was 'Tatt'. 'I think mother went astray. The person she was married to was called Tatt, but he wasn't my father. I met her later on, and she told me. Apparently my real mother's husband was a pretty nasty sort of man, and didn't want to have anything to do with her, other than have sex whenever he wanted it. She was hot—she said—and sometimes he wouldn't give it to her. They lived out in the bush then. He'd be out working, and a couple of blokes would go out ferreting, and would whistle out and she'd go wandering over—and they'd "insert the ferret" of course.'

So when the boy was born, her husband knew he wasn't his child, and didn't want him. She had to get rid of him, and that's how he came to be traded to the Rollasons when he was about twelve months old. They didn't have children, and were looking for some future labour on their farm. It wasn't a happy landing. When he was only five or six, Rollason used to be belted unmercifully: 'I suppose I was always a little bugger, but he [Rollason's adoptive father] would get stuck into me for no reason. We had a bit of an orchard, and he would get one of the suckers off a tree, about four foot long, and thrash me with it. When he'd finished he would have cut the sucker right down to his hand. I had cuts all over my back and they'd be there for a week— great welts nearly as big as your finger. He was a bastard of a man.'

He was also a drunk, and dominated Rollason's adoptive mother, who would dish out punishment to the youngster by giving him a clip under the ear if he got into fights at school. 'I have a memory of him going mad once. We had shifted from Maldon to Campbells Creek a few miles away, and his brother was a blacksmith there. I remember him going through that place, tipping up carts and carrying on. He was drunk then, but for some reason after that, he never drank.' Rollason did at least get enough to eat because, apart from the orchard, they grew their own vegetables and had a milking cow and chooks for eggs and extra meat.

The young Rollason became a loner, and used to wander in the bush, looking at birds and killing lizards. Once he burnt out a paddock trying to smoke rabbits out of their burrows, but without success. By the time he was thirteen, the Rollasons had moved to Bendigo and he was sent to a boys' farm, where he was supposed to learn the basics of farming. 'My first job was on a dairy farm at Dingee, about thirty miles from Bendigo. The manager there was a bit of a standover man, and it was a rugged time. They were certainly tough days.'

Things didn't get better. By the time he was eighteen he had a job at Harcourt, in apple country, twenty miles south of Bendigo, working on another farm. It was initially not too bad, until World War II broke out, and the farmer he worked for took a job in a foundry, leaving Rollason to run the farm on his own, milking up to fifteen cows by hand, morning and night.

Enlisting in the AIF seemed a better alternative, and he joined the 2/29th Battalion and was posted to Malaya.

After the surrender, 'Bluey' Rollason's route to Outram Road Gaol was an unusual one. On the third day at Selarang Barracks, with confusion everywhere, one of the Motor Transport drivers noticed an unattended truck, and drove it to a depot in company with other Japanese-driven trucks, loaded it up with food and returned to Changi, where he delivered his purloined supplies to the kitchen of his unit, Rollason's own 2/29th Battalion. Rollason says: 'The driver wanted to empty that truck and go back for another load. The Japs didn't know what was going on, they were idiots, and would have thought he was supposed to be doing what he was doing. He was risking his bloody self to bring more food in.'

Instead of a pat on the back, one of his officers in the new Australian administration (now working under Japanese command) decided to discipline the driver by banging him up in the brig for a week! Rollason was appalled, and it wasn't long before he was in trouble himself for attempting to steal a radio from an abandoned house at Mt Pleasant, where prisoners of war were working building a road. For that mis-demeanour, the Australian command gave him a fourteen-day stint in the same brig in Changi. Rollason was completely fed up with the Australian officers kow-towing to the Japanese. 'Anyway, I done about seven days of that, and I said, "Stuff this, I'm going through the wire." So I just shot through and spent six months out in the bush then.'

One of his companions was David Henry 'Pop' Davies, a civilian English rubber planter, experienced in local ways. Forty years on, Bluey Rollason could not remember the name of his third Australian companion. 'Pop was an elderly person compared to us, he was an absolute gentleman—a terrific bloke. The other feller was about my age. At first we just cruised around, sometimes camping in a cemetery, sleeping on top of the graves. Then we got the word about two days later the Japs had come in, they must've known someone was in that area. That's the time when they shot a couple of fellows down on the beach—they were out after us, but they missed us.'

The three decided their best chance would be to make camp in a swampy tidal area in the mangroves near the coast. They built a camp with whatever they could scrounge, making a roof out of makeshift *atap*. 'We found all kinds of stuff lying around, including a bed. But we didn't know how high the tides could go, and sometimes you'd wake up in the morning and step out into the water. So we'd build it up a bit higher.'

They did most of their scrounging at night, pinching chooks from both Malay and Chinese houses and stealing whatever they could from gardens—vegetables, sweet potato and tapioca. Sometimes friendly Chinese would give them some rice. They had cooking pots as well. Rollason did catch dengue fever at one stage, but just had to sweat it out and get over it. 'We knew our way around at night. Sometimes we would come across some Japanese camps, we knew where they were and you could hear them yapping away. Even in the day time we'd go up to a road and hide in the bush, and watch for a while, and be over and gone. While you were waiting some of these bloody tree snakes would slither across you—you could just about tickle their bellies, but you got used to that.'

But after six months, their luck ran out. Realising they had been spotted by a local who might have reported them to the Japanese, they moved camp—but not far enough: 'One night the bastards came by boat. They had an interpreter with them to yell out a few things to us. There was a heap of them, and we just had to give ourselves up. We just yelled out where we were, and in they came.'

Their next port of call was the infamous *Kempeitai* headquarters in Singapore. Technically, they had escaped—a serious crime carrying the death penalty—even though they had obviously been living in close proximity to the main Changi POW camp. Rollason remembers they were cuffed about a bit and questioned, but escaped the water and electric shock torture treatments. When they were eventually court-martialled, the sentences were nevertheless severe. Because Rollason's two companions had been out longer than he had, they got ten years at Outram Road Gaol and he got eight. Sadly Pop Davies died shortly after entering his cell. Rollason says: 'I always said that the only bloody good thing old man Rollason did for me was to toughen me up, and that helped bring me through the prison camp, and Outram Road. They couldn't hurt me. What's a few bumps and bruises? I was used to them. Oh, I got my hidings from the Japs, don't worry about that, but you just never let them know they were hurting you. You couldn't afford that.'

When World War II broke out, Sandakan was the capital of British North Borneo (later Sabah), under the administrative control of the British North Borneo Company, an elegant colonial town situated around a shallow but scenic harbour. Further south, on the west coast of the world's third largest island, were two other British protectorates, Sarawak and Brunei—the Dutch laying claim to the vast interior and the southern part of Borneo. Sarawak, presided over by the English Brooke family, the 'White Rajahs', had oil wells, and the protectorates had rich timber resources. All this was about to drop, unopposed, into the laps of the invading Japanese, like the ripest of cherry plums.

British North Borneo was completely without any defence force— except for a hastily assembled local militia, the Borneo Volunteers, comprising one 'combat' platoon which the administration wisely decided not to activate when the Japanese did arrive by sea on 19 January 1942, 27 days before the surrender of Singapore and Malaya. But the Japanese were not seen as liberators from British colonialism— certainly not by the civilian administration, and not by the Chinese, Indians, Malays and indigenous tribes who mainly remained quietly loyal to the overthrown British, and worked bravely and assiduously to resist the increasingly brutal Japanese.

Doctor James Taylor, the hospital superintendent in Sandakan, was then approaching 50 years of age. In April 1983, when Dr Taylor was in his early nineties, he spoke about those troubled times from his Sydney home in Mosman: 'I expected the Japanese to land, because

Kuching had fallen, and we were bound to go. I was actually on my way to the Sandakan gaol for a medical inspection, and I saw the Japanese coming ashore. Earlier, a commandant in Singapore and Member of the Legislative Council came to Borneo and pulled a few maps out of his pocket and said, "Oh you needn't worry, they won't come here. The waters are too shallow." But they came in small boats, you see.

'There was no fighting. Strangely enough the first Japanese I saw was the former manager of the cordial factory, and he knew where to go all right. He had been a fifth columnist of course. And I also recognised a Japanese doctor who came ashore, I knew him quite well. When I was arrested later, he took over and carried on my medical work.'

The Japanese quickly occupied the colonial mansions overlooking the harbour. James Taylor and his wife Celia were ordered to move out of their big two-storey house into a little cottage in the hospital grounds, and he and all the other medical officers were told to carry on their medical work until they could be replaced.

Six months later, in July 1942, the 1500-strong B Force of prisoners of war from Singapore arrived, and Dr Taylor was soon a key figure in the underground network run by Captain Lionel Matthews and his deputy intelligence officer, Lieutenant Rod Wells. He supplied medicines and extra food to the POW camp at great personal risk—even assisting some Australians to escape, and sail to the islands of the Southern Philippines to join guerrilla forces there: 'I managed to get some of the escapees over to Berhala Island, in the harbour, where they could hide out for a time waiting for a boat. This was done through a Chinese contact, Mu Sing. He was from the Philippines and he'd established a contact with the Filipino guerrillas, and we managed to get quite a lot away in a little trading boat. He was the go-between.'

Dr Taylor told me there were even ambitious plans to get Sergeant Macalister Blain—who was a federal member for the Northern Territory in the House of Representatives—away and up to Tawi Tawi, in the Southern Philippines, and have him picked up by an American submarine to get back to Australia and reveal the appalling conditions experienced by prisoners of war of the Japanese. Unfortunately, the underground network was broken the day before he was due to leave Berhala Island and he was arrested and later sent to Outram Road Gaol for attempting to escape.

For six months Dr Taylor had been putting himself at grave risk by organising medical and other supplies into the POW camp at Sandakan. 'I've often thought over in my mind why I got so heavily involved. I saw men dying like flies, just for the need of a few drugs, and I couldn't stand by and not give them some. So I took them from the store and faked the returns, but it never occurred to me to stop it.'

During this time, Dr Taylor managed to send into the camp atabrin, quinine, various M&B preparations, ether, sterilised bandages and iodine, chemicals for radio batteries, some surgical instruments for the Australian medical officers and occasionally even food for the seriously ill.

The complete underground movement collapsed on 22 July 1943. It had operated successfully for over six months, gradually increasing its scope. The first James Taylor knew of its betrayal was a Japanese guard at the door of his cottage, where he and his wife were both arrested early in the morning. 'When I got down to the gaol, I saw the *Kempeitai* there, and people that I knew also arrested, and I knew what had happened. I feared we couldn't go on for too long, and it didn't come as a great surprise because the Japanese had been putting listening devices into the camp, and you had a mixed population living in the region—some were half Chinese and half native, and there was always the chance they would give us away.'

All the immediate suspects were rounded up, and taken to the upper floor of the *Kempeitai* Sandakan headquarters for interrogation. Dr Taylor soon found out that Celia and some of the other European

women were being held in cells on the ground floor. Captain Lionel
Matthews was with the group on the upper floor, which was actually the
first time he and Taylor had personally met despite their collaboration
in the underground network. 'I had a strange feeling about Matthews—
you know, he just looked like Jesus Christ. He was a tall man and a
kind man, and the morning he came into the *Kempeitai* headquarters
I thought that he was very like Christ. It's strange, but it's a fact.'

Others have commented on Matthews' distinctive mien. Known
as 'The Duke', he had won a Military Cross during the action in
Malaya, and was not only a thoroughly professional soldier, but an
inspirational figure for those who worked with him. With no talking
allowed, James Taylor was not able to communicate with Matthews,
even by furtive whispering, as Taylor's hearing was bad: 'I had worked
out my own scheme of what to do and made up my mind to tell them
as little as possible and stick to it. Some of the Asians were beaten so
badly they confessed almost immediately, but I found my way was
better. But when they found out that I was lying, I'd get a walloping.'

The interrogations in Sandakan went on for six months. Dr Taylor
was questioned about three times a week in a separate room with
an interpreter and several other Japanese. On every one of these occasions he was bashed. The first session was the worst.

'When the Japanese thought you were lying, they called on a man
with a stick to lay into you. I was badly beaten, and had black eyes
and bruises. Actually I didn't think I'd come out of it. Next morning,
they took me down to the women's compound and showed me to my
wife and told her to tell me to tell the truth in future. As time went on
I found it was best to tell them as little as possible, and let them find
out certain things—you had to admit something. But on the whole it
paid out.'

At this time the Japanese put an informer in with the European
women to try to get them to say something incriminating, but they

were aware of what was happening and did not oblige. After a few weeks the women, including Celia Taylor, were taken by ship to Kuching, to an internment camp for the rest of the war. Dr Taylor says: 'The Japanese found out about the people we had taken to Berhala Island that were escaping to the Philippines. I think they suspected me for a long time before they caught me, but had no definite proof. They kept harping about that and being in touch with the camp and Matthews. I think it was an accumulation of these things that settled me eventually.'

The trials were held in Kuching, where Matthews and a number of Chinese were sentenced to death for their crimes in being associated with the underground network. 'The only contact I had with Lionel Matthews was to say goodbye. He didn't show fear at all, and seemed unruffled by the whole thing. But it was very serious because he was looked on as the ringleader.'

Before he left Kuching by ship for Singapore and Outram Road Gaol, James Taylor was at least permitted to see his wife. One of his travelling companions was a friend, Gerald Mavor, who had been in charge of the Sandakan Light and Power Company. In fact, on their arrival at Outram Road, they were both pushed into the same cell with a concrete floor, no blankets and no food. Taylor remembers saying to Mavor, 'We've got the real McCoy now!'

Although nearly 50, Taylor said he had youth on his side. He considered himself to be strong and healthy, and was determined to survive. 'I've often wondered why some people died so quickly. I had beriberi and all these things, but I was determined to live anyway. If you had this strength of will you would do better than the average soldier, who was probably not particularly well educated. If you don't mind me saying these things, I've often wondered why the better educated and determined people lasted, helped perhaps by their intellectual strength.'

Taylor needed all the self-help he could summon up. Because he was a doctor, the Japanese would often put him in a cell with a dying man, so that they could write in the records that a doctor had been in attendance. 'It was upsetting. I couldn't do anything, and unfortunately they wouldn't give me drugs or anything like that. You just saw people dying. I even had to be with my friend Gerald Mavor and watch him die of beriberi and starvation. There was nothing I could do to help him. They were all hopeless cases, unconscious most of them, and I can't say that it affected my morale. I'd become very hardened by then to anything at all that happened—being beaten up and interrogated continuously and used to all the sights around me. I became very hard, but I don't think I ever became accustomed to it.'

Taylor kept a tally in his head of all the deaths he became aware of during his fifteen months at Outram Road Gaol from March 1943. There were 1400. That gives an indication of the scale of executions and deaths by disease and starvation at Outram Road during its war-time operations that have never officially been confirmed.

Dr James Taylor was still at Outram Road Gaol when the war ended, and was immediately put into hospital with dysentery. He was there for a month, and during that time his biggest worry was about his wife 500 miles away in Kuching, not knowing whether she had survived the war.

'When I got fit enough to walk, I tried to get word of my wife and it was very difficult to get information in those days—about anyone. I thought, "Well, if I get a chance I'll go over to Labuan and wait there." I managed to find a brigadier who was sympathetic and he got me a seat on a plane to Labuan where I waited around the airport and various places but I couldn't find her. So I thought I'd wait a little longer, and then go back to Australia because I thought she would drift there eventually. Fortunately Celia came in to Labuan the next day on a plane, and we had a very happy reunion.'

# 9

# CHANGI WAS LIKE HEAVEN

One of the thin strands of hope for the Australians at Outram Road Gaol was that if they became so sick that their deaths seemed imminent, there was an outside chance the *Kempeitai* administration might return them to Changi for hospital treatment. This was not a manifestation of any humanity on behalf of the Japanese—they didn't care whether their charges lived or died—but it was a bureaucratic concern. This was one aspect of being a prisoner of the *Kempeitai* that worked in Outram Road inmates' favour.

As Rod Wells recalled: 'If you were an ordinary prisoner of war on a work party, and a guard hit you with a wooden stick and broke your neck, nobody worried about killing a prisoner accidentally because you were one of thousands—if they killed a few, it didn't matter. But once you were arrested and charged under the *Kempeitai* judicial system and were sentenced to a term of imprisonment, trial records were kept, and in a way you became more precious than prisoners of war in general. You were put in Outram Road to serve a sentence, and it was skin off their nose, if you like, if you didn't. So if you became seriously ill, it was more convenient to send you to Changi rather than have you die in the gaol. Of course while you were there, your sentence was under suspension and your time away from Outram Road wasn't counted. So in a way, that was an advantage. I'm sure none of us would have survived if we'd been put in there to die.'

Some tried to fake symptoms to get to Changi, but that was a huge gamble. Sick people were put on half rations, or not fed at all—an absurd tactic by the Japanese based on their bizarre belief that if a prisoner became sick, it was his fault. The punishment was to cut his food.

Like everyone else, Major John Wyett sat rotting in his cell during the latter part of 1943. Unlike the conventional prisoner-of-war situation where officers received extra pay and did not have to do the hard physical work that killed so many of the other ranks, even officers of field rank like Wyett received no extra privileges at Outram Road. To keep his mind active he first tapped on his cell wall with a button from his prison shirt, and made contact with a British major next door, who also knew Morse code. After some rewarding nights swapping stories about their war service and life in general, the tapping was heard by the guards. Wyett and the major were bashed, and all the buttons on their clothing were removed—together with those of everyone else in the entire gaol.

Meditation seemed the only safe alternative. Wyett says: 'During this period of long contemplation I had what appeared at the time to be a great idea. Why not design an internal combustion aero engine to run on solid fuel such as cordite, suitably modified to drive a piston without bursting the cylinder. This would have the effect of turning a 4-stroke engine into a 2-stroke, thus doubling the power for the same engine weight. The jet engine had not yet been developed and I felt that this idea would have great use in aircraft design. This exercise involved a great deal of mental effort as there were no writing materials nor any reference books. Fortunately I could remember most of the atomic weights and the formulas for such explosives and went over and over the various calculations in my mind so that I could memorise them in order to proceed the next day from the point where I left off.'

Wyett became quite enthusiastic about the way it was all working out when a thought struck him and collapsed the project. The simple fact was that an aeroplane does not carry its own oxygen for the engine to work. A few more calculations showed him that the great weight of oxygen used by the aircraft engine is obtained freely from the air. So that was that. At least, Wyett, reasoned, it had given his brain cells a workout.

One day, John Wyett noticed a few small creamy grey creatures crawling on his skin and a closer inspection showed that they were lice. When he examined his miserably thin blanket he found it was literally lousy with vermin, so he set about picking them out. 'A roar from the guard and a bash over my head stopped the process which I then had to approach more cautiously. I would collect three or four lice at a time and feed them alternatively to a couple of spiders high on the wall in the corner of my cell. By the time I had cleaned out my own lice and those in the blanket, the spiders were getting quite fat and we were good friends.'

Meanwhile, Wyett had been trying to think up another worthwhile project, and finally decided that the world of music lovers needed a decent and reliable record changer. Most records in those days were the ten-inch and twelve-inch 78 rpm type, and what changers there were did not treat the records at all gently and were unreliable. Wyett became very keen about this idea, and thought that the invention might even work. But it became difficult to develop without the help of a few diagrams. 'One day, when I was putting my bed boards up against the wall, I dislodged a small piece of plaster. It was just what I needed to draw with. When I had worked out a section of my apparatus in my mind I would wait for the guard to pass, turn one of the boards around and sketch a rough drawing with my piece of plaster, and turn it round again before he completed his round.'

Then, disaster struck. Wyett became so absorbed in his working drawings that he forgot about the ever-present guard, who caught him in the act, rushed in and bashed him and erased his sketches. As things turned out, Wyett admitted to me ruefully, he would have been too late with his automatic changer because, as coincidence would have it, a friend of his in Hobart, Eric Waterworth, had been working on a similar idea, and by the time the war ended had been approached by a manufacturer to market it!

While Wyett's mind might have been functioning efficiently, his body was not. Quite soon after he went into solitary confinement, signs of beriberi began to appear because of the meagre diet. As the weeks passed, the flesh fell away from his bones and he grew thinner and thinner. His stomach started to swell and the telltale signs of beriberi appeared—oedema in his legs and arms where pressure from a finger would cause a deep depression in his skin and last for quite some time. Then Wyett noticed something curious: 'It was usually at this stage that a few yellow soya beans would be included in the rice and after a few days of these there would begin a copious flow of urine and a reduction in the swelling of my limbs and abdomen. The effect was quite dramatic considering the few beans involved. It was then that the supply stopped. Within a few weeks the swelling would return and so would the beans. It all pointed to a policy of calculated beastliness and starvation.'

At that time, prisoners were allowed out of their cells in small batches, three or four times a week, to empty slop pails and have a brief wash under a tap. As the weeks dragged by, Wyett could see the dramatic deterioration of all prisoners. They were becoming more and more emaciated and things were looking so grim that on one of these occasions, he demanded to see the commandant of the Allied prisoners in the gaol, a *Kempeitai* sergeant: 'Rather to my surprise, he appeared a few minutes later—a lean individual with a long, thin moustache on a narrow, swarthy and cruel-looking face. He was wearing black jack-boots and carrying the usual heavy Japanese sword. As he approached, and I only just had enough strength myself do to this, I picked up one of the chaps standing nearby and, holding that light, thin frame in my arms, I confronted the scowling commandant.'

He knew that Wyett was a senior officer, and was angry at being challenged so publicly. When Wyett demanded more food and told him that the conditions in the gaol were a disgrace, he became furious. Flinging his arms about he shouted an order to the guards, who immediately hustled everyone back into their cells. Wyett's protest did not achieve much, certainly not as far as he was concerned because he received no food at all for the next couple of days.

Another untreated infection was ringworm, which affected some very seriously. There was a particularly nasty case in the cell opposite Wyatt. It struck first at the prisoner's legs and gradually spread over his whole body. As he lay in his cell suffering the intolerable itching of the spreading infection, he received no medical attention. He was simply left there to rot.

Eventually the unbearable pain and irritation overcame his reason and his maddened, incoherent shouting, together with his moans, echoed throughout the gaol day and night. After some days, the shouting became weaker and soon faded altogether. The moaning then turned into a series of weak croaks as the unfortunate man lay there, alone in a foul mess of urine and excrement. Finally, no further sound came from that loathsome cell door. Wyett said a cold chill seemed to creep through the gaol. The man was dead, released at last from his pain and suffering.

The next day after the body had been removed, a guard unlocked Wyett's door and beckoned him out. He was confronted by the unlovely

sight of the commandant standing there leering at him. Wyett was
given a bucket and a scrubbing brush. The door of the dead man's
cell was thrown open and he was forced to go down on his hands and
knees and clean up the mess. 'The scene before me in that ghastly
cell beggared description. The poor devil had discarded his clothes
in his frenzy of pain, and torn large pieces of his tormented skin and
flesh from his limbs and body. These were now lying scattered in that
stinking mess all over the floor. I was sickened in mind and body at
the sight and by the unbelievable and cynical cruelty of it all, as I went
about the revolting and degrading task of cleaning up the fetid mix of
ordure, blood and rotting human flesh.'

It was not long after this incident that Wyett's beriberi became
worse, and signs of the scaly skin disease pellagra began to appear.
Pellagra is a chronic disease prolonged by a deficiency of nicotinic
acid in the diet leading to gastrointestinal disturbances, skin erup-
tions and nervous disorders. It is something that doctors would never
see in a normal society, or perhaps only in areas of Third World
famine. But it was endemic at Outram Road, inflicting great pain,
misery and personal degradation—even death—in its advanced
stage. More worryingly, within a few weeks Wyett's eyesight, already
fading, went altogether and he was completely blind. 'I found it a
strange experience that somehow did not worry me much. I could
still think reasonably clearly and never doubted that all would be
well in the end. Oddly enough this proved to be the case sooner
than I thought. After about a week, a glimmer of vision began to
return and gradually improved to the somewhat fuzzy state it had
been before. I was then able to examine my legs and body, which
were covered with scaly skin very like the scales of the fish. From
them oozed a clear, yellow and sticky fluid which soaked my shorts
and, when dry, stiffened them so hard I could stand them upright
on the floor.'

When dysentery started it seemed the final blow. Wyett rapidly became weaker and finally was unable to stand. He lay there on the cement floor of his dismal cell, swollen with beriberi, his body covered in pellagra scales and now infested with scabies. He found himself gradually drifting into a semi-conscious dream world, while a kaleidoscope of early events in his life passed through his mind in a meaningless procession.

One of the earliest dreams was of him as a very small boy in Beaconsfield, Tasmania, where he was born. He was sitting with the family dog outside his kennel, sucking the piece of charcoal that he had fished out of the dog's water bowl where his mother had placed it to keep the drinking water pure and sweet. The young John had been roundly scolded for eating the dog's charcoal and the memory of it had stayed with him ever since. 'The next incident that came to mind must have occurred when I was about the same age. I'd crawled out of bed early one morning and found a slice of bread, spread with a blue paste, lying beside the fireplace where my father had placed it the night before. I was about to eat it when there was a howl, and the bread was snatched from my hand by my father, who had just got up and spotted me. Pretty rough treatment, I suppose, that may have been just as well because it was put there to poison a rat.'

Finally this kaleidoscope of memories began to fade and then became jumbled to the point where they made no sense, until they ceased altogether. Wyett had never heard of the phenomenon of an out-of-body experience, yet what he went on to describe was eerily similar: 'My mind and body seemed to separate into some sort of dichotomy where the real me floated off, leaving the rotting carcass lying on the ground like a discarded garment. I felt myself fluttering off and then returning, always departing and then coming back for a brief time, only to leave my body yet again. Everything was hazy and intangible. Reality had gone out of my life, leaving me in a state where nothing seemed to matter any more. I was interested in my situation but in an ethereal and insubstantial way as a detached observer, without any sort of personal or emotional involvement. I was living in a Nirvana all my own. My emaciated, disease-riddled body was something to be observed rather than experienced. Yet I was cold, so cold, in the all-pervading warmth of that tropical climate.'

Wyett's well-fed spiders in their corner seemed to glow intermittently as if in an effervescence of golden light, which waxed and waned about them. That was when he decided to go up to join them, and sat there with his two old friends, his only companions in the dreary loneliness of that grim, grey and silent cell. (Madness is the final stage of pellagra.) 'I had no idea how long I was in that state of suspended animation—probably not more than a week or two as I doubt I could have lasted much longer before the temporary and intermittent separation between soul and body became permanent. My fluttering spirit seemed to be in an agony of indecision as to whether it should let me go, or re-join my body, and I have a distinct recollection of a moment of clarity when I told it to stop being stupid and come back. There was thus a brief reunion of my body and spirit as I was removed from my cell and put on a truck along with several others to be taken to the hospital at Changi.'

There was, however, one final act of bastardry inflicted on the barely conscious Wyett, courtesy of the implacable hatred of Outram Road Gaol's commandant. He was handed a bowl of watery soup with a number of red and green pods floating in it. Starving as he was, he drank it without a thought as to what they could be.

'On the way to the camp a burning pain started, and by the time I arrived I was in agony because of the effect of the hot chillies on an already inflamed gut. From then on, everything was a blur and even the move to Changi was an event to be observed rather than experienced. I believe that my removal to hospital rather than being left to die on my cell floor was due to the farsighted attitude of the *Kempeitai* in covering their tracks against any future reprisals.

'All remained hazy and indistinct until I felt myself being lowered into a hot bath. The ever-present pain and irritation of the scabies, the pellagra and all the associated skin complaints faded, and were replaced by a feeling of utter bliss. I think that bath marked the end of my visits to the spirit world, as I became more and more aware of my surroundings and of the care and attention I was receiving. My spirit was returning and I was being made whole again.'

Private John McGregor, who, with Lieutenant Penrod Dean, had the doubtful honour of being one of the first Australian residents of Outram Road Gaol in May 1942, later wrote in his memoir that the year 1942 to 1943 was 'The Black Year' at Outram Road, where the treatment of prisoners was the most bestial. Starving men were left in solitary confinement in filthy cells that were never cleaned, coping as best they could with treatable diseases that were allowed to take their course by an uncaring gaol administration. All the while they were being slowly starved—some to death. It took enormous willpower to overcome the hopelessness of this situation. McGregor and his neighbour Chris Neilson were two outstanding examples of stubborn courage—at least they had the distraction of being able to communicate with each through their cell walls by Morse code.

McGregor has left a vivid, disturbing, but quite remarkable account of survival against the odds at Outram Road in *Blood on the Rising Sun*. How any mortal could live through such a combination of horrors is astounding—yet he was not alone.

By August 1942, McGregor had dysentery so badly that he had to secure himself to his overflowing toilet bucket, wedged into a corner of his cell, for three days and nights during the worst of it—knowing that had he fallen off he might not have been able to extricate himself from the stinking mess of human excreta, blood and stomach lining which surrounded him. When that crisis subsided, the Japanese guards—clearly relishing the humiliation of the white man—insisted he clean up this mess with his bare hands and put it back into an emptied *benki*. He was then kicked and bashed for good measure, and left lying on the floor of his still filthy cell.

> Sometime during the night I rallied. The mosquitoes were there, the lice troublesome and the bugs hungry, but I knew them as my friends because they carried no swords, nor wore heavy boots. The light from a guard's torch waved to and fro across my face, then a voice telling me to lie down and sleep. These guards were unbeatable. If it so happened that a prisoner was asleep when a new guard came on duty, he was aroused just in order to prove that he was not yet a corpse. But if a prisoner was sitting up, or even awake at the time of inspection, then he was promptly ordered to go to sleep. The Jap assumed, of course, that if the prisoner was awake in the middle of the night it was obvious that he had something on his mind, such as an attempt at escape. In either case, the poor prisoner was at fault.

In a tropical climate there are many illnesses which inevitably follow in the wake of dysentery and malnutrition—diseases which, if unchecked, can kill. Aware of his frail condition, McGregor began to plan his survival strategy. Even in his debilitated state, he thought it necessary to start an exercise program to try to retain what fitness he had—made doubly difficult by the constant daily surveillance and rules about sitting to attention all day. The night gave more freedom to move so McGregor exercised when he could, thrusting his arms upwards and outwards, counting, quietly singing and reciting— anything to help keep a grip on his sanity.

He was barely over his dysentery attack and eating again when he became aware of a slight swelling in his hands and feet, as well as numbness. Beriberi was on the way. This deficiency disease causes the kidneys to fail in their ability to discharge liquid. Oedema builds up first in the extremities of hands and feet, leading to death if untreated. McGregor was aware that beriberi was induced by eating polished rice, the only type they were given. It was Hobson's choice, really: eating rice would bring on beriberi, but not to eat the miserable daily ration of rice would kill you by starvation. Beriberi could have easily been fixed by using unhusked rice or providing a vitamin-B substitute, but this was not the *Kempeitai*'s way. McGregor wrote:

> I elected to eat whatever my dish contained, to enjoy it as best I could, and to remain alive as long as possible. A dead man could no longer fight, but I was a long way yet from being incapable of fighting and would remain so while I was able to retain a grip on myself both physically and mentally.

As the weeks dragged on, however, McGregor's condition slowly worsened. His legs and hands were swelling rapidly, despite his walking on the spot in his cell at night, heaving his heavy feet up and down and holding his hands above his head to try to get some relief. He even tried running on the spot until utter exhaustion overtook him, and he collapsed on the cold concrete floor:

> For the next two months I fought this terrible disease and held it in check, but early in the new year I began to notice that my eyes were growing dim. Whether this was an aftermath of beriberi or malnutrition I wasn't sure, but in the months which followed an eye condition known as retro-bulbous neuritis developed sufficiently to render me almost blind. However, strange as it

may seem, this growing dimness of sight, itself a major blow, was not my main worry at that moment. The advent of malaria further added to my travails, to be followed by a symptom which I quickly recognised as the second stage of beriberi. At night I would massage my burning feet for lengthy periods of time, then I would run on the spot until completely exhausted, all in a mad attempt to drive the burning sensation from my swollen feet just long enough to permit me to snatch a few moments peaceful slumber on my cosy bed—the bare concrete floor.

Then he realised that the scourge of pellagra was taking hold. McGregor was constantly taking stock of the state of his body, which was by now filthy; the hair on his head and face was long and matted; his feet and hands were heavy with accumulated fluid; his skin was dry and hard, leading to an uncontrollable itch; semi-paralysis of his legs was setting in; malaria was a constant; his vision was decreasing daily; and he still had diarrhoea. Now he had to face up to pellagra:

Sores quickly broke out all over my body, even on my face and scalp. As the disease assumed greater control my fingernails dropped off, teeth loosened yellow pus forced its way through pores whenever I made the slightest movement. As I walked around the cell this pustulous matter would eject itself from the soles of my feet and cause a sticking sensation. The yellow pus in my body built up to such alarming proportions that it couldn't all escape through the myriad number of skin fractures, but would simply dribble through my pores whenever movement of any kind caused any kind of friction. If I rubbed my hands until they became warm, the pus would run as freely as from a tap. The rubbing together of my hands would bring about movement in my elbows, shoulder, and neck, so providing further outlets for this sticky and evil smelling substance—this putrid mess was slowly but surely draining the life from my already overburdened body.

Unbelievably, things got even worse. Scabs were beginning to form on those parts of McGregor's body where pellagra sores had become firmly established, and were building up and enlarging as layer after layer of pus was forcing its way through the affected pores, finally to settle and dry. He was not encouraged by seeing a corpse being carried out on a stretcher from a nearby cell, and immediately realised the prisoner had died of pellagra. McGregor saw with horror that the dead man's naked body was completely encased in an inch-thick yellow scab, so completely that the only part of his body not covered were the two small holes where his eyes would have been. McGregor believed that the sight of that scab-encased corpse being taken out was by far the worst case of human ill-treatment that he saw in his whole time at Outram Road Gaol. It did, however, spur him on to even greater efforts to combat his own diseases.

I continued to draw the pustulous substance from my body by constantly ringing my hands, and in this unorthodox way causing the fluid to be both centrally contained and ejected, so preventing skin breakages occurring elsewhere. I would deviate from this filthy practice occasionally to watch the little pockets of pus forming beneath the skin of my still softened palms, later to expand in size until it all converged into one huge blister. Then, in triumph, I would bash my hands against the wall to effectively put an end to at least another cupful of this loathsome disease. Whitlows formed on the tips of my fingers, now without nails, but a smart smack on the floor and they were gone. There was no feeling left in my body now, the pellagra having, thank

God, wholly contributed to this respite. The bugs in the cell aggravated, the lice bit, and the Japs smirked and carried on with their unceasing tide of mental and physical terrorism, but I felt nothing, nor did anything have any meaning other than the fight I was having with life itself.

Scabies appeared, and the paralysis in McGregor's legs became more pronounced. Scurvy joined in the attack, and the already uncontrollable itch grew even worse. But nothing was as bad as the ravages of pellagra.

Fortunately I never contracted blood poisoning. This was impossible because I had no blood. Believe me, when I say I had no blood, there was none in evidence whenever a Japanese sword sliced my unprotected body, nor when I tore huge pieces of flesh from my withered frame at night because of an uncontrollable itch associated with both scurvy and scabies. My blood had turned to pus, obviously, so much so that there was now no feeling. At night saliva ran from my mouth unnoticed, and I would feel no pain when I clawed at the huge weals of proud flesh which pockmarked my entire body. I would even fail to wake when the nervous system took charge of my limbs and set them kicking and bashing away at the wall or floor, and the fiery pain in my feet had either burned itself out to make way for the third state of beriberi, paralysis, or it too had been swallowed up in the only consoling feature of advanced pellagra—complete immunity from pain.

Deliverance was finally to come, not through the likely agency of death, suicide or firing squad, but by transfer to the Changi prisoner-of-war camp on the morning of 19 July 1943. On this great and memorable day, with three other Australians and four Englishmen, McGregor was led, unshackled this time, out of the gaol and into a waiting truck. On arrival at Changi, the near corpses from Outram Road were unceremoniously dumped on the hot bitumen of the Selarang Barrack Square, remaining there undetected until someone noticed the heap of huddled humanity and notified the hospital staff.

I remember a doctor picking me up like a child and hurrying with me across the square in the direction of the Australian section of the hospital. No sooner had I been placed upon a bed, somebody was offering me three boiled lollies, someone else was ready with shaving gear, and others just gaped and marvelled that life would still exist in so battered a human frame. I remember the giver of the three boiled lollies, Major Adrian Farmer, from Perth, apologising for not having something better to offer. And then I broke down. Coming out of hell and into a haven such as this was more than any human being was able to bear. I literally cried like a child, tears running freely into my filthy matted beard, so overcome was I by the kindness which surrounded me.

I muttered uncontrollably about Japs, about the prison, and the treatment, and about my mates. My nerves were certainly playing tricks, so much so that I was beginning to fear that after all, I had lost my reason. The doctors must have thought of this possibility also because they quickly hunted the well-wishers away and had us isolated, issuing strict orders to the effect that we were not to be disturbed until we had completely settled down to the new environment. God, what must have been the doctors' first impressions of us? Four naked Australian soldiers, thin and gaunt, bodies filthy and unwashed, covered with scabies and infected sores, limbs badly swollen, skins dry and parched, and the face of each completely hidden beneath a shaggy mass of matted and vile-smelling hair. Hell, what a sight.

Under the care of Changi's skilled doctors and surgeons, John McGregor experienced a major overhaul. He had an operation for haemorrhoids, pterygiums (a benign growth on the conjunctiva) on both eyes were removed in an effort to boost his failing eyesight, and he was fattened up with the best food the camp could offer. But he knew full well he was on borrowed time—just a few months, with luck. Every week, a Japanese medical officer would arrive from Outram Road to see who was fit enough to return to continue their sentences. The Australian doctors became adept at blinding the visiting Japanese medicos with medical jargon, and stressing the parlous state of their patients' health. When McGregor put on some weight and was obviously cured of his multiple diseases, the doctors made much of his blindness. Eventually the Japanese doctor asked if McGregor's sight could be returned. When they said no, the Japanese said, in that case, he might as well return to Outram Road Gaol! So McGregor went back to finish his sentence.

His former cell-neighbour, Chris Neilson, had better luck, and managed to stay in Changi for just over a year, once he had been revived. He was also blind when he got to Changi but got his sight back, although he had no central vision in his left eye for the rest of his life. 'Whenever our doctors saw the Japanese medicos coming, they'd find some way to convince them we were still crook. We weren't allowed to be in the ordinary hospital wards, we had to lay out on the hospital verandah in the boiling heat, and we weren't allowed to go to concert parties or anything like that. They trained us to control our reflexes, so you could be hit in the right spot and your leg wouldn't jerk or jump. If they had enough warning, they would inject something and blow a scar in my eye up, or give us the sweats to simulate malaria, so

I was lucky enough to stay in Changi for quite a long time. But you always knew you'd have to go back to Outram Road at some stage.'

Changi was fortunate in having so many good and experienced doctors, but as John Wyett says, that was a happy accident: 'The 8th Division had been allotted two field hospitals in anticipation of a build-up in Singapore of combatant troops from the Middle East. We got the non-combatants but not the fighting men, with the result that we were weighed down during the campaign by this imbalance. In the end, however, under prisoner-of-war conditions the two hospitals proved to be a godsend because we had more doctors of greater seniority than otherwise would have been the case.'

Somehow the doctors seemed to be more successful at keeping officers in Changi and most never returned to Outram Road Gaol, whereas other ranks did go back. But even with the officers, some ingenious strategies had to be employed. In Wyett's case, the nerves controlling the muscles of his feet had degenerated, with the result that he could not walk, because his feet flopped about uselessly. With care and physiotherapy he was able to walk again, but his left foot was stronger than his right. Using a stick, Wyett had to flip his right foot into position at the beginning of each new step. 'One day Dr Charles Osborn said to me, "John, if you get better too quickly the *Kempeitai* will take you back to Outram Road, and I doubt if we could pull you through a second time. Keep dragging that foot, I don't want it to get better yet." Colonel Cotter Harvey, our senior physician, came in at this point and objected strongly, resulting in a heated exchange between physician and surgeon. "If John does that there will be a permanent degeneration of the muscles of the foot and there is every chance he will be left with a disability for life."' Osborn resolved the argument by saying, 'Better a man alive and limping than a dead John.' That settled it, and although Wyett's foot became a little stronger he continued to limp and drag it even after he returned home.

About this time, Jack Macalister—who was to have been the pilot of the escape plan Wyett and he had devised—was also brought to the Changi hospital in a bad way. His condition gradually improved with the medical treatment and a better diet. Two of Macalister's regular visitors were Dr Charles Huxtable and a fellow RAAF officer, Arthur 'Tink' Tinkler. During one visit, Huxtable said to Macalister, 'You're beginning to look too fit. You'll have to be careful or those damned *Kempeitai* will take you back to Outram Road.' In this case more heroic measures would be taken than encouraging the degeneration of Wyett's right foot. A bizarre plan was hatched to break Macalister's leg, to incapacitate him—hopefully not permanently.

Wyett recalled: 'Having decided what should be done we then spent the rest of the evening discussing how to go about breaking Mac's foot. Finally Charles said, "Tink, do you think you can get hold of a sledge-hammer?" Tinkler said he could because he saw a party of engineers using one a few days ago. Charles then announced that he had a small quantity of cocaine, not enough to do the job properly but he thought it might help deaden the pain a bit.'

One dark moonless night, Huxtable and Tinkler took Macalister out to a drain with a concrete edge where Huxtable injected his scanty dose of cocaine into Macalister's leg. While waiting for it to take effect he explained to Tinkler, who held the sledgehammer, exactly where he should hit the shin. Macalister managed to suppress any cry from the pain of the blow, but was half fainting from the shock, until he was brought back. 'Charles began chuckling quietly to himself in the darkness. Eventually he said, "If the Australian Medical Association ever got to hear of me deliberately breaking a patient's foot with a seven-pound sledgehammer just to keep him in hospital, I'd be banned from ever practising again." At that point Tinkler said that it wasn't a seven-pound sledgehammer but a ten-pound one. I winced involuntarily and Mac passed out!'

Although this unusual assault on his leg did gain Macalister more time, he was eventually taken back to Outram Road and stayed there till the end of the war—apparently the only Australian officer to make the return journey from the sanctuary of Changi hospital.

Chris Neilson's time came late in 1944. He was moving around freely when the Japanese arrived unexpectedly, and that was that. But his exit from Changi and arrival at Outram Road Gaol were light years away from the tranquillity of more than a year in Changi. Just as the Outram Road guards were about to march him away, an Englishman called out to him. Neilson says: 'I'll never forget it: "For Christ's sake, I've got a mate in Outram Road. He was one of a group that tried to go through to Burma. They executed most of them, but for some reason this bloke and another one wasn't. Please, when you get back in there, give him a message that I'm still alive."'

Suddenly, Neilson pushed his Japanese guard aside—a brave move under any circumstances—and walked over to the Englishman. 'It throws them for some reason, they don't understand if you push them aside. They are so arrogant, and so obsessed with their power they can't understand any prisoner of war doing anything like that. I said to this Englishman, "You'd better give me the story quickly because this bloke will belt the piss out of me."'

The Englishman, who introduced himself as 'Tich', explained that he had been part of a group working on the Burma side of the railway and most of them came down with cholera. He said his mate thought he had died, but when the British said they couldn't carry him any further, a group of Australians came past and carried him into a bush hospital, and he survived. The two men had been brought up together in London, and it was vital that he knew Tich hadn't died. Neilson said he'd do his best, and walked back to his furious guard: 'He pulled his sword out. I said, "You're not game". Major Clark said later they waited for about four minutes for the guard to slice my head off.

I knew he wouldn't. He had to deliver me back to the gaol or *he* would have been beheaded. I was awake to all those tricks. He put his sword back into its scabbard and took it off his belt, then whacked me with it—knocked out one of my teeth and smashed my conk [nose]. It had to be reconstructed later. He put the handcuffs on me so tightly my hands swelled up, and as soon as we got to Outram Road I was put in the black punishment cells for thirty days.'

When Neilson got out of the black cells, he found an utterly different Outram Road Gaol from the one he had left the previous year. Solitary confinement had ended. With more prisoners coming in than the gaol could handle, most of the tiny cells had two prisoners, and some had three, with barely room to lie down and sleep. But at least they could talk to each other. Even the food was a bit better—not much, but any improvement was welcome. There were also more chances to get out of the cells, and work on various jobs. Neilson says: 'They still didn't trust me and sent me out with another bloke to work in the prison garden, an Englishman. He said, "Are you the bloke they call The Rebel?" [I said,] "Yeah." He said, "I'm going to get out of this. I'm going over the wall." I said, "Do you want to get everyone here executed? They'll execute everyone of us if one bloke escapes, or even tries to escape. If you start having a go, I'll call the bloody guards, and that's an order."'

Neilson asked what his name was, and realised it was the man the Englishman in Changi had asked him to find: '"You're the bloke I'm looking for. You've got a mate called Tich. I copped a bashing and 30 days in the black cells for talking to him." He said, "Tich died of cholera in Burma." "No, I've just met Tich in Changi. He asked me to find you and say he was still alive. He said you were brought up together, joined up together and were in Shanghai together. Tich was picked up by the Australians and taken to Kanburi [Kanchanaburi] and fixed up." He quietened down then and was satisfied, and said he wouldn't try and escape any more. I think knowing that gave him the will to go on and actually saved his life.'

For Chris Neilson, sharing a cell turned out to be a mixed blessing. There was a sudden influx of about 80 Indians into Outram Road Gaol, probably charged with trying to escape, although Chris thought it was more probable 'the poor buggers were just hungry and lost'. The man he shared with was a Gurkha, who spoke not a word of English. Chris knew no Urdu. (Unlike other Indian units, the Gurkhas remained true to the British cause and so endured intense hardship.) This man was crippled, and Chris, from his experience in gymnasiums as a boxer, knew enough to massage his legs, although he didn't think the man would survive. Somehow the Gurkha made it clear he thought he was dying and that he wanted Neilson to pray for him. Although an atheist, Neilson did his best to go through the motions: 'I started mumbling a lot of mumbo jumbo, and was doing the sign of the cross, because I remembered that from convent school. Suddenly I saw the Gurkha's eyes open wide, and I looked around to see the camp commandant, the interpreter and a couple of guards looking in. They charged me with ridiculing this bloke's religion! I got three days in solitary with a bashing every hour, no food, and a bit of water twice a day. So I decided that's the last time I pray for any bugger, including me!'

Teenage prisoner Bill Young had better luck when Rod Wells shared his cell for five weeks. Wells, realising that Young had not had much education, started giving him lectures on the basics of atomic physics. Young says: 'Rod would be surprised, I'm sure, if he knew that I still remembered many of the talks he gave me on the structure and nature of the atom. As a very young boy I had never been encouraged to go to school and this certainly agreed with my own feelings then. To show my Irish, the only times I went to school I wagged it. So when Rod came with his university-gained knowledge, I sat at his feet—literally.

'Both of us at that time were ignorant of just how important those little itsy bitsy atoms he was describing were to play in our safe deliverance from Outram Road and from the little yellow creeps keeping us there. While he was explaining things to me like atomic weight, valency and the nucleus, the atomic bombs that would save our lives were about to be dropped on Japan.'

No prisoners at Outram Road expected anything other than harsh treatment by their *Kempeitai* guards. But some were worse than others. Their Japanese names eluded the Australians and they were known by their nicknames. Bill Young says: 'There was "Hitler" (nice fella), "Attila the Hun" (lovely bloke), "Fatgut" (gracious), "Himmler" (nature's gentleman), "Lughead" (just great), "Owl Face" (he had a mother), "Black Bastard" (what a kind man) and then there was the "Postman" (he only knocked once), who was in a class of his own.'

The Postman combined brutality with psychological torture. There would only be one knock. Perhaps there would be another knock, or was it the wind? The prisoner sat, stiffly at attention, waiting for what he knew was about to happen. Young wrote:

> You knew in your heart he was out there enjoying himself, keys dangling in his hands, waiting for the exact psychological moment—which came with the noise of that great key turning in the lock. But the door would remain closed, with everything silent except for your own heartbeat.

With a crash, the door would swing open, at last revealing the black silhouette of The Postman. He would walk in slowly, standing to the side and a little behind his seated cross-legged victim—who at least knew that the waiting was almost over:

> Softly he speaks in Japanese, 'It won't be long now'. You hear the sound of the keys rattling as they are brought up, way up,

making your body tense up. But the wait goes on. You try willing your hair to grow thicker and stronger—a safety helmet. Hope comes sneaking back, perhaps he's in a good mood.

BANG, down come the keys, crashing into your poor, weak unprotected skull. The blood runs down your forehead, and through the pain-wracked tears streaming from your eyes, you watch his departing figure.

It was always the same when The Postman knocked.

In April 1944, Bill Young was out on gardening duty in the Outram Road garden, tending the paw paw trees dripping with their luscious golden fruit—of course, only for the Japanese guards. He noticed an older *Kempeitai* sergeant standing on a bank looking down on them: 'To the Japs, rank is very important and the gap between them is jealously guarded. I once saw the punishment meted out to a 2-star private by a 3-star private, for showing a lack of respect. The 2-star private was a bloody mess when it was over.'

Young noticed that the sergeant standing on the bank had a bearing, a presence, an air of authority without the usual arrogance they had become used to in their captors. Another thing that made this man stand out from the rest of the *Kempeitai* was his age. He was white-haired, slow-moving, and seemed to Young's youthful eyes to be elderly. But he had a sense of presence and stayed watching while the prisoners had their scabies bath. Young christened him 'The Old Bloke', and for some strange reason had a hope that, somehow, because of him, things might improve.

Bill Young said later that none of them could have guessed that this moment marked a turning point in their years of imprisonment. The changes that took place were modest, but significant for their survival.

First of all, they were given buckets of disinfectant and were told to scrub their cells out and also give their own bodies a scrub. A spoonful of fresh vegetables appeared on their rice and, at midday, they were allowed to eat together at a long bench built for the purpose, in the passageway. This was an undreamed of luxury.

Young remembers one memorable morning when 'we were taken outside the prison gates and along a creek bed to a place where vines and scrub grew thickly. Imagine our surprise when we were told by gestures and mime to partake of the vine. Apparently the leaves were rich in vitamin C. We didn't need a second invitation as back in time we went and became like our primitive ancestors—leaf eaters. Cripes! They might have been rich in vitamin C but what a horrible taste! I happened to look up and there standing on the bank of the creek was the old Japanese sergeant. The look on his face was one of compassion.'

The old man was not at Outram Road Gaol for long. But one day Young saw him walking through the prison, not as a sergeant but as a full-blown captain. His three stars now sat on a thin blue line, and the ribbons on the handle of his sword were no longer brown but blue. To cap it all he was wearing highly polished riding boots and his tunic was ablaze with medals: 'He marched off to who knows where—a Japanese officer with credit. The pitch-black days of despair and the torment of those long, lonely hours spent in a solitary cell were at last coming to an end.'

# 10

# SURVIVING VICTORY

Towards the end of 1944, the war was going badly for the Japanese. They knew it, and so did the Allied prisoners of war from news reports clandestinely gleaned from the secret radios in Changi. Word even got to Outram Road Gaol, from prisoners being returned to the gaol from the Changi hospital, and even from the horse's mouth in early 1945 when American flyers, who had been shot down near Singapore, were put into Outram Road before they were executed.

Inside the gaol even the emaciated prisoners were seen as a labour resource for the increasingly desperate Japanese. Solitary confinement was no longer obligatory because the gaol was bursting at the seams. At first, work consisted of gardening around the gaol—if you were lucky, because there was always the chance of scoring some extra food even if it were only a snail or two—and, less appealingly, picking hemp from old, worn mooring ropes so new ropes could be manufactured.

About a hundred prisoners sat in four lines in the gaol courtyard teasing out hemp fibres from the old rope with their bare hands, and putting it into a pile in front of them. They then sorted them into bundles of twenty or so hemp fibres and spun them into long thin cords, which were then spun into a new hawser with the aid of a big wooden wheel. Bill Young reckoned that rope-making was a dying art, and wished it would die: 'Every now and then the guard would come on an inspection tour down through the lines of prisoners sitting cross-legged at their work. Woe betide the poor coot whose work didn't come up to scratch. We got over this problem by placing our bundles over the top of some teased out hemp and making the pile look nice and big. This worked well providing some lumdrum or other didn't put too much teased hemp under his own pile and make ours look that much smaller so we copped it from the guards.'

Gossip in the gaol made Young aware that in several of the cells there might be some of the Allied pilots who had been shot down. Young was on *benki* duty, in company with a new guard. When they came to a cell with one of the downed pilots in it, he made up some excuse, dashed back to his cell and retrieved a precious pencil stub and a piece of paper, and scurried back into the pilot's cell. 'I shoved the pencil and paper into the hands of this poor fellow who was lying down and I could see he had been badly burned. There was only time to greet him and ask him to write down all he could about himself and the war news—and that I would collect the paper when I returned his bucket.'

Later, Young managed to get back inside with only enough time to shake the injured pilot's hand and wish him good luck. At the door he turned and waved to the big man, obviously of Maori heritage, lying bandaged and lonely in the corner of his cell. He never saw him again. Back in his shared cell with Allen Minty—a former friend from the Sandakan days—he carefully unfolded the scrap of paper with its news: 'My friends call me Habbie. I am a Kiwi pilot and was flying a Hellcat fighter from an aircraft carrier on a raid at Palembang when I was shot down . . .'

The note went on to describe the success of D Day, and the subsequent fighting going on in Europe, the sinking of the German battleship *Tirpitz* in Norway, as well as the Allied victories in Russia. The news was tapped urgently along 'The Wall' using Morse code. Later, The Wall also reported the sad news that the injured Habbie had been sentenced to be executed.

On 4 November 1944, Bill Young turned eighteen—'Old enough to join the army', remarked the lad who had enlisted at fifteen. And what a birthday surprise he had when a flight of American B29 bombers dropped their lethal load on top of the naval base storage yards, causing great thunderheads of thick oily smoke to rise up into the sky. His mate Jimmy MP Brown yelled out, 'How do you like them apples, Nippon?' Both boys laughed and shouted their delight—then took the opportunity to dig some yams out of the garden in the absence of their frightened guards. Not long afterwards, the B29s came back again. Young says: 'Their noise came up behind us like the accumulation of a thousand storms. Then they were upon us. I counted 125—big, glimmering, threatening, beautifully swarming, avenging angels of B29s.'

The Japanese had been expecting air raids, which was why hemp-picking for the Outram Road workforce was diverted into the more urgent (for the Japanese) job of digging tunnels into the hills of Singapore and Johor as air raid shelters and storage areas—and also where they planned to make their last stand when the Allied forces invaded. This was extremely dangerous work, particularly as the men were down to half their normal body weight, weak, starved, and suffering from a raft of tropical diseases. The tunnels were dodgy affairs, not properly shored up. The roofs often collapsed without warning, killing or injuring the emaciated workers. The earth and rock were carted out of the tunnel by makeshift railway tracks over which skips full of the spoil were pushed by the slave labourers—a situation ripe for more accidents. However, the workers were slightly better fed, and although they were taken to work in chains, they could talk and plan.

There was also the unexpected bonus for prisoners thought to be mortally injured in an accident: the most convenient way for the Japanese to handle them was to have them transported to Changi to be cared for by Allied doctors. Before the work parties, the option of convincing the Japanese medicos that a man was so sick he was going to die and should be sent to Changi was more long-term and hazardous. Chris Neilson had managed to fake being so ill and unable to eat that he succeeded in getting back to Changi in 1943. Some others who tried that ploy failed. But you could be luckier in the tunnels where Neilson, back from his first Changi respite, was now working.

'There was a little bloke called Joe Smart, an Englishman,' Neilson explains. 'He was working and I says, "What's the matter, Joe?" "Oh," he says, "I'm bloody crook." It was obvious he was passing blood, amoebic dysentery. Well, as we got back about 50 feet into this hill, there was a slight incline, then it flattened off where the tunnels went T-shaped. As the loaded skips were coming down, I took a ride down with him to empty the skip and bring it back. On the way down I said, "Joe", and as he turned around I gave him a shove. He landed pretty heavy, and broke his pelvis. That saved his life. He got out to Changi and that's where they kept him for the rest of the war.'

Neilson decided to try this tactic himself, and staged a fall that he reckoned a Hollywood stunt man could not have bettered. The Japanese rushed over, while he pretended to be unconscious. The guards were all concerned because Neilson was regarded as a good worker. The guard in charge said, 'We need this man, he's a good mining worker. We need him bad—got to get him right.' As they tried to pour coconut oil down his throat, Neilson was trying to work out how an unconscious man should choke.

'After a couple of days they decided to take me back to Outram Road. They weren't too sure whether I might be putting up a trick so they left the cell door open. It was tough, but once you started, you had to keep going. They left the door open, and they put my food on the front step. Now that was the hard part. You're starving bloody hungry, and the food is there, six foot from you, and the *benki* bucket is in the other corner. So when you had a piddle, you just piddled yourself. That food stopped there. And when I'd see a Nip, just around the corner, having a look in, I'd kid I was trying to crawl to it, and all of a sudden I'd let out a yelp of pain and pretend to faint again. After three days they were satisfied that I was crook. So they let a *toban*, as they call it, a servant, come to change my pants, bring me food and help me onto the *benki* bucket.

'After a couple of weeks, with this bloke feeding me all the time, they brought the Jap doctor in—he was going to have a look at a few others to see if they could go to Changi. So he went to move me, and of course I threw another mickey and fell back, as if I'd fainted with the pain in my hips. He was satisfied. I heard him say in Japanese, "Yeah he's got something broken there, better send him out." I'll never forget it. They put me out and left me lying on a stretcher in the yard. And one of the Nips called my number, 551. Then he said in Malay, "You're not sick. You want to go to Changi where there's good food." Anyway, out I went.'

Neilson was transported on a flatbed truck, and dumped on the ground outside the Changi gates. Major Clark asked him how he was, but he needed to know if the Japanese had gone. Then Colonel Glyn White, who had also picked up Neilson when he had first come from Outram Road a year and a half earlier, arrived. He said, 'Neilson, you bastard, you cost me ten dollars. I said you'd be out in three months. It's three and a half!' This time they managed to keep him in Changi until the war ended.

A big Queenslander, Private Herb Trackson, was also working in the tunnels. He had tried to escape from Sandakan but was betrayed by locals, and—as it happened luckily for him—was sentenced to four years at Outram Road, which meant he missed the death marches. Trackson didn't mind working in the tunnels so much because of the slightly better food, but he too decided to get back to Changi by faking an accident. While working with some Englishmen he got them to pull some earth over him with their *chunkels* (hoes) as though a part of the roof had collapsed. He was first taken to the Japanese hospital in Singapore, where the medical staff were so revolted by his body, which was covered in sores and scabies and encrusted with dirt from the tunnels, that they did not touch him at all, but asked what was wrong with him. Through an interpreter he said he had hurt his back, could not walk, and had no feeling in his feet. Happily for Trackson he was transported to Changi and was carried inside, away from the sight of any Japanese.

'Someone asked me, "What's the matter digger?" I said, "Have the Jap guards gone?" When they said yes, I jumped up off the stretcher and said, "Well for Christ's sake, give me something to eat!" Then the doctors came to interview me, and they were amazed how I got away with it. They put a screen around me and four days later they told me that I had gone to pieces . . .'

Herb Trackson had a nervous breakdown. But he recovered quickly with extra food, and although the doctors kept an eye out for visiting Japanese doctors and had Trackson turn on an act with his 'bad back', only six weeks later he was back at Outram Road and working in the tunnels again until the end of the war. He said he 'looked like a big pig' to the other prisoners when he got back to the gaol.

Private Bert 'Bluey' Rollason was working in the tunnels, but the soles of his feet became so sore he couldn't walk, so he said he couldn't leave his cell. His rations were immediately cut in half: 'You got bugger all rations to start with, so half of half is not much, I tell you.' But his attempt to get back to Changi failed: 'Oh, I got that bloody weak. One morning when the guard came to let the other tunnel workers out to go to work, I thought to myself, "There's only one way I'm going to survive, and that is to get out of this cell." I called a guard over and told him I wanted to go to work. This particular guard called me "Eskimo". I had red hair and freckles and they didn't believe I was an Australian, so I told them I was an Eskimo. He brought up another guard and pointed to me. "Eskimo die soon." I said to him, "Eskimo no die you bastard" and I told him to let me join the working party, limping around as best I could, and after a couple of weeks with the extra food I came good.'

Bill Young also worked in the tunnels and saw that some injured workers were sent back to Changi. He knew that the Japanese were strangely spooked by the sight of blood and decided to fake an accident. Young says: 'I tumbled on a heap of dirt and bit my bloody tongue for a supply of bloody blood, in order to have a good supply to spit out at the end of my fall. Nearly bit my tongue in half, and stayed moaning and groaning in my cell for a week, but the Japanese doctor must have gone on strike—not even a house call. If I'd known the war was nearly over I wouldn't have tried that caper! Me mouth was as sore as a coot for weeks after.'

There was no Changi for Young, and it was painful to eat his meagre rice ration. He stayed at Outram Road until the end of the war.

Private Stan Davis had better luck in the tunnels. There were two Australians named Davis in Sandakan, and Sapper Eric 'Mo' Davis might have been involved with the underground movement. The confusion of names was enough—presumably in the interests of *Kempeitai* thoroughness—to land both Davises two years at Outram Road Gaol. Stan Davis, later to be a master builder in civilian life, was unimpressed by the amateur way the Japanese attempted to shore up the tunnel roofs with heavy baulks of timber. Sure enough, the tunnel Stan was working in collapsed. 'I was whacked across my chin by a big five inch by five piece of heavy timber. It stung a bit, but that was all.

Luckily for me there was some blood and that panicked the Japanese. I was a bit stunned, but conscious, and made out I was worse than I actually was. I've known blokes put *chunkels* through their feet to get taken back to hospital but in this case, my mate Frank Martin said, "How are you going mate? Keep it up, I think you'll get to Changi." They threw me on a stretcher down to the Singapore Hospital, and I heard the Jap doctor say the magic word "Changi". And I stayed there until the end of the war.'

In June 1945, Rod Wells decided that his health had reached the point where he had to take an immediate gamble on being shifted to Changi. If he waited for the Japanese to make the decision, he feared that he would die at Outram Road, or within days of getting to Changi. Like Chris Neilson and Stan Davis, he collapsed at work, took the beatings and refused food. After the Japanese doctor made his inspection, Wells heard 'the lovely words "641, Changi"'.

Dr Glyn White was one of the team of Australian doctors who worked on the men brought in from Outram Road. 'I was only about seven stone at that stage myself, but with Rod it was just like picking up a weeny little baby. He was unrecognisable. You could count the surface anatomy of every bone he had in his body, he was so emaciated. He just relaxed as soon as I got him in my arms. He was almost too weak to speak, but he still had a smile. You could see the smile under his whiskers, and his eyes were all deeply sunken. He just looked awful. It was one of the most emotional episodes that I had the whole time I was a prisoner of war.'

Like Trackson, the medicos managed to keep Wells in Changi until the surrender, then less than three months away.

Towards the end of 1944 and on to 1945, the executions at Outram Road Gaol continued apace—sometimes a single execution, at other times in groups. Both occasions were marked with a welcome extra issue of small burnt rice cakes to the Allied prisoners. Teenage prisoner

Bill Young, bored in his cell, was grateful for any diversion, and he likened the executions to sitting outside the Civic Theatre listening to the sounds of a Hopalong Cassidy movie to which he was too poor to buy a ticket. Young says: 'There would be a pistol shot, followed by a long silence—footsteps again, and then more silence. Another shot, and I'd call out, "Good shooting Hoppy, I think you got the varmint."'

Sometimes the Japanese executed their own varmints, and senior officers were not spared, usually executed for failing higher command's expectations of success in a battle. While on *benki* duties, Young noticed a Japanese army guard in full battle dress standing outside a particular cell on the second floor, which was most unusual. Young thought there must be a high-ranking officer in there, as all his meals were brought to him on a tray, and he had regular visits from the *Kempeitai* commandant. He caught another glimpse of him being marched away to his court martial, a middle-aged man, 'his uniform covered in fruit salad' and the red ribbons of a field officer, probably a general.

The Wall carried a frenzy of tapping in Morse code speculating on the general's fate. His crime must have been particularly heinous because the high-ranking officer was refused the 'honour' of a beheading, and was shot by a firing squad. Later, Young, out on a working party, saw where guards had dug into a bank beside the gaol to make an enclosure and saw a row of small stools arranged in a line—the front stalls—and behind, two hard-backed chairs, the 'dress circle', where *Kempeitai* officers had watched the execution in relative comfort. Young recalled: 'The call to attention began the sideshow of sound effects. This carrying on outside wasn't just a sideshow, it was a full-blown circus. I've always loved a circus. Crouched down in my cell with an ear to the outside wall, the sudden sharp crack of a volley of rifle fire made me jump, and the penny dropped. "They've shot the bloody general!"'

In September 1943, during a special operation code-named 'Jaywick', Australian commandos from Z Special Force voyaged from Australia in a 70-foot wooden ship, *Krait*, a former Japanese fishing boat. They sailed undetected to the waters off Singapore, paddled 31 miles in collapsible canoes and successfully infiltrated Singapore harbour, placing limpet bombs against the hulls of Japanese ships, sinking or badly damaging seven of them. They escaped unscathed— later returning to Australia. The Japanese were mystified and thought it must have been a local conspiracy. They arrested, tortured and executed Chinese, Malays and already interned Europeans who, of course, knew nothing about what had happened.

A year later, buoyed with this success, another Z Special Force group tried a sabotage attempt, again led by the first leader of Operation Jaywick, now Major Ivan Lyon. This time the operation was code-named 'Rimau'. They travelled to Indonesia in a British submarine to the uninhabited island of Merapas, from where they commandeered a Malay junk, *Mustika*. This time they were not so lucky, and the force of 23 men, six British and seventeen Australians, was attacked and captured by the Japanese in October 1944. Remarkably, Lyon and six other men did manage to paddle into Singapore harbour and sink three ships. Only ten commandos survived—nine Australian and one British—and they were imprisoned at Outram Road Gaol. Early in July 1945, the ten survivors were put on trial for espionage, found guilty and executed.

The 'Rimau Ten' were beheaded on 7 July, barely a month before the war ended. Bert Rollason was the last to see them alive. He was on roster to collect and empty their *benki* buckets, but was only able to exchange a few words with them. 'A little army bus arrived, and they were all handcuffed and tied up, and as they got into the bus they were talking and carrying on, and appearing to be quite cheerful. I did get a chance to say goodbye to them.'

The Japanese claimed that the Rimau Ten had been well treated before their executions, but Rollason, who was given the job of cleaning up their cell, found the blood-spattered walls mute evidence that they had been savagely bashed before being taken away to be executed.

One of the last *Kempeitai* atrocities relating to Outram Road took place four days after the war ended on 15 August. Nine Allied pilots and aircrew held at Outram Road had been captured after having been shot down while attempting to bomb the oil fields at Palembang. One was the injured New Zealand pilot 'Habbie' (Lieutenant John Kerle Tipaho Haberfield), who had given Bill Young news of the progress of the war. *Kempeitai* officers, in full ceremonial dress, decided to avenge the insult to their divine emperor that these pilots represented, despite the unconditional surrender already ordered by Emperor Hirohito. The 'Palembang Nine' were taken to a beach near Changi, beheaded, their bodies put into a boat and set adrift. These *Kempeitai* officers were later arrested, but committed suicide in captivity before they could be brought before a court.

In Changi, the prisoners had radios and knew what was happening in the outside world. But they could not predict how the Japanese would react, and there was evidence that the Japanese were going to be bad losers. Former officer George McNeilly says: 'Towards the end of the war we wondered why they were excavating big pits just outside the gaol walls, and we were going out daily to dig them. Then some men discovered that the pits were being built for us to be machine-gunned into [in the event of an Allied invasion] so they told their friends and soon the whole camp knew.'

Sadly that is when some men, who had hung on through all the privations of three and a half years, finally cracked. A number committed suicide in a particularly horrible manner, only days before their actual liberation. They threw themselves down toilet boreholes. Sydney Piddington was a member of the Changi Concert Party:

'The Australian command asked us to run the radio and get hourly reports, which we did. As it became more and more dangerous it was a rule not to tune in until right on time. However, I tuned in about five minutes early and heard the last few bars of Paul Whiteman's band playing *Rhapsody in Blue*. Then I heard the first news of the dropping of the bomb on Hiroshima.'

Unlike their comrades at Outram Road, those Allied troops in the main base camp, Changi, were soon aware that the war was over. Sergeant Stan Arneil recalls: 'There was a young fellow dropped onto the aerodrome and he looked like a pirate. He must have been about six foot three. He seemed to be as wide as an ox, in great health, with a revolver and all that sort of thing—and he looked absolutely beautiful.'

Chris Neilson thought so too: 'You would have thought he was Flash Gordon. He looked the part—he'd have given Flash Gordon a hiding. He strolled in amongst us and we were all cheering like bloody hell. A Jap raced up to meet him. Evidently they had been told that he would be coming in on his own. This Jap came up, bowed and said, "I will take you to the commandant of the Changi prison camp." This bloke just went WHACK! and lifted him under the chin. He said, "You take me nowhere, you bring the bloody commandant to me," and he gave him a kick in the arse as he ran away. The next minute, up came the commandant at the double. Oh, it was lovely! You should have heard us cheer. He rushed up and started bowing, and this bloke said, "Never mind about that bloody crap. Look at those skeletons over there—you're responsible." Oh, did he tear into him!'

The commando had entered a military time warp. Since 1942, the army had abandoned the tunics and gaiters, and adopted loose camouflaged jungle uniforms. Blancoed belts and shiny brass work were no more. Officers were not saluted as rigorously either. But Colonel Black Jack Galleghan's rigid regime in Changi had remained frozen in time.

While the Japanese in charge of Changi had obeyed their emperor's order immediately, the *Kempeitai* at Outram Road did not quickly acknowledge the new realities. The prisoners had been confined to their cells for two weeks, without knowing why, but they sensed change of some kind was in the air, and thought it best to play it safe. They feared the *Kempeitai* were more likely to kill them than open the Outram Road gates.

Bill Young was sharing a cell with two Tamils, whom he did not find congenial. One was ridden with venereal disease and close to death, and the other was unfriendly and hostile to the white man. Young's scratches on the wall told him it was 15 August 1945. Two events marked that particular day: 'The first came with our rice, or rather the bowl of water that came with it, but it wasn't water, it was milk. Milk from a can, but for all that, still milk, and didn't it taste great. I licked at mine like a cat and made it last as long as possible. Bloody marvellous it was, nectar of the Gods. The second thing was my two Tamil companions must have felt a stirring of the possibilities, and from being a "white bastard", I had now become a "sahib" to them. Such are the fortunes of war.'

Then, an anti-climax: for four long days, the only sounds heard were the steady flip-flop of the guards' sandals as they slapped their way along the concrete passageways. On 19 August, the key of Young's cell door turned silently, and the door swung open. The prisoners cautiously stepped out, down the two steps and into the passageway. Young saw two guards—but their swords had gone. Then he heard the sudden shouted command, 'Come!': 'This was the command we had heard for so long which brought us out of the cells for the last time and told us we were free at last. But the word "come" was too late for so many of my mates.'

Out from the cells, on both sides of the block, the prisoners stumbled and shuffled, still afraid to believe the evidence of liberation that was unfolding. They wanted and hoped, but they were cautious. Young says: 'I went over to my old cobber MP Jimmy Brown, saying, "This is it!" Always the super pessimist, Jimmy replied, "Naw Billy, don't give me more bull about the Yanks landing at Penang."'

The prisoners were herded up to the chief warden of the gaol, who sat behind a table near the exit door. Speaking through an interpreter, he said, 'Today we are sending you back to Changi prisoner-of-war camp. But you must come back later, to complete your sentence.' Young recalls, 'At long last we were in the tunnel, with the main gates swinging open as we came out into the light of a free world . . .'

At Changi gaol, four days of freedom had already been experienced, but many found it difficult to relate to people from an almost forgotten world. Stan Arneil says: 'It was quite odd. We had gone into the army as kids really, with an average age between 21 and 22, down to 17, and I remember two nurses came. They were absolutely delightful and we were sitting in a long 150-yard hut on our bamboo slats. These two nurses walked right through the hut and spoke to every man there and I don't think one person replied. It was absolutely lovely to see these beautiful women. They were clean and fresh, they had lovely cheeks and their hair was nice, and we just sat and looked at them.'

Many prisoners did not know how vulnerable they were. Leon de Castries recalls that it was too ridiculous for words to keep them in the camp. De Castries and two mates got transport into Singapore city and went straight to the wharves. The Royal Navy already had corvettes and frigates pulled up there and as they stood on the wharf, the sailors began throwing loaves of bread to them. De Castries says: 'We hadn't tasted bread and we were tearing into it. Then a few of us were invited on board, and that was a tragedy. They invited us into the wardroom and they sat us down to a meal. Of course we just couldn't take this western food straight off. There must've been half a dozen others in their boardroom, and one fellow actually died on the wharf getting back. Our stomachs couldn't take it. They had contracted to such an extent that we couldn't eat meat. We were actually served up meat!'

Two of the earliest visitors to Changi were the Supreme Allied Commander, South-East Asia Command, Lord Louis Mountbatten, accompanied by his wife Lady Edwina Mountbatten. Some of the prisoners just released from Outram Road had started to come in, and one of Mountbatten's officers looked at them, and said, 'They'll die.' Chris Neilson remembers one of the doctors saying, 'Oh no, we've had them a lot worse than that, they'll live.'

They then brought forward Chris Neilson, not long out of Outram Road, and paraded him in front of the Mountbattens, clad only in a small loin cloth to reveal not only his emaciated state, but the stab wounds from the guards' bayonets and other injuries, including whip lashes and sores. He was skeletal at six stone—half his normal body weight. Neilson says: 'I only had this little thing on, you know, like Tarzan wears, just to cover my old feller, and I was asked to drop that and turn around. I said, "No way in the world". And Lady Mount-batten said, "Oh don't worry, just treat me like a soldier." I said, "That's impossible, you're a woman," and I kept my hands over my front while they turned me around and counted all the bayonet jabs that had started festering.'

Neilson said that he and some of the other Outram Road inmates should be sent back there to pick out the bad guards, and put them under similar conditions—and halve their rations. One of Mount-batten's officers said, 'Christ, they'll all bloody die if you halve the rations.' Neilson responded, 'You don't want them to live, do you? We were on less than half rations and we didn't die.'

Mountbatten personally ordered a British Gurkha officer, a colonel, to take Neilson back to Outram Road Gaol to identify the guards who might be war criminals, and also those not so culpable. Neilson was very keen to do this, because he particularly wanted to get his revenge on the Korean guard he called The Groper who had busted his hands and given him a depressed fracture of the skull. But he said nothing about this to his escort.

Back at Outram Road, the guards had been stripped of their clothes and, wearing only skimpy loin cloths, had been locked into the filthy cells where they had imprisoned the Allied prisoners of war, while their identities were established. Among them was the brutal *Kempeitai* sergeant who had run Outram Road Gaol for most of the war. Much to his chagrin, Chris Neilson was unable to find The Groper, but he was able to identify one of the few humane guards, whom he had called The Frenchman, who had actually smuggled vitamin B tablets to him on occasions at great risk to himself.

One guard he did spot was Very Special, the Outram Road executioner, whom he had first encountered during his torture sessions at the YMCA building shortly after his escape attempt in 1942. Very Special had beaten him savagely, then later at Outram Road he used to tell Neilson how he was looking forward to cutting his head off with 'one chop'. Neilson's death sentence was commuted to three years of solitary confinement, but Very Special continued to bait him. Because he had never broken him, he had respect for him, which he expressed to the British officer when Neilson asked to go into Very Special's cell, saying in Japanese that Neilson was a 'very brave man'. This didn't cut much ice with Neilson, who decided that a spot of instant justice was in order. 'I said, "They're going to hang you, you bastard. Do you remember telling me about the girls at Bondi you were going to have?"'

Despite his emaciated state, The Reb, knuckle man and pugilist to the end, suddenly delivered one of his vintage left hooks and hit Very Special hard enough to knock him to the ground. 'When he hit the floor, I couldn't resist it and picked up the four by four by ten inch wooden "pillow" and hit him over the head. I thought I cracked his skull, but it must have only knocked the hard-headed bastard out, because he did turn up later at the war crimes trials. The British colonel went screaming bloody mad, and said, "Christ! British justice must prevail. These men have got to have a trial.'" Neilson had to promise not to do anything like that again, or the gaol tour was off.

Back in Changi, Neilson met up with Herbert James 'Ringer' Edwards, a survivor of the Thai-Burma Railway who had little reason to feel benevolent towards his Japanese captors. In 1943, Edwards and two other prisoners had put their stockmen's skills to good effect by killing some skinny yak cattle to provide some protein for themselves and their mates. They were caught and sentenced to death by crucifixion. Edwards and the others were bound at the wrists with wire, suspended from a tree, and beaten with baseball bats. Edwards managed to free his right hand. The wire was then driven through the palms of both hands. He hung in that way for 63 hours. Some of his friends managed to smuggle some food to him, but both his companions died. Incredibly, Ringer survived, to return to Changi and eventually Australia after the completion of the railway. (Novelist Nevil Shute used Edwards as the basis for the character of Joe Harmon in his 1950 novel *A Town Like Alice*, later made into a film and a television mini-series.)

Neilson and Edwards were keen to give a bit of their own medicine to the Japanese, and were particularly infuriated to see a *Kempeitai* corporal stacking Japanese rifles in a heap in the grounds of Changi gaol. Both men knew how brutal the *Kempeitai* had been and, on the spur of the moment, Ringer said, 'Hey, hold this bayonet.' As Neilson held the bayonet in front of his chest, 'Ringer pushed the bastard onto it', killing him instantly.

The Australian military police arrested Edwards, and Neilson was put under guard in a hut. Who should happen to walk through this hut but Lady Mountbatten, who recognised Neilson from their earlier encounter.

'Lady Mountbatten said, "What are you in for?" I said, "Oh we were out chasing a few Nips to give them a bit of a hurry up like they gave us. And our officer found out and we've been charged." She said, "How many of you?" I said, "Two. Ringer, me mate, he's up in the tower under guard." She said, "I'll be back." She demanded to be taken to see Ringer Edwards, and asked what he was in there for. They told her the story and she said, "Go and release that man immediately. They should be paid for killing these bastards." Then she said to Ringer, "How would you like to come down and see Mountbatten's flagship?" He's the only man in the AIF who visited Mountbatten's bloody flagship. [Laughs.] He was a tough man, Ringer. Eventually he pinched enough cattle to finance himself into a farm.'

Strangely enough, the enthusiasm of Australians to take revenge on the Japanese for their often bestial treatment over three and a half years melted away when the war actually ended. The savage action by Chris Neilson and Ringer Edwards, although understandable in view of what they went through, was an aberration.

Private George Aspinall, the man to be known as 'The Changi Photographer', had a more typical attitude. He said there were a number of dead Japanese found at the back of Changi gaol down at the beach: 'Whether they were shot by Chinese or by our people, we don't know. But we were so pleased, so elated, that the whole thing was over and we would be going back home, I don't think a lot of us were looking for revenge.'

Sergeant Jack Sloan said it never occurred to him to bash a Japanese just because he was a Japanese. 'I knew enough of them to realise that their code of conduct was completely foreign to us. We were aware that some of the occupation forces had made it possible for people to take action if they wished. A story going around was that one Australian was given the opportunity and he took it, but in doing so broke his wrist. It's debatable whether that was worthwhile.'

Private Eddie Henderson realised that guards who had ill-treated them were taken away and new guards brought in. The Japanese knew it was all over and probably wanted to avoid incidents. 'The Australian attitude, I think, is that you can't kick a dog while it's down and they looked so beaten and so subservient that we couldn't do anything to them. But if it had been the ones that had ill-treated us, we probably would have been into them.'

Even Australians in far away prison camps in Japan, like Gordon Maxwell, were surprisingly benign in their attitudes to their defeated captors: 'Some of our fellows did catch one of the Jap guards and they put him in the guard room in the little solitary confinement cell for a couple of days, but the novelty wore off and they just let him go.'

When revenge did occur, it was usually an isolated instance. Private Ray Myors was still in Thailand when the war ended: 'We were down at the bank of a river in Bangkok and this particular fellow and a couple of his mates were a little bit high and the worse for wear from drinking *lau*—the local brew, a type of wine spirit which was the only thing available. When he saw this party of Japanese coming across the river in a canoe about 20 feet long, this fellow on his own without any assistance from anyone, just swam out on the river and tipped it over. Then one after another he held the Japanese under until they drowned. He got his fair share of commentary from our point of view because we didn't agree.'

Dr Rowley Richards thought it was quite incredible that so little revenge was extracted: 'Despite the threats that many prisoners of war had made against the Japanese, when they had the opportunity, they did nothing. While there were some who claimed that they dealt with a few, I personally doubt it because the bad Japs who knew that they were going to be in trouble just plain shot through—they disappeared.'

Major John Wyett was fit enough to be with the senior officers in Changi who welcomed not only Lord Louis Mountbatten, but General

Sir William Slim, Commander of the Fourteenth Army, fresh from his victories in Burma and the architect of the plan to drop commandos into Changi to prevent the massacre of prisoners of war he expected the Japanese to carry out. Wyett says: 'I was able to join our two Commanders, Colonel "Eb" Holmes and Colonel Fred Galleghan, with several others of the staff. We all looked reasonably presentable, if still a bit skinny, when we met the two visitors with their respective staffs. The contrast between the leaders was most striking. Slim expected to see a crowd of dishevelled and half-starved prisoners and had dressed accordingly. He and his staff were all in battledress, Slim wearing a black beret with a bullet hole through it, memento of a near miss by a Japanese sniper in Burma, and a cotton shirt which had seen better days, sagging off his shoulders with the weight of his badges of rank.'

Lord Mountbatten was immaculate. Wyett had heard the apocryphal story of when his ship was sunk in the Mediterranean. Legend had it he was still clutching his waterproof uniform box when rescued and came on deck shortly afterwards pristine as ever. He certainly was sartorially splendid when he greeted the British and Australian commanders in Changi, with his white shirt setting off the coloured ribbons of his decorations and gold braid, beautifully laundered white shorts, white stockings and highly polished black shoes. The Changi commanders appreciated Bill Slim's thoughtful gesture in choosing battle dress, and took it as a compliment.

Two days later, Wyett was chafing against the restrictions forbidding them to leave the camp. He and an officer friend, Bill Anker, managed to 'acquire' a jeep and decided to go AWOL and do some sightseeing. Exhilarated by the new sense of freedom and the wind blowing in their faces, they noticed a sign indicating an office set up to co-ordinate the evacuation of the POWs, so they went in. There was a Red Cross section, and while talking to the officer in charge, Wyett noticed a large map pinned to a board behind his desk showing the location of the various prison camps. He was intrigued to see that Changi was marked 'Luxury Camp' and presumed they must have reached this conclusion through Japanese propaganda!

Driving on, Bill Anker found out that the Japanese troops were being concentrated in an area along the Bukit Timah Road, so they decided to go there. They were greeted with the extraordinary sight of thousands of Japanese soldiers moving slowly and in an orderly fashion into their allotted positions. Some cast listless and incurious glances at the two Australians as they mingled freely among them in order to get a closer look at the uniforms and equipment. 'However, not all of them were uninterested,' Wyett recalls. 'A tap on my arm caused me to turn, and there was a Japanese major staring at me and saying in quite good English, "One of these days you will finish your sentence." I did not remember having seen this arrogant Japanese before, but obviously he knew a good deal about me. He would not have been *Kempeitai* because their officers had "done a Gordon Bennett", as the troops used to say whenever anyone attempted an escape. The Jap officer melted away into the crowd as Bill came over to join me, and we stood there, two lone Allied officers surrounded on all sides by a veritable sea of Japanese troops. Seething inwardly at this offensive remark, I said to Bill, "I think we'd better get out of here before I murder someone."'

The two Australians drove down to the docks where HMS *Sussex* was lying alongside, having come in as part of the invasion force. They went aboard, not forgetting to salute the quarterdeck, and were conducted below to the wardroom by two of the officers. Seating Wyett and Anker at a table, they said, 'Don't tell us what you would most like—we know.' Wyett remembers, 'With that they disappeared and came back beaming, bearing a freshly baked loaf, a huge slab of butter and a pot of jam. I cannot remember having had a more enjoyable meal before or since. When one has not tasted any of these everyday foods for so long they become gourmet delights, and have remained so.'

Simple gastronomic pleasures were yet to come for Bill Young and the other Outram Road Gaol alumni, still in their dank cells, four days after the war had officially ended. But on 19 August, they were freed at last and taken by truck to Changi Gaol. There Young was reunited with his great friend Paddy O'Toole, who had survived his stint on the Thai-Burma Railway and whose 'great lovable Irish face' beamed its welcome as he picked up the frail stick that was all that was left of Young, and carried him into the hospital. Young says: 'It was so strange. We didn't even want to go over to the battalion, or even mix with anyone else but ourselves. The others felt the same and we all stayed together.'

Young had fixed it that a friend at Outram Road, John 'Becky' Sharpe, an English soldier, was taken with him to Changi Hospital. 'I didn't think the Poms would feed him as well as we could.' With the war over, journalists and photographers came in to Changi, and Young said that Sharpe was propped up in bed to be photographed for the *Illustrated London News*. The shot of his amazingly emaciated frame was cabled all around the world, complete with cheeky gap-toothed grin. It only takes about a week to lose that skeletal look with proper food, but people who saw that photograph now and then marvelled that any man could recover from such a starved state. Others at Outram Road were in similar condition.

Later, after a quick medical once-over and some limited food to eat, the Outram Roaders wandered out beyond the now open wire, and down to Changi Beach.

'We sat there, and we stayed all night,' Young reccalled. 'A great big moon came up, and the world was at peace. We watched the sea washing across the sand—you wouldn't see a more beautiful sight, with this great beach around us and the palm trees and this huge moon that came up out of the sea, up and up and up. All of us just looked up at the stars we hadn't seen for so long, because there was a light that burned every night, all night. For over two years I'd sat in different cells in Outram Road, each one the same, and never, ever seeing the night sky.

'And that was the greatest night I have ever seen. I've had some good nights, but there will never be a better night than that one. All of us there, we all felt the same. No one wanted to go, we just wanted to sit there—the huge moon and millions of stars—the sounds of an ocean at peace. No one wanted to talk, we didn't need to. The night said it all for us. We just marvelled and wondered, each tucked up in private thoughts. That was our introduction to peace.'

As the dawn of their first full day of freedom broke, Young—still a teenager—took a stick and scratched a message in the sand, soon to be covered by the incoming tide: 'There is absolutely nothing we cannot do, given the time, eventually.'

# 11

# THE LEGACY

The war had ended suddenly and unexpectedly on 15 August 1945 and most surviving prisoners of war wanted to get home quickly. The Allied command created an organisation to expedite their return, Repatriation of Allied Prisoners of War and Internees (RAPWI), which could hardly produce quick results, with former prisoners in camps in Indo-China, Thailand, Burma, Java, Sumatra, the Netherlands East Indies, Ambon and British North Borneo. About 2700 Australians were distributed through Japan, Korea, Manchuria and Hainan. Then there were nearly 6000 Australians on Singapore island and Johor in Malaya. Apart from the tyranny of distance, shipping and aircraft were scarce.

However, even if transport was immediately available, many of the prisoners of war were so weak and ill that it would have been inadvisable for them to risk the rigours of a sea journey. Finding them in those distant camps and carefully feeding them limited meals to restore their health and stamina were necessary measures before they could travel.

The frustrated ex-POWs immediately re-dubbed RAPWI as 'Retention of All Prisoners of War Indefinitely'. Many did not get back to

Australia until late October from distant collection and assembly locations in a number of countries. Of the 22 000 Australian servicemen and women who had become prisoners of war of the Japanese, only 14 000 came home.

Post-traumatic stress disorder was not recognised in those days. Most returning POWs simply wanted to leave the army and get on with their lives. But their lives had changed drastically, not only because of what had happened to them, but because they had been in a time warp for three and a half years. Some soldiers reported missing in action had remained so to their loved ones and families until the war actually ended. Some wives, believing their husbands to be dead, had formed new relationships. There were returning prisoners who only discovered that one or both of their parents had died once they were back in Australia.

Australia had changed too. Women, who had entered the workforce during the war, had enjoyed freedoms they were loath to give up when the servicemen returned. Even the radio sounded unfamiliar, with jazz and crooners like Bing Crosby being universally popular, including on the ABC, as Aunty loosened her corset.

Some simply could not cope and often took to alcohol to drown their sorrows. And there were instances of distraught ex-POWs killing their unfaithful partners and then themselves. Many, though, were simply grateful to be home and were able to resume normal life, seemingly shrugging off the trauma they had been through. More than half a century later, former prisoners of war still vividly recalled the unfamiliar luxury of simply being home. For the first few weeks ashore, one returnee found he could only sleep for a few hours. He would rise, well before dawn, quietly make himself a cup of tea, then wander the streets as the dawn broke. Other members of his family would ask, nervously, if he was all right. He found it difficult to explain his pleasure as each morning he rediscovered his freedom and delighted in doing the simple things that confirmed the reality that he was home at last.

Historian Hank Nelson drew attention to the age factor:

> Prisoners who had enlisted at twenty years of age were coming home at twenty-four or -five. They had missed the years when their vigour was at its greatest; when they would have played their best sport; when they would have selected a career; and when they would have married. They were all conscious of the distorted pattern in their lives. They felt a need to try and catch up; some were uncertain that they could do so.

The long-term physical and mental costs of imprisonment on individuals are difficult to determine. It seems likely that when the body weight drops by more than a third, when conditions are so bad that a third of the prisoners die, and when there is intense stress for more than three years, then there will be lasting wounds. Hank Nelson said, 'Perhaps the extent of recovery is more surprising than the frequency of illness.'

The survivors of Outram Road Gaol were doubly traumatised, having endured physical torture and being denied the companionship of their fellow prisoners in Changi, or even the comradeship of the forced labour camps of the Thai-Burma Railway. Cooped up in compulsory solitary confinement, their survival depended on the resources of their own minds to stave off boredom, and even their return to Australia in late 1945 was, in its own way, another psychological challenge to cope with.

## CHRIS NEILSON

On his repatriation, Chris Neilson spent fourteen months in Brisbane's 112th Australian General Hospital, which, in 1947, was renamed

Repatriation General Hospital, Greenslopes. On top of all his other medical problems, which included continuing dysentery, a perforated bowel and a depressed fracture of the skull, he had picked up hepatitis on his way back from Singapore. He was in hospital for so long that he could hardly bear to face the outside world: 'You'd walk down the street and think someone was looking at you, and you'd glance down to see if your fly was open or you'd pissed yourself or something.'

He was too ill to attend the Tokyo War Crimes Trials from 3 May to 12 November in 1946, but did send testimony from his hospital bed to help convict the worst war criminals encountered at Outram Road Gaol. There were two Outram Road survivors included in the ten Australian witnesses at the trials—Lieutenant Gordon Weynton (who had been part of the Sandakan underground movement, had helped to build the secret radio and was sentenced to ten years at Outram Road) and Lieutenant Penrod Dean, who served two years.

There was minimal psychological care for the returned prisoners of war, although it was sorely needed. Neilson, and others like him, were told to forget all about the bad things that had happened to them and 'put it behind them'. Neilson, whose bullshit detector was well honed, reacted characteristically when a psychologist said to him, 'You've got to forget about it completely': 'I said, "You stupid bastard, if you were there for five bloody minutes, you'd never forget it all your bloody life."'

Unable or unwilling to talk about their experiences with friends and family, the former prisoners of war sought out the company of their comrades—as did the survivors of Outram Road Gaol.

'I think that's why most of us used to keep together,' Neilson explained. 'So many POWs in Brisbane would go down to the boozer together. You couldn't assimilate for a while, you know, you couldn't get used to the way of thinking. It took a good while. I think most of them would agree with that. The first few months they might have gone out with a woman, but very soon after they were back with their mates because they seemed to be the only ones they could converse with. You only felt safe when you were with your mates—like "Ringer" Edwards—even if we got drunk and got into a lot of trouble. But it was the only time I felt really secure.

'For instance, down at the Pacific Hotel, a sailor came in—a poor bloody sailor, he'd be as big as me—and he bumped me and me beer spilled over. I said, "God strike me. Haven't you got enough room?" He said, "I'll make bloody room, you bastard, if I want it." I said, "You'd better start making it if you call me a bastard." He swung and I just— bang! I had to take him to the hospital and he got eleven stitches in his gob, bled all over me. Later my mother said, "Oh Gawd, you haven't been fighting again?"

'I know this, I couldn't go into a bloody cafe. If I was as hungry as buggery do you think I can go in there and order a meal? Had to find some bugger looked like he was hungry and ask him to have a feed with me. I couldn't do it on my own.'

There were strange disconnections. Neilson's three brothers had been soldiers too. They had all been infantrymen, one had been a forward scout and 'had killed hundreds of Japs'. But it took Neilson three years before he could talk to them about what had happened to him in gaol.

In the 1980s, Neilson was living in a war service retirement home in Collaroy with his wife, Mavis, and still having nightmares about Outram Road. It was the same for many other POWs of the Japanese. 'The worst nightmare in my book was the one you lived with all the time in Outram Road. The guard would say, "551, today I come to cut your head off." Often in the dream they would come without the Holy Man, who would have been there had they been taking you out to be executed. They played so many tricks, trying to break you. In Outram Road, McGregor and I worked out if they did come in to our cells with the Holy Man, we'd each grab the latrine bucket and chuck it over his head and hit the first bloke with the wooden "pillow". But always the dream seems to end at the door. They didn't come in.

'If you have a bad dream—anyone will tell you this—get up and walk around. Don't lay in bed. Get up and walk around and you'll forget about it and go back to sleep. Don't just stay there, because it'll come back again.'

While Chris Neilson was living in Cairns with his parents he met Mavis, his future wife, and they were married in 1948. Shortly after they met, he came down with a bout of malaria, and told Mavis that he had been offered a job in Borneo with the Shell Oil Company, and talked to his parents about it. Mavis sensibly said it was no good going to Borneo if he was still getting malaria! 'So we got married, and I said this is no good, I simply have to get a job. So in 1948 I went down to the wharf, and there was an old Swede there who was a splicer of wires and ropes—which was my trade actually. He said he was leaving, and asked me if I'd take over his job. So I worked for Howard Smiths then for the next ten years, doing all the wiring and splicing. I spliced wire down there to lift a 50-tonne train off a ship.'

But in 1958 he had to go to Brisbane for an eye operation. Dr Bernie Clark, who had looked after him in Greenslopes repatriation hospital, told him, 'Never front a Board—they'll put you on a TPI [Totally and Permanently Incapacitated] pension': 'Well, I couldn't afford to go on a TPI in those days. Anyhow, I came down for a simple eye operation and they did put me on a bloody TPI! I think I was the only bloke in Queensland that I know of that asked to be boarded to get off a TPI the minute he got on to 100 per cent pension. When they asked me why, I said, "Well, I'm bloody buying a house, I've got to buy a boat, I live across the water. Jesus Christ, what's twelve quid a fortnight going to do for me, I get one pound an hour splicing wire in the big mills over the weekend. I'm just starting to get ahead. I simply can't afford it."'

Chris Neilson was unable to work for six months, but he did get weekends off while on compo. Then he went back to work full time.

## HERB TRACKSON

Former prisoner Herb Trackson had his demons at home too. Solitary confinement had affected him deeply. 'You always seem to be frightened of something. As far as my case goes, I could not bear to be on my own. I had to have someone with me, or someone around me, even if it was strangers. To be in a room by myself was just impossible. I'd have to get out or make an excuse to go and see someone.'

His wife, Frances Trackson, said in 1983 that he had still not conquered that phobia: 'He still doesn't like being on his own. He says he's over it, but I don't think he is, because if he goes out and I'm left in the house, and I go down to the yard and I'm talking to somebody there, he's around looking for me before he'll settle down to anything.'

Herb resumed his trade as a butcher, which at least kept him in contact with other people. But he simply wasn't able to return to an empty house after work if Frances wasn't there. He'd go looking until he found her.

## KEN BIRD

Ken Bird had escaped from Adam Park camp in June 1942 with Chris Neilson and three others, only to return to the camp when Bob Green became too sick to continue. (Bird gave the inspiring mime with a phantom butler laying out his dressing gown in the Outram Road Gaol yard during the scabies bath treatment, convulsing his fellow prisoners and deeply puzzling the Japanese guards.) Bird was one of the survivors who turned their backs on the army system as soon as he got home, and he didn't even apply for a service pension at first.

Bird had met his wife-to-be, Greta, at a dance three weeks before he sailed for Singapore: 'She could dance, and I was training her for the [ballroom dancing] championships. The very first night I saw her I thought, "Christ, she's beautiful", but I didn't get a chance to see her again before I went. A mate said, "Lay off you bugger, she's too good for you." But I was dead lucky. I came home and married her. I didn't really know whether she was happy about it or not, because she had just finished three years with the RAAF. Greta was only about seven stone and I was fourteen stone when we got married—I didn't want to squash that poor girl!'

Ken Bird recovered his health and strength quite quickly, began work as a fisherman, and he and Greta had four children. It was only when he began having problems in the 1980s that a friend, who discovered that he did not have a pension, insisted he fill out the required papers. The Department of Veterans Affairs eventually granted him a full pension with back pay. 'So I gave the kids a thousand each, and Mum [Greta] and I went off for a trip around the world on $25 000. So now we've got money that we don't need, and we give the kids some every now and then.'

Four years after he returned to Australia, another of the escapees, Reg Morris, presented Bird with the copy of a paper that proved that Colonel Oakes had turned the five Adam Park escapees over to the Japanese—information which was received with great joy by historian Don Wall, who knew the facts of the escape and betrayal but needed hard evidence.

Neilson didn't need any paperwork to know what Oakes had done to the escape party. He harboured a fierce resentment at the injustice of what had happened and, as soon as he was fit enough, he set out to find where Oakes was living, acquired a gun (he was a crack shot), and headed off to shoot him. He found Oakes on a property in North Queensland, and staked out the house. To his dismay, a young woman with several small children walked out of the back door of the house, and Neilson realised that Oakes, a World War I veteran, must have had a second marriage.

He waited till Oakes appeared, and shouted to him from the scrub that he had come to shoot him for betraying the Adam Park escapees to the Japanese, but he had seen his wife and young children and could not do it. There seems no doubt that Oakes, a man with a distinguished World War I record, had failed badly in turning his own men over to the Japanese. Hank Nelson sighted a sworn statement in the Australian War Memorial made in May 1946. Driver Reg Morris wrote that Oakes had questioned the men on their forced return to Adam Park 'and saw fit to hand us over to the Japanese'. No official action was ever taken against Oakes for the betrayal of his own men.

## FRANK MARTIN

In an interview in 1992, Frank Martin spoke by phone from Queensland. He described himself as being in 'good form'. (Martin was one of the Sandakan prisoners of war implicated in the underground, and sentenced to three years at Outram Road.) He too still suffered from nightmares, although not as badly as immediately after the war. His attitude to the Japanese remain unchanged. 'Hatred is a terrible thing, you know, it does you more harm than it does the person that you hate. But I have no time for them at all. There's nothing I can do about it, and there are many Japanese of course up here on the Queensland coast. I certainly don't express my feelings to them in any way. A lot of people up this way, because they are making money out of them, say "Oh yes, they were all young fellows, you know, at the time and all these young people here had nothing to do with the war." But fifty years ago the young ones were the bastards. I still can't meet a Japanese today. I had a very nice home on [the Gold Coast], and I've sold it because I got a Japanese neighbour, even though I built the house.'

After the war, Frank Martin was in hospital for quite a long time, and then got a job in real estate. He considered how his Outram Road experiences had changed his outlook on life: 'Any religion that I had in me I got rid of, for the simple reason you used to see all the different religions. They all seemed to be praying to a different God, and there always seemed to be a terrible lot of Gods, and no God seemed to be doing much for anybody at all. I was a loner before the war, and have been a loner ever since, but in little ways Outram Road Gaol affected me. I don't like going into a small room because it's too much like a cell. That's why I've always lived in a fairly big house. I've only been to the pictures about twice, I think, in fifty years. I just can't get in and be confined in a place like that. Little things, that are stupid in a way.'

On hearing that Herb Trackson still couldn't be in a room by himself, Martin said he was the opposite: 'I'm better off by myself.' The only time he ceased to be a loner, strangely enough, was in the Sandakan camp where he had a good friend he could talk openly to: 'People you could trust, and they trusted you—which you don't find so much today. I used to double up on the work gangs, when I didn't need to if a mate of mine wasn't able to work. That was the kind of friendship you had. The only one I ever keep in touch with from the army days is Stan Davis, in Sydney. We ring each other from time to time and keep in touch. I don't drink and I don't smoke, so there's no percentage in going to RSLs because everybody wants to relive the war and there's more in life than to listen to bloody drunks and half-drunks.'

What does he do to relax? 'I read the financial pages. My wife had a couple of unsuccessful eye operations, she can't read and she's a very intelligent woman. We have some shares, and I read the financial pages to her. We do our shopping, go driving and go out to dinner. We've got a swimming pool, and we both swim in the summer twice a day. We seem to get through. We only had one son, he was born in 1936, and he became a journalist. He died suddenly in 1978. We have two grandsons—he was married to an American, it was a broken marriage.'

Frank Martin made a conscious decision not to go to POW reunions after a few occasions, which included not only those who had been prisoners of the Japanese, but the Germans and Italians as well. 'A terrible lot of them are "professional prisoners of war". It seems to be the only thing that ever happened to them, and they're going to make sure it's going to be with them the rest of their lives. So that was a conscious decision not to be involved. I'll be 82 this year [1992] and I've still got all my marbles, and you know, no problems really.'

## STAN DAVIS

Stan Davis was interviewed at his home in May 1983. He was then a successful builder, running his own company in Western Sydney, and, by his own admission, seemed to have had no trouble in throwing off the traumas not only of Sandakan but of Outram Road Gaol as well. He had built one of his own large project houses on top of a bare hill near Campbelltown in Sydney's west, with 360 degree views, in which he lived alone: 'People are amazed at me. I said, "Well, the rabbits, they're good company." It doesn't worry me living alone. I love company, but I've got a lot of solace in my own thoughts. I am very gregarious. I love going to the office, I love my people—I kiss all the girls every morning and have a joke with the boys. My work gives me a lot of things to do.'

Wrongly identified as being part of Lionel Matthews' underground group in July 1943, he had been tortured and interrogated in Sandakan by the *Kempeitai* for six weeks, then put in the cages at Kuching for five months, starved and forbidden to talk to anyone, before being sentenced to two years at Outram Road Gaol in Singapore, despite it being clear to the Japanese that he had nothing to do with Matthews' underground network. That was *Kempeitai* 'justice' writ large.

The good news, of course, was all this meant Davis was spared the death marches, which would have undoubtedly killed him. To Stan

Davis, Outram Road—if not rest and recreation compared to what he had been through—was something that he could cope with. He was a big-boned, tall man, and always had a positive attitude. Davis said that his namesake, Sapper Roy Davis, who was also implicated in the underground and received a sentence of two and a half years at Outram Road, died in there because he 'gave up the ghost'. Stan Davis finished up at 8¼ stone—bone weight for a man of his stature. Roy Davis, Stan said, was also a big man and 'a perfect physical specimen' when he went in. 'But he lost the will to live, and died very quickly.'

Perhaps the most enduring legacy for Stan Davis is his hatred of the Japanese, despite going to Japan on a business trip several years before my meeting with him. If anything it hardened his attitudes. 'I have no time for them really, and I shouldn't say that. The women seem nice and gentle when you go to Japan. But the men are arrogant. I couldn't shake hands with a Japanese.'

## PENROD DEAN

Without doubt, Penrod Dean walked out of Outram Road Gaol the fittest of any Australian prisoner of war after two years, most of which had been spent in charge of the food distribution to the cells of his compatriots. Despite his claims to have been more equitable in his distribution of the meagre rations than the 'trusties' who did that job before him, there is evidence that he returned to Changi close to his normal weight, although he claims otherwise in his memoir.

Chris Neilson attests that on one occasion he saw Dean in the corridor stuffing a plate of rice and tinned fish into his mouth— the ultimate banquet other prisoners could only dream about in those miserable circumstances. Dean owed his position on the tucker trolley as a trustie because of his ability to pick up the Japanese language from his guards, who also used him as an interpreter.

After the war, he elected to stay in the army while he sorted out what he wanted to do. His first assignment, on getting back to Australia, was to be put in charge of a prisoner-of-war camp for captured Italians in Wongan Hills, north-east of Perth! Dean wondered who was so dopey to give him such a job. That only lasted a few weeks; he was discharged from the army, and he and his wife, Bunny, built their 'dream home' in the affluent Perth suburb of Dalkeith. He went into business, opening a drapery shop in Mossman Park, and as trade picked up he added another store a few kilometres away.

In October 1946, Dean was one of ten former POWs asked to give evidence at the Tokyo War Crimes Trials and he went to Japan, as previously mentioned, where his language skills and familiarity with Japanese culture led to several sightseeing tours during time away from the trials.

Dean had not been a popular figure at Outram Road Gaol, and his privileged status with the Japanese guards as well as his easy access to food were resented. There were several matters I wanted to discuss with him in 1992, when he had moved from Western Australia to retirement in Dromana, Victoria. Dean replied to a letter I wrote to him, saying that he was writing his own account of his POW experiences and did not wish to engage in any discussion with me until his own book was finished. When *Singapore Samurai* was published in 1998 I wrote again, detailing some of the issues I wished to raise with him, including his claim that he taught John McGregor Morse code (Chris Neilson said he had performed that service, and that Dean didn't even know Morse code), and also his claim that he left Outram Road weighing six stone four pounds. Neilson said: 'As a Justice of the Peace I swear this is the truth. Dean came out to Changi in April or May 1944 and looked out of place because he was about eleven stone and a very fit bloke.'

There were also discrepancies in the description of Dean's escape from Changi with John McGregor, who curiously failed to mention in his own account how Dean (with McGregor's alleged help) had performed acts of sabotage while on the run in the jungle, acts that he made much of in *Singapore Samurai*. However, it was never possible for me to raise any of these matters with him, as once his book was published, Dean did not respond to any of my letters.

Although Dean was a controversial character, he began his time at Outram Road Gaol experiencing the bestial circumstances of imprisonment. He thought through a strategy for survival very early on, and by learning Japanese and earning trustie status with his captors, he was able to walk out of Outram Road fitter than any other Australian prisoner of war from that punishment prison. He claims to have done his best to distribute the food more fairly than was the case before he took over that role. Other inmates disagree. But who can judge anyone who emerged from that place?

## JOHN MCGREGOR

John McGregor never wavered in his friendship with Penrod Dean. He died in the early 1980s, so he never read Dean's book, aspects of which may have surprised him. Both were Western Australians. John McGregor's wife, Nan, did not share his high opinion of Dean. She disliked him intensely, thought him a social-climbing upstart, and no good friend of her husband. She believed he was an attempted deserter before the surrender in Singapore, had failed in action, and had to escape from Changi as soon as he did because the men of his 2/4th Machine Gun Battalion were out to get him.

McGregor believed to the end of his days that Dean had saved his life by giving him extra food at Outram Road, but that was not enough to save his sight. He went blind at Outram Road. He was taken to Changi for treatment by Australian doctors, but was returned to Outram Road until the end of the war because the *Kempeitai's* attitude was that, if his sight could not be restored, he might as well return to gaol to serve his time.

As John McGregor died before he could be interviewed for this book, his experiences are drawn from his self-published book, *Blood on the Rising Sun*. McGregor never recovered his sight.

### BERT 'BLUEY' ROLLASON

There is nothing like a Depression upbringing to toughen up a bush kid, and Bert 'Bluey' Rollason seemed to shrug off his Outram Road Gaol experiences on his return to Australia in 1945. While he admitted he was plagued by dreams, they gradually lessened: 'You'd get ones where you'd see the old planes coming in and the Japs' heads hanging out and having a look at you—but not now.'

On his return to Bendigo, he 'just fooled around for a while' and then went rabbit trapping. Eventually he did a rehabilitation course in carpentry, and for the rest of his working life worked in the building trade. Unlike many other ex-POWs, he was not particularly interested in seeking out his 8th Division comrades to talk over their experiences: 'I never worried about them. But I was working at a job once and a bloke came up to me and said, "Oh, I'm president of the ex-POW club in Bendigo, you'd better come." So I went to a few of their meetings, but they were a bit cliquey for me, I didn't think much of it. They started to yap about what had gone on during the war, and it didn't interest me, so I dropped out.'

He got married after the war, and had five children. Reflecting on whether his POW experience had changed him in any way, he said he thought it had. 'They reckon I'm a surly, niggly old bastard now.' That certainly reflects his attitude towards the Japanese, post-war: 'I just take no notice of them. In your mind, you'd end up trying to strangle one of them. I'm not about to walk up and shake hands with one. But I suppose if I had to, I would. The younger generation wouldn't know much, but the older ones—well, who knows, they were told to fight us I suppose, but they were cruel. I still know people who won't buy Japanese-made stuff.'

In 2013, still living in Bendigo, Bert Rollason was then one of only two survivors of Outram Road Gaol still alive. He was about to turn 92.

## DR JAMES TAYLOR

James Taylor was nearly 50 years of age when he was arrested by the *Kempeitai* in Sandakan in July 1943, tortured, interrogated, and, in company with the other members of the Sandakan underground network (which he had bravely supported), sentenced to a fifteen-year stint at Outram Road Gaol. After the war, he was miraculously re-united with his wife, Celia, at Labuan. They were both dressed in others' cast-off clothing, frail and ill after their experiences in captivity and effectively penniless.

When interviewing James Taylor in April 1983 in his Mosman home in Sydney, he was in his early nineties, and his daughter said that his health was failing. His long-term memory was very good, however, and he gave an excellent and insightful account of his experiences in Sandakan and Outram Road Gaol.

He said that he could have taken the job as Head of Medical Services in Borneo immediately after the war, but could not get any guarantees about superannuation, so he and Celia decided to return to Australia and start again: 'I joined the Repatriation Department and was sent to the Lady Davidson Home in North Turramurra, where ex-servicemen with tuberculosis were treated, and after a year there I went over to the Concord General Repatriation Hospital where I eventually became the Principal Medical Officer.'

Dr James Taylor was the only civilian detainee from Outram Road interviewed for this book, but his experiences were closely tied to the survivors of the Sandakan camp. He was a remarkable man. Middle-aged when arrested, he endured torture and interrogation in Borneo, as well as being subjected to unspeakable humiliation and cruelty at

Outram Road when the *Kempeitai* administration callously put him into cells with dying men, with no opportunity to practise his medical skills other than offer solace. Despite this, and starvation rations as well, he maintained his optimism and dignity. It was quite special to have the opportunity to speak to him in his nineties.

## JOHN WYETT

On 6 November 1945, the immaculately dressed 'El Supremo' Lord Louis Mountbatten, Supreme Allied Commander, South-East Asia Command, and General William Slim (in his familiar khaki 'bush shirt') arrived at Changi Prison to meet the senior Australian and British officers who had been in charge of the Allied prisoners of war on Singapore island. The group included John Wyett as a former staff officer to General Gordon Bennett. Wyett remembers Slim's first words as he stood and surveyed the emaciated but surprisingly well turned-out Australian and British officers assembled to meet him: 'Gentleman, this must be one of the bright spots of the British Empire. After what you have all suffered I expected to find you ragged, dispirited, dejected. I am amazed and I congratulate you one and all.'

Wyett felt that, coming from a distinguished leader and soldier like Slim, who was much admired and respected, this was a great compliment, and they were all rather overwhelmed by it. He reflected that compliments had been a scarce commodity during the previous three and a half years.

Despite fronting up to Lord Mountbatten and General Slim, Wyett was far from well. He found his mental acuity slow, and struggled to find words that should have been familiar. He was limping badly, and walked with a stick because the Australian doctors' efforts to keep one of his legs from healing (to make sure he did not go back to Outram Road) had been too successful. He had a 'dropped' foot that was hard to control.

After some weeks in Singapore he was pleased to hear from Dr Cotter Harvey that he had been granted a berth on the hospital ship SS *Manunda*, which was due to sail for Sydney. On board, Wyett found himself in the completely new world of a large ward with gleaming white walls, comfortable beds and spotless white sheets. It was all quite unbelievable, while the sense of unreality was heightened by the presence of quiet, smiling nurses in their neat uniforms, and a deep sense of calm and tranquillity. It all seemed too good to be true, and as he lay there he felt every muscle of his body relaxing on the first night at sea as he sank into a deep sleep.

'The bathroom was a veritable Aladdin's cave of treasures with cakes of soap, a razor that was actually sharp, a hair comb, a full-sized towel and a face washer. For three years I did not have a towel and managed quite well with a small piece of cotton rag on those occasions when I was allowed to wash at all. The habit has become so ingrained that I still use the squeezed-out face washer to dry off and the towel only to finish; it is still one of those little luxuries. No wonder everyone thought we were all mad.'

Meals were provided often and in small serves because their stomachs had shrunk and could cope with only a little food at a time. Their digestive systems needed to adapt to the nutrients that had not come their way for so long. The ex-prisoners were thoroughly exhausted and even the mild stimulation of ordinary conversation and the simple social exchanges of everyday life tired them quickly.

At least they were on their way home, with the first stop scheduled to be Darwin. But as they sailed down the north coast of Java, the ship was ordered to divert to the war-time base of Labuan to pick up some evacuees. Spirits sank, particularly when it was realised the evacuees had in fact already left. This meant the ship was short of fuel, and Australia seemed as far away as it had been in Singapore. Wyett befriended an Australian pilot, Flight-Lieutenant Anderson,

at the air base at Labuan. He was also chafing at the bit to get back
to Melbourne to see his fiancée. Wyett convinced him he should fly
a group of sixteen returnees in his amphibious Catalina aircraft to
Australia. Anderson said, 'Christ, you'll get me shot,' but somehow it
was arranged.

They made it safely to Darwin, and flew on to Brisbane. Their
flight ended in Sydney, where the mainly Tasmanian contingent took
a train to Melbourne. The next day, 3 November 1945, they boarded a
priority flight to Launceston, where the system claimed Wyett again,
putting him into a military hospital that had been established in
Campbell Town, just south of Launceston. It was half-hospital and
half-rehabilitation centre, run by an old friend of John Wyett, Colonel
(Dr) Douglas Parker. One reason for the last hurdle to getting home
was that the ex-POWs might be carrying some kind of exotic tropical
disease that could infect families and friends.

While Wyett was being checked out, Parker came to him, a problem
clouding his usually beaming face. Seating himself on Wyett's bed, he
said that he needed his help because he had an order from headquarters telling him to commission a court of inquiry. Would Wyett do it
for him? 'I took the paper he was holding and sure enough he was in
a spot of bother. The auditors had found discrepancies in some of the
hospital supplies and equipment and these had to be accounted for.
I smiled to myself as I read, thinking of the massive losses of supplies
and equipment we had incurred in Malaya—but now we were back
in the trivia of the peacetime world with a vengeance and this was
no laughing matter for the Commanding Officer of the hospital. So
I said, "OK Duggie, leave this with me and I'll fix it."'

It did not take him long to finish Parker's court of inquiry, and the
report was duly submitted to the Headquarters Tasmania Command,
accepted, filed and forgotten, as Wyett had guessed it would be. In
preparing it, Wyett had found a few discrepancies but nothing of

great importance, and he was able to provide a variety of facile explanations. He had learnt the technique during his days in the Royal Australian Naval Reserve when 500 mattresses went missing. The officer in charge was able to satisfy the inquiry by writing underneath the item 'Eaten by rats'. This was accepted despite the fact that the mattresses concerned were made of coiled steel wire. It was an explanation to go on the file, and that was the main thing.

Back in Hobart at last, Wyett accepted the offer of a job with Cadburys, the chocolate maker, which is still operating in Hobart. He could choose his own job and selected 'advertising manager', because he knew absolutely nothing about it. But he reasoned he could use his army staff training and military skills to get by, and this worked.

In 1962, he went to Sydney for General Gordon Bennett's funeral, his feelings mixed because of his own experiences of Bennett's curious and eccentric behaviour during the last stages of the Malayan Campaign and his final misjudged action in deserting his own troops: 'His was the sad case of a man with high ideals fallen victim to his own ego, yet because of his fine record in World War I, he was fully deserving of the military funeral which the army gave him when he died on 3 August 1962.'

Interviewed in detail on two occasions, in April 1984 and March 1988, Wyett was strangely reluctant at first to talk about his experiences, but became more forthcoming as the interview went on. He eventually wrote his own book, *Staff Wallah: At the Fall of Singapore*, published in 1996 by Allen & Unwin.

Wyett lived into his nineties, despite the lifelong spinal injuries incurred during his interrogations, first at the *Kempeitai* headquarters and later at Outram Road Gaol itself. He wore a neck brace from time to time, which gave some relief from the pain, but felt that taking pain-killing drugs permanently would dull his mind, so he simply put up with it.

## BILL YOUNG

In 2014, Bill Young is one of only two living survivors of Outram Road Gaol. He is 88 and living in Sydney. Having enlisted at the age of fifteen, he was still a teenager when the war ended. He had missed the Sandakan Death Marches because of an escape attempt, but had endured torture, unspeakable cruelty and deprivation, both in British North Borneo and at Outram Road.

He contemplated what his life would have been like if he hadn't joined the army. 'People often say to me, "I'll bet you were sorry you joined the army." And I say to them, "Look, no way, it was the best thing I ever did." Because looking at me, in my head was an abyss. I don't know what would have happened. There would have been no discipline and that's necessary. I suppose all kinds of things could have happened. But I would have been like a feather tossed on the waves. Where would it have been tossed? Where would it go? I just put it down to the fact that the army and the battalion became my school-room, and the soldiers in it were my teachers and life itself has taught me a lot along the line. I read a lot and that's been a great help for me, but without that start, that army start, and that knowledge of meeting such marvellous people, I might have fallen by the wayside.'

But Bill Young had been badly damaged by his war experiences, more so than he realised. He was not alone, of course, and he certainly knew that. Shortly after returning to Australia, one of his POW friends told him his parents had an orchard. Young was shocked to hear that his friend had later gone into the orchard with a .303 Lee-Enfield rifle and blown his brains out. When we spoke in 2012 about his friend's suicide, he was still quite emotional about it and able to quote part of a poem that Sergeant Eric Hatfield had scratched on the wall of his cell, shortly before he was executed at Outram Road Gaol in December 1943. Young had occupied Hatfield's cell nine months later, and memorised the poignant verses. Hatfield had not composed them

himself, but they must have meant a great deal to him, and that was
how Young remembered his late friend, by quoting from the poem by
a New Zealand poet, Thomas Bracken:

*Not understood, we move along asunder,*
  *Our paths grow wider as the seasons creep*
*Along the years, we marvel and we wonder*
*Why life is life, and then we fall asleep*
*Not understood.*

(Hatfield had escaped from Changi with two friends in late 1942,
and managed to join up with Chinese communist guerrilla fighters
in southern Malaya. He took part in sabotage actions against the
Japanese with the Chinese, and amassed excellent intelligence, which
he wanted to pass on to Allied forces by attempting to escape by sea
in mid 1943. But he was caught by the Japanese, interrogated by the
*Kempeitai* and sentenced to death by decapitation.)

Robbed of his youth, Bill Young's adjustment to normal life was
traumatic—he says it took him 40 or even 50 years to get over what
had happened to him. When he first arrived back in Australia there
was no psychiatric assessment or care. 'All they could think of was
to give you a carton of cigarettes. I had more cigarettes than I could
poke a stick at. They would give you medicine and pills for one thing
and another. They gave me bomb after bomb, trying to get rid of the
hook worms and parasites that were inside me, and finally they'd say,
"Oh Billy there's no more worms inside you," and you'd think, "Oh
that's lovely."'

Young's beriberi was more difficult to get rid of. It's a condition
not often seen in western society. In some cases, prisoners of war with
beriberi on the Thai-Burma Railway, and even at Outram Road Gaol,
found that their testicles swelled up grotesquely to the size of footballs,

so that they couldn't walk, even if their swollen legs had allowed it. Doctors used to bring in medical students to look at Young, whose legs—fortunately not his testicles—remained stubbornly swollen. One of the symptoms of beriberi is that the flesh turns spongy. You can push your finger onto the flesh, and the indent stays there for some time. 'I had a type of beriberi that was very difficult to treat, apparently. It lasted for months. I was an exhibit for doctors. I got used to them coming in and saying, "Oh, Mr Young, do you mind if I show Doctor So-and-so?" And they would press the flesh on my legs and say, "Yes, that's beriberi."'

One of the most distressing legacies of all those years of malnutrition was impotence. Bill Young, at nineteen, should have been in his prime: 'As a young bloke I suffered for a long time. I couldn't do anything sexually. I had to be treated for years. A lot of POWs suffered in the same way. That's why a lot committed suicide—as well as the difficulty of coping with ordinary society [were] the sexual expectations of being a husband or a father.'

Finally discharged from hospital, Young was apprenticed as a cabinetmaker in Tasmania. But he was still mentally fragile. One day he was making a wardrobe, with long mirrors on its front doors, when for no reason he suddenly picked up a hammer and smashed the mirrors. The RAPWI people realised that he must still have problems, so they put him into a convalescent home in Claremont, just north of Hobart, to recover from his nervous breakdown.

At 26 he married, and had four children. But by the late 1970s, the marriage had failed, by mutual consent: 'My ex-wife is a schoolteacher and she was comfortably off. We had a house. I left her all the stuff and I took $10 000, got a car and a little caravan, and took off caravanning around Australia from 1977 to 1979 and eventually managed to relax.'

Arriving in Sydney in 1979, Young asked about a caravan site at a beachside park at Ramsgate, near Botany Bay. He booked for two weeks, and stayed for five years, later moving into a rented room in the same suburb. It was at Ramsgate he joined his first RSL club, where he met other 8th Division ex-servicemen and began talking for the first time about his own war experiences. His landlady encouraged him to start writing his memories down, and his electric typewriter led to a computer and drawing lessons. He learnt to draw on a computer screen with his finger, and began a remarkable series of images based on his memories of Sandakan and Outram Road. He self-published a book in 1991, *Return to a Dark Age*, illustrated with his own black-and-white drawings.

He thinks he started to get rid of his demons during his caravan trip, and the healing process continued at Ramsgate: 'Joining the RSL club was part of that. I had a group of friends and we used to have our own table. Good fellows they were, nice fellows, and I joined a fishing club and one thing and another and over the years that helped too— getting over those awkward things.'

In 2013, Young was living alone in a unit in the south Sydney suburb of Allawah. In 2012, Anthony Hill published a book about his life, *The Story of Billy Young*, which also featured his drawings, some-thing that pleased him enormously. At last, he is at peace with himself.

'I've got no qualms or worries, I'm not frightened of death or anything like that, which is a good way to be. Some people get so messed up about it all. I've gone through all that, worked it all out, apparently. It's a bit like the fellow who worked out the Rubik's cube. Someone said, "How did you do it?" And he said, "Buggered if I know!" I've reached the stage now where I've reconciled myself with life and I'm quite contented when it ends.'

## ROD WELLS

As a kid, Rod Wells grew up on a country property in northern Victoria. He developed an early interest in crystal set radios and technology in general, so that when I first met him at his house in Rushworth, Victoria, in June 1982, I should not have been surprised when he proudly showed me around his completely self-sufficient property, powered by solar and wind with back-up batteries, water provided by rainwater tanks and a dam, and an ingenious composting sewerage system. What I did not realise, when we began our interview in his exceedingly neat and well-ordered study, was that I put him under a great deal of stress (so his wife Pam told me later) by littering his pristine desk with my tape recorder and notes for the entire interviewing session. I could see that he was uneasy about something, but at the time—and I did not pay this much attention—I thought it might be the interviewing process.

His compulsive neatness and sense of order, Pam believes, might be a lifelong trait and not necessarily related to his experience at Outram Road. However, that did affect him in a number of ways, which we talked about in that first session. 'I'm certainly over fastidious with cleanliness. I shower in the morning and use up most of the hot water in the house and, I know it is very silly when I think of it, but I will soap up and rinse a second time and go through the whole thing again just to make sure I haven't missed something after the first wash.'

This cleanliness obsession extended to his clothes, particularly his underwear: 'I can't stand any underwear on if it has any scent about it. I even smell it when I take it off to see whether it is all right, and do the same with my socks. I know it annoys Pam, but I can't stop. When I am travelling, I take a small bowl and a plastic bag with soap powder, rather than send things to the laundry where they might not be properly washed. So I wash my underwear and shirt in my room and hang them up to dry overnight.'

After counting every grain of his meagre rice ration at Outram Road, there have been enduring fixations about food. When he first came home, he could not leave anything on his plate: 'Every piece of whatever it was had to be eaten. I still have that tendency, but it has changed to whatever is the best food value. If there is a piece of meat and, say, a piece of pumpkin, I'll leave the pumpkin and eat the meat. I love potatoes, but I'll leave the potato and eat the meat or the half egg or something that's better food value for me. I still do it subconsciously.'

Pam Wells recalls that, in 1946, not long after getting home, the Royal Australian Signals Association sent Wells to Adelaide to see Lorna and David Matthews, the wife and son of Lionel Matthews, who was executed in Kuching for his role in leading the underground network in Sandakan. David told her later it was like 'meeting a very old man' who had walked towards them on two walking sticks. Pam said that her husband would have been 26 at the time.

Taking advantage of a rehabilitation scheme for returned service men and women, Wells started a bachelor of science degree at the University of Melbourne in 1946, graduating in 1949. He decided to take up teaching, and in 1950 was the head science master at Shepparton High School. But his nerves were still on edge, and he found teaching school students a strain, so, in 1951, he re-enlisted in the army to do a post-graduate course at the Royal Military College of Science in Wiltshire, at Shrivenham, in the United Kingdom. Pam believes this was one of the happiest times of his life; his brain was fully occupied and he met staff and students with brilliant abilities. There were also lots of extra-curricular activities, including photography, theatre and sport. After graduating from the RMCS in 1953, he worked for two years with the UK Ministry of Supply in the field of research and development with signals and radar.

Returning to Australia in 1955, Wells joined the Department of Supply, and was the technical staff officer in telecommunications and radar for all of the armed services in all Australian states. He also worked on development projects for the Colombo Plan and South-East Asia Treaty Organisation (SEATO).

Always keen to acquire new qualifications, he returned to England in 1956 where he worked with the Atomic Energy Commission at Aldermaston, and also studied nuclear physics at Cambridge University. He was one of only two Australian army officers chosen by the British to work for them, providing telemetry systems for their atomic bomb tests at the then Maralinga Rocket Range in Australia.

In 1960, he resigned from the regular army—by then he was a Lieutenant-Colonel—and joined the Defence Department, where he became an Australian Secret Intelligence Service (ASIS) officer, and worked with the British intelligence agency MI6, as well as the CIA. (The ASIS has been in operation for 60 years, but in 1972 its existence had remained a secret—until Australia's gaffe-prone prime minister, William McMahon, unwittingly mentioned it in public, so it wasn't a secret any more.)

Wells's secret intelligence work kept him travelling overseas most of the time, using his communications expertise, particularly in South-East Asia, Africa and the Middle East. His knowledge and affection for Malaya were particularly useful during the Malayan Emergency, the Indonesia–Malaysia Confrontation, and the threat of communist infiltration in Malaya in the 1960s and 1970s.

In 1978, he set up a private consulting service at Rushworth until health problems forced his retirement in late 1987.

Because Wells's travel often took him to Singapore, he saw Outram Road Gaol for the first time since he left it in 1957 while travelling to Britain on an RAF Hastings transport aircraft. He managed to get into Changi prison with some difficulty because there were political detainees there. He also called at Outram Road Gaol, where he was forbidden entry by a Sikh guard, and only allowed through the gate but not into a cell, which he particularly wanted to see.

Ten years later he flew into Singapore again, still hoping to see Outram Road Gaol. This time he had a friend with a few strings to pull, Major Peter May, a Royal Artillery officer with the British High Commission. May knew what Wells wanted to do and suggested lunch at his house at noon. They set off from the High Commission in his car, but Wells was surprised to see they were driving up Tamplin Hill Road, and asked where they were going. May said, 'You'll see in a minute; we have a job to do.'

Over a rise Wells was astonished to see that Outram Road Gaol (which had been scheduled for demolition in 1912) was finally gone—all except for a tiny section of wall sitting on a foundation. What followed had taken some tricky negotiation. May had heard of the demolition, but also knew Wells was due to visit Singapore. He contacted the Department of Works and asked if a small section could be left for a personal reason, but got nowhere. 'It was typical of Peter,' Wells recalled, 'he went straight to the top—the prime minister of Singapore, Mr Lee Kwan Yew—and explained the situation. The PM instructed his works minister to leave a small section of Outram Road Gaol until the nominated Wednesday. Peter told me to put a pick in the ground and dig the remaining piece of wall—I think it was near the north-west corner. The Chinese foreman said, "You are here this morning to demolish the remnants of your old home, so put the pick in the ground and dig it out." I did that, and I felt a bit emotional—a tear came to my eyes, I don't know for what reason, because I should have been so pleased to see the damn place go. Peter said, "Enough of the past, let's go home and have a gin and tonic."'

On a later visit, Rod Wells saw that a housing estate had been built near the old gaol, and thought it a good omen that children were running around playing on a site that had seen some of the saddest, most brutal and vile behaviour that was ever visited on human beings. 'So to see life and smiling children there was a great thing, like a good phoenix rising out of the ashes.'

(In 1975, when Wells returned to Kuching, he revisited the Cathedral School where the Japanese court had been, and stood on the spot where he had said farewell to Lionel Matthews. In Kuching, unlike Singapore, he was taken inside the gaol and saw his old cell, which had been greatly enlarged.)

# THE LAST WORD

It has taken me nearly 30 years to finally write the story of Outram Road Gaol, using the testimony of the ten survivors I personally interviewed, and the memoirs of two others. In the course of a long career in journalism and oral history, I have sometimes been asked a question I dread: 'Who was the most interesting/fascinating person you ever interviewed?'

I usually deflected it as gracefully as possible, but when that question arose after the prisoner-of-war radio documentaries went to air, I suddenly had a flash of what for me passed as inspiration: 'It is someone that you would never have heard of—his name is Chris Neilson, a former Australian prisoner of war of the Japanese, and he is a survivor of a dreadful military prison in Singapore called Outram Road, a place of punishment and death.'

One of the great bonuses of the field of oral history is that you are not often talking to famous people or 'tall poppies'. You are mostly interviewing so-called 'ordinary' people who have extraordinary stories to tell. Chris Neilson is such a person. For all prisoners under-going solitary confinement at Outram Road Gaol while being slowly starved to death, it was essential to hold on to the will to live. People forced to sit at attention all day on the cold concrete floors of their cells (and bashed by guards if they didn't) had various stratagems for keeping their minds active. Some recalled music that they liked in their heads, or tried to recall poems they might have been taught at school, or recalled their childhoods in detail. Some, with technical knowledge, designed new inventions in their imaginations.

Chris Neilson was not well educated and he had to adopt other methods of surviving. Basically, he goaded his captors and tried to get the better of them verbally and mentally, even if it invited bashings, which in Chris's case seriously injured him on more than one occasion. At least, he maintained, it broke the monotony and gave him a sense of moral superiority.

So Chris Neilson is the 'most interesting person' I have ever interviewed. Chris, and others like him, who are not in any sense famous, are unique. It has been a privilege to be able to help reveal their stories.

Chris Neilson lived into the twenty-first century, and into his nineties, which is remarkable considering the chronic ill-health that dogged him for life following his imprisonment. He spent his last years at a retirement home in Collaroy, Sydney, where he had cared for his wife, Mavis, who died several years before him. Neilson knew I would one day write this book, and he was delighted with the prisoner-of-war radio documentaries which, in the early 1980s, helped to raise public awareness of what the Allied POWs of the Japanese had been through. He also happened to hear the radio interview on air when I nominated him as the most memorable interviewee of my professional life. That surprised and delighted him.

I ended his *Survival* radio documentary, which I titled 'Just One Stubborn Bugger', with one of his own statements that I thought summed up not only his personal approach to survival, but spoke for all the others who somehow walked or were carried out of that dreadful hell-hole, Outram Road Gaol, their bodies damaged, but their spirits unbroken. So, Chris Neilson deserves to have the last word.

'I've said it before and I'll say it again, I'm no bloody hero, just one stubborn bugger, that's all. You've got to put your pride into it. You want to make your people, perhaps, think you're a hero. But you're not really. Anyone can be a hero. It depends on how you look at it. But I think the main thing is, when you're frightened—it's all right to be frightened, you know—don't let any other bugger see. That's the secret. Yeah, you can be frightened, I've been frightened, but I was the only bugger who knew it.'

# BIBLIOGRAPHY

Tim Bowden (producer), *Prisoners of War: Australians Under Nippon*, 16-part series, ABC Radio, 1984

Tim Bowden (producer), *Survival*, 10-part series, ABC Radio, 1987

Thomas Bracken, *Not Understood: And other poems*, Gordon & Gotch, Wellington, 1908

Penrod Dean, *Singapore Samurai*, Kangaroo Press, Sydney, 1998

Frank Desprez, 'Lasca', oral recording made by Harry E Humphrey, The Public Domain Review, <www.publicdomainreview.org/2013/08/22/frank-desprezs-lasca-read-by-harry-e-humphrey-1920/

Peter Firkins, *From Hell to Eternity*, Westward Ho Publishing Company, Perth, 1979

Rosalind Heard, *Keep the Men Alive: Australian POW doctors in Japanese captivity*, Allen & Unwin, Sydney, 2009

Anthony Hill, *The Story of Billy Young: A teenager in Changi, Sandakan and Outram Road*, Penguin Books, Melbourne, 2012

John McGregor, *Blood and the Rising Sun*, self-published, Sydney, 1980

Hank Nelson, *Prisoners of War: Australians under Nippon*, ABC Books, Sydney, 1985

Lynette Ramsay Silver, *Sandakan: A conspiracy of silence*, Sally Milner
    Publishing, Burra Creek, 1998
Nevil Shute, *A Town Like Alice*, Heinemann, Melbourne, 1992
Don Wall, *Sandakan: The last march*, self-published, Sydney, 1998
John Wyett, *Staff Wallah*, Allen & Unwin, Sydney, 1996
Bill Young, *Return to a Dark Age*, self-published, Sydney, 1991

# INDEX